AF538860

V.S. NAIPAUL

Critical Essays

V.S. NAIPAUL

Critical Essays

VOLUME–III

Edited by

MOHIT K. RAY

Published by

B-2, Vishal Enclave, Opp. Rajouri Garden,
New Delhi-110027
Phones : 25413460, 25429987, 25466842

Sales Office
7/22, Ansari Road, Darya Ganj,
New Delhi-110002
Phones : 23273880, 23275880, 23280451
Fax : 91-11-23285873
web : www.atlanticbooks.com
e-mail : info@atlanticbooks.com

ISBN 81-269-0352-X (Vol. III)
ISBN 81-269-0166-7 (Set)

Printed in India
at Nice Printing Press, Delhi

Contents

PREFACE

The immediate occasion for bringing out a third volume of *V.S. Naipaul: Critical Essays* is the jubilant reception of the first two volumes and the concomitant demand for more essays on Naipaul. This volume is an humble effort to meet the demand.

The special distinction of this volume is the full text of the Presentation Speech delivered on the occasion of awarding the Nobel Prize to Sir V.S. Naipaul, and the Press release of observations of the Permanent Secretary of the Nobel Foundation.

The luminous essays in this volume together offer a fairly good idea of the essential Naipaul: his mind and art, his visions and re-visions and the flickerings of the innermost flame that gives shape to his writings.

I thank all the contributors for their perceptive essays and I thank my colleague Professor Rama Kundu for her valuable assistance in readying this volume.

I am grateful to the Nobel Foundation for giving me permission to print the full text of the Presentation Speech. I am also grateful to Creative Books for the essays by Professor Jadgish V. Dave and Shri Kamal Mehta, reprinted from *Critical Practice*, Vol. 9, No. 1 and to Professor Hiren Gohain for the article reprinted from *Frontier*, Sept. 29—Nov. 2, 2002.

I am particularly grateful to Dr. K.R. Gupta, Chairman, Atlantic Publishers and Distributors, New Delhi, for the confidence evinced in me, and for seeing the volume through the press.

Mohit K. Ray
Editor

On Naipaul

THE PERMANENT SECRETARY, THE SWEDISH ACADEMY

THE NOBEL PRIZE IN LITERATURE 2001

V.S. Naipaul

The Nobel Prize in Literature for 2001 is awarded to the British writer, born in Trinidad, V.S. Naipaul

> "for having united perceptive narrative and incorruptible scrutiny in works that compel us to see the presence of suppressed histories."

V.S. Naipaul is a literary circumnavigator, only ever really at home in himself, in his inimitable voice. Singularly unaffected by literary fashion and models he has wrought existing genres into a style of his own, in which the customary distinctions between fiction and non-fiction are of subordinate importance.

Naipaul's literary domain has extended far beyond the West Indian island of Trinidad, his first subject, and now encompasses India, Africa, America from south to north, the Islamic countries of Asia and, not least, England. Naipaul is Conrad's heir as the annalist of the destinies of empires in the moral sense: what they do to human beings. His authority as a narrator is grounded in his memory of what others have forgotten, the history of the vanquished.

The farcical yarns in his first work, *The Mystic Masseur,* and the short stories in *Miguel Street* with their blend of Chekhov and Calypso established Naipaul as a humorist and a portrayer of street life. He took a giant stride with *A House for Mr Biswas,* one of those singular novels that seem to constitute their own complete universes, in this case a miniature India on the periphery o. the British Empire, the scene of his father's circumscribed existence. In allowing peripheral figures their place in the momentousness of great literature, Naipaul reverses normal perspectives and denies readers at the centre their protective detachment. This principle was made to serve in a series of novels in which, despite the increasingly documentary tone, the characters did not therefore become less colourful. Fictional narratives, autobiography and documentaries have merged in Naipaul's writing without it always being possible to say which element dominates.

In his masterpiece *The Enigma of Arrival* Naipaul visits the reality of England like an anthropologist studying some hitherto unexplored native tribe deep in the jungle. With apparently short-sighted and random observations he creates an unrelenting image of the placid collapse of the old colonial ruling culture and the demise of European neighbourhoods.

Naipaul has drawn attention to the novel's lack of universality as a form, that it presupposes an inviolate human world of the kind that has been shattered for conquered peoples. He began to experience the inadequacy of fiction while he was working on *The Loss of El Dorado,* in which after extensive study of the archives he described the appalling colonial history of Trinidad. He found that he had to cling to the authenticity of the details and the voices and abstain from mere fictionalisation while at the same time continuing to render his material in the form of literature. His travel books allow witnesses to testify at every turn, not least in his powerful description of the eastern regions of the Islamic world, *Beyond Belief.* The author's empathy finds expression in the acuity of his ear.

Naipaul is a modern *philosophe,* carrying on the tradition that started originally with *Lettres persanes* and *Candide.* In a vigilant style, which has been deservedly admired, he transforms rage into precision and allows events to speak with their own inherent irony.

The Presentation Speech

THE SWEDISH ACADEMY

The Nobel Prize in Literature 2001

The work of Sir V.S. Naipaul presented by Horace Engdahl, Ph.D., Permanent Secretary of *The Swedish Academy*, Member of its Nobel Committee.

Prize citation: "for having united perceptive narrative and incorruptible scrutiny in works that compel us to see the presence of suppressed histories."

Dr. Horace Engdahl delivering the Presentation Speech for the 2001 Nobel Prize in Literature at the Stockholm Concert Hall.

Your Majesties, Your Royal Highnesses, Honoured Nobel Laureates, Ladies and Gentlemen,

In the Middle Ages, master craftsmen worked in full view in the street or in an open workshop, so that prospective buyers could see that the materials they use were genuine and that no defects were hidden beneath a luxurious surface treatment. Similarly, as a mature writer V.S. Naipaul has allowed us to scrutinize his craft and the conditions surrounding it. He has candidly described how, as a beginner, he neglected to obtain knowledge of what he saw and falsified his experiences in order to live up to the perception of literature he had gained through his British schooling.

He knew at an early age that he had to write, but not what. His first book, *The Mystic Masseur,* appears very bold when read in the light of his confessions about the awkward beginnings of his own career as a writer. The masseur/charlatan is the author's shadow and caricature, to which he exorcistically transfers his bizarre traits and imagined failures, something like Sartre did with the autodidact in *La Nausée*.

Naipaul was born on the West Indian island of Trinidad as a descendant of immigrant workers from India, in a milieu where peoples and cultures from four continents mixed. In his case, moving into literature presupposed irrevocably breaking away from these origins. Yet it was not until the moment when he decided to explore what he had abandoned that his writing took off. His childhood street set the tone for him. At first it was playful and immediate, but the subject grew in his hands. In the book that made him famous, *A House for Mr Biswas,* he lent the profundity of the major novel to the wing-clipped characters in a Caribbean backwater and granted them dignity. Mr Biswas, who bears traits of Naipaul's father, gained a place in the English literary gallery of immortal tragicomic heroes.

Naipaul's subsequent works examined, in ever wider circles, the forgotten historical circumstances that explain the author's background. He became an explorer, not of the wilderness but of societies—everywhere at home and a stranger, a Ulysses whose only Ithaca was his desk. Perhaps he is a witness from the freely circulating humanity of the future.

Naipaul has been praised for writing the best English in the market, and that may well be, but his view of style is reminiscent of Stendahl's, who believed a writer has failed if the reader remembers the words he has written: what should remain are his ideas. Naipaul is no worshipper of fantasy or utopia, no creator of alternative worlds. Dickens's ability to describe London with the open gaze and simplicity of a child is his declared ideal. He continues a critical direction in literature that distances itself from myth and expressive hyperbole. His text is permanently unrelenting, like a chill wind that will not stop blowing.

In *Reading and Writing,* an essay of great value in understanding his works, Naipaul relates his steadily growing doubts about the novel, the grand genre of the West. He describes how while working on his history of Trinidad, *The Loss of El Dorado,* he found in the archives traces of the native tribe that had given its name to the small city where he spent his first years, and how his perception of reality suddenly expanded. "Fiction by itself would not have taken me to this larger comprehension," he writes. The technique he adopted while working on *El Dorado*—unearthing from the documents the life stories of seemingly insignificant individuals—returns when he works with the notes from his journeys. The various literary forms he has tried—fictional narrative, autobiography, feature story and historical documentary—have eventually merged into a unique genre, "prose in the style of Naipaul." By this innovation, he has enlarged the territory of literature.

One experience that seems to have been crucial to his literary method is his first encounter with India. He saw traces of a history that had been concealed from view when the champions of independence had to deny the misfortunes that had preceded the English: six hundred years of Muslim imperialism that deliberately destroyed the memory of earlier civilisations and plunged the Hindus into a helplessness similar to that of the American Indians. He studied R.K. Narayan's novels in the Indian setting and saw that their world is built around an emptiness that the author is incapable of dealing with: the forgotten defeat that turned people into dwarves among monumental ruins. Only an intact culture provides the background knowledge that makes the novel a reasonable form, Naipaul argues. He found that he had to cling to the authenticity of details and voices and abstain from fabulation, while continuing to give his material a literary shape. He became a collector of testimony.

This method presupposes the courage to seek out human phenomena that frighten every normal observer, the author included. But even when he reports from places where no hope seems to exist, the author's empathy makes itself felt in the acuity of his ear. He says he finds every person interesting, at least for the first few hours. He distinguishes individual fates beyond the dutiful idealization that controls our perception of the earth's ill-fated nations. He wants to understand the principle of every person's life, the decisive thing that makes him what he is. He records the relationship between pretension and reality, two contours that never really cover each other and never completely diverge.

Decay and disappearance are a fundamental theme in Naipaul's writings—but without grief, rather as something that makes existence bearable. The English landscape that he discovers in *The Enigma of Arrival* is the ruin of an age of greatness, and at last he feels at home! He says that even as a child, he has pondered that he was born into a world past its climax. Yet his books are not negative. His phrasing embodies an absence of resignation that keeps melancholy at bay and shares with the reader the pure joy of intelligence.

Naipaul has praised the West for having recognized the right to individual endeavour and for its diffidence. The core of his devotion to European civilisation is that it was the only one of the alternative cultures that made it possible for him to become a writer.

Sir Vidia! Your life as a writer calls to mind what Alfred Nobel said of himself: "My homeland is where I work, and I work everywhere." In every place, you have remained yourself, faithful to your instinct. Your books trace the outline of an individual quest of unusual dimensions. Like a Nemo piloting a craft of your own design, without representing anyone or anything, you have manifested the independence of literature. I would like to convey to you the warm congratulations of the Swedish Academy as I now request you to receive the Nobel Prize in Literature from the hands of His Majesty the King.

1

The World, the Text, and the Caribbean Writer: Representation in the Work of V.S. Naipaul

RAFE DALLEO

> How can the history of this West Indian futility be written? What tone shall the historian adopt? [...] The history of the islands can never be satisfactorily told.
>
> —V.S. Naipaul, *The Middle Passage*

The representation of history is always a contested site. In the post-independence West Indies, these battles become magnified through centuries of slavery and one-sided tellings of history. Men and women from the islands have, for more than half a century, been writing their own versions of West Indian history, both as fiction and non-fiction. V.S. Naipaul, in the passage reproduced above, raises the salient questions: how is the history of the West Indies to be represented? How are we to get at the truth? Asking these questions raises many issues: whether history should be told from above or reconstructed from below; which genre best suits history writing in the West Indies—traditional history, the novel, or something else; the relationship of history and West Indian fiction; the role of imagination in narrative reconstructions of the past; and the possibility of realism, a style of writing in which words directly and unproblematically represent things. When documents from the past are scarce and frequently one-sided, efforts to reconstruct history ethically and accurately become especially acute.

I contend that these considerations have guided V.S. Naipaul's career since its beginning. His examination of the representation of history is limited neither to his only book of explicit historical writing, *The Loss of El Dorado* (1969), nor to his non-fiction travel narratives, journalistic pieces, and autobiographical reflections. In his first three published books, all fiction, Naipaul pushes the limits of genre as he tries to determine the form appropriate for representing the reality of an East Indian in the West Indies. *Miguel Street* is not quite a novel, but is more than a collection of stories. The narrator of *The Mystic Masseur* is never certain where his tale ends and Ganesh's begins; and Ganesh's tale itself combines a blend of "autobiography" and "spiritual thriller" (*Mystic Masseur* 119).[1] Not until his fourth book, *A House for Mr Biswas*, does Naipaul settle into a style which resembles that of the realist novel.[2] The style is overwhelmingly descriptive, assumes and produces a coherent narrative world, and no longer features the potentially unstable narrators of the earliest works. This style moves even further towards "objectivity" in Naipaul's subsequent writing, whether fiction or non-fiction, as a journalistic style comes to replace the early exploration. It is only with *A Way in the World*, Naipaul's major work of the 1990s, that the author returns to the earliest books in order to re-examine his previous assumptions about reality and style.

A recent collection of essays entitled "Sisyphus and Eldorado: Magical and Other Realisms in Caribbean Literature" posits a divide between social realism and magical realism, in the Anglophone and Hispanic Caribbean respectively. I will use these terms as a model for discussing Naipaul's career. The volume's title refers on the one hand to Orlando Patterson's novel *The Children of Sisyphus*, as an exemplar of West Indian social realism. On the other hand, El Dorado alludes to the Latin American continent as site of myth and legend. In his preface, Kamau Brathwaite writes (in his distinctively anti-realist video style):

> [...] the 'differences' between these two orientation—and it's more that than fixed position and there's also, need I say, overlap at times & places between & among these 'orientations'—are (however) significant & go beyond, I think, any bias of preference or fashion or zeitgeist & is telling me that in the Caribbean, the

> Sisyphean tradition, w/whatever individual & timely xceptions, is very much a part of our history & structure, and represents our 'reality' of stasis & emprision—the literature of the negative catastro phe; while MR/dorado represents (again w/cautions & qualifications) the optimistic creative rascal of (New World) encounter—the dream & pressure of metaphor breaking out of the prison s/hell to par ticipate in a literature (in both cases also orature) of optimistic catastrophe—catharsis—illuminated manu uscript of blindness. ("MR" 16)

Brathwaite hints, here and elsewhere in this essay, that the tradition of Sisyphus, of realist protest writing, is simply "Caliban using Prospero's language to trace him in great detail, in a way, but not getting/going beyond that into the image of Sycorax & 'beyond' even that unto Setebos at the mud of the making of nature & its transcription into human consequences" (11). Brathwaite's notion of tracing Prospero has three possible meanings: either tracing Prospero's books, that is copying his style; or tracing Prospero's figure, that is representing Prospero as the cause of the present situation. In Jamaican parlance, it also means to curse.[3] Yet perhaps these three meanings are not entirely opposed. As in *The Tempest*, Caliban's attempts to curse Prospero have generally come in Prospero's language; attempts to write protest literature have generally used the style of social realism to trace oppression in great detail. Other Calibans, like the early Naipaul, have tried to trace Prospero's style in writing their novels. Eventually, Caliban comes to find that Prospero's style, the style of social realism, cannot represent certain things. Getting beyond realism implies a broadening of vision, a move away from protest towards offering imaginative solutions.

Using Brathwaite's paradigm, I classify Naipaul's post-*Biswas* poetics, the style he employs during the middle period of his career beginning with *The Middle Passage* until at least *A Bend in the River*, as the poetics of Sisyphus. Brathwaite's argument, that protest literature is locked in an unproductive dialogue with the colonial past, a dialectic without synthesis, is a familiar one. He adds an original twist, suggesting that protest literature's limitation is its dependence upon the techniques of social realism. Although few would consider Naipaul a "protest writer," his descriptive style is based on the same poetic assumptions as protest literature's: charting the injustices of colonialism in great detail, without offering alternatives or solutions. These approaches, while perhaps motivated by different ideological positions, could be regarded as different sides of the same coin.[4]

The Jamaican section of *The Middle Passage* is the first occurrence in Naipaul's writing of a description of the "children of Sisyphus" without the lens of fiction and the novel. He describes the slums of Kingston, the infamous "dungle" where Orlando Patterson sets his novel, in relentless detail: "Hovels of board and cardboard and canvas and tin lie choked together on damp rubbish dumps behind which the sun sets in mocking splendour" (*The Middle Passage* 216). The passage continues in this vein for most of the page, turning a meticulous eye to the sights of the dungle. These types of physical descriptions are common in Naipaul, whether he is describing landscapes or people. Naipaul's descriptions of landscape might be called naturalistic, representing in physical presence the values of the society and culture of which they are a part. In *A Bend in the River* and *In a Free State*, the landscape is chaotic bush, just like African history; in *The Enigma of Arrival*, on the other hand, ordered and manicured gardens are characteristic of British civilization. In his description of the dungle, Naipaul emphasizes the abject chaos, filth, and hopelessness which mark the life of poor Jamaicans. By investing so much energy in description, Naipaul manages to elide discussions of the causes of this destitution. For Naipaul, excessive moralizing clouds the writer's ability to be true to reality; these descriptions are simply the unromanticized truth.

Even in this early passage, with some excavation, we can see where Naipaul's discourse reach its limits. Naipaul, in trying to trace Froude and Trollope's style of travel writing, realizes that there are parts of the West Indian reality which this discourse cannot represent. Before launching into the description cited above, Naipaul gives this disclaimer: "The slums of Jamaica are beyond description. Even the camera glamorises them" (216).[5] To call something "beyond description" and then spend the rest of the paragraph describing it is a curious strategy. Naipaul is still uncomfortable with his position as objective observer. As Naipaul refines his style, he will no longer foreground the inadequacies of his discourse: in *The Loss of El Dorado,* as we will see, or in the African-set novels, he gives up on trying to represent the unrepresentable Africans, slaves, or Amerindians. Yet these margins will return to encroach on the center. These margins become central to *A Way in the World,* in the "unwritten stories," those stories which the author has never been able to write, and even now, can only "partly" work out (*Way* 47). I will return to these stories at the end of this paper.

The traveller persona of Naipaul's middle period goes hand-in-hand with this poetics of Sisyphus. Thus this persona, standing at a remove from his surroundings, observing rather than participating, becomes the dominant form of narration for all of Naipaul's writings in this time period, whether fiction or non-fiction. Gordon Rohlehr, in a 1980 interview, notes that "A lot of [Naipaul's] recent work has a kind of journalistic finish. It is journalistic" ("Space" 106). After experimenting with narration and form, Naipaul during the late 1960s and 1970s uses, variously, omniscient narration, as in *In a Free State,* journalistic objectivity, as in *The Overcrowded Barracoon* and *The Return of Eva Perón,* or the icily detached first person of *The Mimic Men* and *A Bend in the River.* Perhaps the best example of the vision of history which Naipaul adopts during this time period is his only extending foray into history writing, *The Loss of El Dorado.*

Selwyn Cudjoe has justly taken Naipaul to task for assuming an entirely European view of history by relying so heavily on European accounts of New World events and representing only Europeans as historical agents. Cudjoe uncovers the absences of Naipaul's version of history (the unrepresentable) in order to show the assumptions upon which this ideology rests. In particular, Naipaul's reliance on Western documents and therefore Western ways of seeing short-circuits his ability to say anything more about the substantial African population than "the slave is silent, faceless [...] he has no story" (*Loss of El Dorado* 376). This version of history reveals the "limitations of colonial discourse" (Cudjoe 118) for describing colonial history:

> He was unable to penetrate deeply into the Negro culture and psyche and for that reason the African remained unreal, residing only within Naipaul's imagination. Because Naipaul was unable to locate the African in his 'real social world,' he was unable to reveal him as a fully constituted colonial subject. As a consequence, his work, particularly as it relates to the African person, is of limited value. (119)

Cudjoe has no trouble arguing that Naipaul's depictions of Blacks are unsympathetic and unconvincing; whatever Naipaul himself thinks of Africans, his acceptance of a Western vision of history handicaps his ability to write history otherwise.[6]

During this period, wherever Naipaul travels, he interprets whatever is around him through the words of other writers, giving the impression that, as he says at the beginning of an article on Argentina, one could "outline it like a story by Borges" (*Return of Eva Perón* 101). By relying so overtly on the texts of other writers, Naipaul assesses these texts as representations of the "real" Argentina or Trinidad or Zaire or India. He generally goes to great pains to show the limitations of the perspectives of these writers, not to imply that writing cannot represent reality, but instead to show that *his* style of writing is better suited to that task.

Visiting India, for example, Naipaul spends a great deal of narrative space analyzing the literary works of Narayan, Anantamurti, and, of course, Gandhi. In Gandhi, he finds "no attempt at an objective view of the world [...] the absence of the external world" (*India* 106): one example of this flaw is that "landscape is never described" (106). He concludes, questionably, that "it is less easy for Indians [than for Europeans, who are always Naipaul's implicit measuring stick] to withdraw and analyze" (108). Whatever the value of what Naipaul says about Gandhi, or of Indians in general, these sort of comments, which appear in virtually all of Naipaul's travel accounts, offer a window onto the system of writing the Naipaul privileges. Objectivity, description, analysis, and the dialectical interplay of the external world on the individual are the characteristics which Naipaul, writing in the 1970s, prizes above all others. As Erich Auerbach shows in *Mimesis*, the Western world believes these techniques to have reached an apogee in nineteenth-century realism.

Even as Naipaul's fictional style becomes increasingly detached and journalistic during the 1970s, we can see hints that he is moving away from documentary-based research as the privileged mode of history writing. *A Bend in the River*, for example, features the character Raymond, a European writing a history of Africa. Reflecting on Raymond's work, the narrator, Salim, comments with disappointment that "the article about the race riot [...] turned out to be a compilation of government decrees and quotations from newspapers" (*Bend* 180). His reservations are not because the newspapers are incorrect, but simply because "they left out a lot of important things—often essential things—that local people would know and gossip about" (181). Thus Salim "was always hoping that Raymond was going to go behind the newspaper stories and editorials and try to get at the *real* events" (181; my emphasis). Salim's final judgment sounds like an indictment of Naipaul's own attempt at writing history in *The Loss of El Dorado*: "He stuck with the newspapers; he seemed to want to show that he had read them all and had worked out the precise political shade of each. His subject was an event in Africa, but he might have been writing about Europe or a place he had never been" (181). During the late seventies, ten years after his attempt to write traditional history, he has come to regard fiction as having more access to reality than documentary history: in the (ironically non-fictional) essay "Michael X and the Black Power Killings in Trinidad," Naipaul writes that "facts can be realigned. But fiction never lies; it reveals the writer totally" (*Return of Eva Perón* 67).

It is within this context of Naipaul's career, constantly navigating its way between fiction and non-fiction, that *A Way in the World* revisits all of these concerns. This latest work is a significant break from what has come before, both in form and content. It is also marked by remarkable continuity: *A Way in the World* goes back through all of Naipaul's previous writing, to show how central the questions of history and writing have been to Naipaul's novels as well as his non-fiction. This book represents Naipaul's most extended meditation on the representation of history and reality. Happily,

Brathwaite's metonymy for magical realism, El Dorado, is the central metaphor in Naipaul's two major explorations of the process of history writing. In many ways, *A Way in the World*, which reviewer Paula Burnett nicknames "Finding El Dorado," can be read as a counterpoint to *The Loss of El Dorado*. The later work defies classification as realist novel; the British edition avoids the title novel altogether, subtitling the book "A Sequence." *A Way in the World* goes back to the beginning to discuss the process of writing *Miguel Street, A House for Mr Biswas, The Loss of El Dorado*, and other key books in the development of Naipaul's aesthetic. It also returns to the scenes of many of his earlier books, especially *The Loss of El Dorado*, as if to right (or re-write) the mistakes of the past.

As mentioned above, Naipaul's writing in the three decades leading up to *A Way in the World* is sometimes experimental in form, but rarely questions its own ability to represent reality. Yet after decades of narrators fully confident in their access to truth, *A Way in the World* features a decentered narrator who begins by observing that sometimes we can see only "a fragment of the truth" (*Way* 11).[7] The narrative is fragmented, proceeds in fits and starts, and jumps from one locale to another, from one century to another, from one period of Naipaul's life to another. This is a new form for Naipaul, a new style, a new discourse, and Naipaul finds that his new form allows for new content; those who could not be represented in *The Loss of El Dorado*, Amerindians and Afro-Trinidadians, take centre stage in *A Way in the World*.

In a recent essay, Sandra Paquet makes the intriguing suggestion that Eric Williams' *Documents of West Indian History* can be considered as a precursor to contemporary fictional representations of Caribbean history, particularly Lamming's *Natives of My Person*, Benítez-Rojo's *Sea of Lentils*, and Naipaul's *A Way in the World*. She explains that all four of these texts present a method of writing Caribbean history which emphasizes fragmentation and discontinuity, and avoids the hierarchical and linear formulations of European history writing. She describes *A Way in the World* as employing a "poetics of El Dorado" which relies on parodic and mythic language rather than the "objective" discourse of traditional histories ("Documents" 770). Through intertextual references to a variety of West Indian historical documents, *A Way in the World* examines a series of attempts to express New World realities in writing, from Raleigh and Miranda to Lebrun (C.L.R. James) and Naipaul himself. Paquet ultimately concludes that all of these texts feed on the interplay of history and fiction in a West Indian context, uncovering fiction as an "ideologically and culturally conditioned way of reading history" and history "as an ideologically and culturally conditioned artifice."

From these observations, we can see how *A Way in the World* practices a poetics of El Dorado, in its presentation of history as episodic, its blending of styles and of genres, and what Brathwaite would call its imaginative efforts to re-present/ re-construct Sycorax, in the form of Amerindian and slave characters whom traditional historical accounts have omitted. This poetics is developed through a variety of readers and writers who appear as alter egos for Naipaul himself: Leonard Side, Foster Morris, Lebrun, Walter Raleigh, Fray Simón, Francisco Miranda, Blair, and of course, the narrator himself. *A Way in the World* is an interrogation of each of these men's view of the world and his inadequate efforts to represent Trinidad and its environs. All of these men contain elements of Naipaul, and seem to represent aspects of his career, a garden of forking paths, some of which Naipaul took, and some of which he chose not to take. Including himself, the young copier of colonial documents (22-23) and naturalistic drawer of landscapes (28), in this lineage of attempts to find a language for talking about Trinidad gives the elder Naipaul a chance to both defend and repudiate his earlier positions.[8]

Naipaul begins this exploration of himself by revealing his changing attitudes towards Leonard Side, and the "idea of beauty" which Side represents: "It was his idea of beauty that upset me, I suppose [...]. That idea of beauty—mixing roses and flowers and nice things to eat with the idea of making the dead human body beautiful too—was contrary to my own idea. The mixing of things upset me. It didn't upset him" (9). What is remarkable about this passage is its past tense. Naipaul is narrating a story from his first return to Trinidad, and the reactions of this young British colonial to the land of his birth. At this point in his career, purity is an ideal for which to strive: purity of thought, purity of form in writing. Forty years later, this passage, and this book as a whole, attest to Naipaul's complicated re-orientation with respect to Trinidad, to history, and to reality. He is finally willing to come to terms with the creolization which characterizes Trinidadian society.

This new attitude towards being, as fragmented, mixed, and constantly in process, is reinforced by setting and space. The book's setting is constantly in flux, beginning in Trinidad, taking detours to England, the United States, West Africa, and East Africa, before ending on an airplane transporting Blair's body back to Trinidad. The action never dwells in any of these places; each is a brief stopover, a return or a departure always recalling or anticipating another place. The longest stretch of action takes place in and above the Gulf of Paria, between Trinidad and Venezuela during the longest chapters, chapters six, seven and eight. As the narrator himself admits, "at one time I thought I should try to do a play or a film—a film would have been better—about the Gulf" (247). Chapter six is set on Walter Raleigh's boat in the middle of the Gulf; chapter seven on an airplane flying over the Gulf; and chapter eight, titled "In the Gulf of Desolation," takes place in Trinidad, and traces the movement of Venezuelan Francisco Miranda throughout the world. More than anywhere else, *A Way in the World* is set in the Gulf, a particularly in-between space, between islands and continental bush, reality and fantasy: "The Gulf, with its confused currents, between an island and the estuary of a continental river, had always been part of the fabulous New World. Columbus had found salt water and fresh in it, and—thinking himself only between two islands—had never known why" (224). The Gulf, an impure space of creative mixture, becomes microcosm for the entire New World.

In a discussion set in the Gulf, the long interrogation of Raleigh identifies the source of the difficulty of Raleigh's attempt to narrate the New World:

> A deliberately difficult book. It's only here that I understand why the book is so difficult. It's a deliberate mixture of old-fashioned fantasy and modern truth. Everything you write about this side of the Gulf, the eastern side, the Trinidad side, everything is correct and

> very clear, every name, every tribe, every little Indian port. Real knowledge, real enquiry. On the river side, it's a different story. When you get down to the main Orinoco, you write about a strange land of diamond mountains and meadows and deer and birds. It's beautiful, but only like a painting. The book's like the work of two different men. (*Way* 175)

These metafictional passages (another comes on page 183) from the surgeon's interrogation of Raleigh identify the poetics of Sisyphus and El Dorado with islands and continent respectively, just as Brathwaite does. The Gulf lies between these poetics. The writer's location in Trinidad, on the edge of the West Indies and at the margins of the Spanish-American empire, leaves him between these two styles. Raleigh's writing becomes difficult and confused because of its inability to effectively negotiate this divide. Naipaul's self-awareness presumably makes him better able to derive energy from the interplay.

By thinking outside of European models of history the elder Naipaul can write the "unwritten" stories which eluded European travellers to the New World, as well as the younger Naipaul. These "unwritten" stories enact the imaginative reconstruction of the world of the Amerindians and African slaves during colonialism which Naipaul had never before attempted. They are that which the poetics of Sisyphus, social realism, obsessed with tracing Prospero, cannot represent. While *The Loss of El Dorado* saw only the dearth of documentation about the lives of these peoples, *A Way in the World* follows Wilson Harris' lead in using the imagination to fill in the gaps left by European history. Naipaul describes this evolution away from reliance on a Western view of history and towards imaginative reconstruction: "historical documents [...] gave me a sense of the crowded aboriginal Indian island [...]. A sense, rather than a vision: little was convincingly described in those early documents, and few concrete details were given. In my mind's eye I created an imaginary landscape for the aboriginal peoples living" (213). By contrast with the journalistic Naipaul, who assumed his descriptions of the world to be precise and unproblematic, this imaginative vision requires the admission of its own incompleteness, the realization that Amerindians possess "ideas I couldn't enter, ideas of time, distance, the past, the natural world, human existence" (213-14).

The central figures in each of the three "unwritten" stories lack this crucial self-awareness. In the first story, the revolutionary travelling into the Guyanese interior fails to realize that in his project he is retracing the steps of generations of European conquerors before him. As a result, he also fails to understand that his way of seeing the Amerindians is no different from those European ways of seeing. These are what Naipaul refers to as "certain historical ironies" (48).

Naipaul, ironically, gives the revolutionary traveller moving up the river no name but "the narrator," yet allows him no chance to narrate; Naipaul will not surrender the privilege of narrating this story. Thus there is a curious distance created between the Naipaul who narrates and "the narrator," who is narrated. Naipaul can see and describe the Amerindians; "the narrator," trapped in European ways of seeing, cannot. We can have a passage in which Naipaul states: "a woman comes down the zigzagging yellow ramp with a basket of food for the man with the shotgun: various things in tins and wooden bowls, separately tied up in cloth." Yet this description could not have been given by "the narrator," who sees only "blank faces, the stillness of the staring people" (49). The narrator is in his own mental world; as he eats, rather than considering the people around him, he loses himself in abstraction, "thinks of all the world's staples" (50). He not only finds it "impossible to enter [the Amerindian] way of perceiving" (58); in the end, his complicity with his European predecessors is made explicit. His is only the latest betrayal of the Amerindians.

"A Parcel of Papers, a Roll of Tobacco, a Tortoise," Naipaul's unwritten story of Raleigh's second trip to the Guianas, plays with the historical fact that while Raleigh's troubled and troubling account of his trip has become a central document in the history of the region, the account of the Amerindian who accompanied Raleigh back to England has never received equal hearing. Naipaul's retelling portrays Raleigh as progressively losing his grip on reality, obsessed only with writing down his confused narration of his voyage (209-10), while Don José, the silenced Amerindian, gives an even and thoughtful version of the same events. As Naipaul puts it, "the narrative is now his" (188), even if that is not how European history will remember things.

The last "unwritten story," that of Francisco Miranda, follows the form of the Raleigh story, the action moved along almost exclusively through long passages of dialogue. The narrative is overtly monologic; the discourse, whether Miranda's voice, Hislop's, or someone else's, is all European. Well-crafted, this discourse elides the slaves, referring to them obliquely when speaking of "human turpitude" (276). Hislop realizes that his ability to frame that sentence so precisely "comforts" (277) him, as the younger Naipaul's precisely crafted prose must have comforted him too.

Yet the shadows at the margins undermine the central narrative. Miranda's daily routine is constantly interrupted by the incomprehensible rumblings of slaves, speaking in their native African tongues. Later, "where there had been Africans in the grounds, speaking an African language, there were now Chinese" (329). In Miranda's writing, these figures appear fleetingly and are quickly forgotten; for the more sophisticated writer of the story, they linger as the unrepresentable margins of European discourse. Their presence reminds us of the insufficiency of Miranda to represent New World reality. As Miranda himself notes, "There were no Negroes in Tom Paine or Rousseau. And when I tried to be like them [Paine and Rousseau] I found it hard to fit in the Negroes. Of course, I knew they existed. But I thought of them as accidental to the truth I was getting at. I felt when I came to write that I had to leave them out" (341). If he cannot understand or account for the majority of the inhabitants of Trinidad, how can he expect to represent them, either in writing or as the leader of their revolution?

A Way in the World does manage an attempt to represent these people. Paquet notes that in indicting Raleigh's and Miranda's representations of the past as lies and partial truths, Naipaul is implicitly recanting his own use of their narratives in writing *The Loss of El Dorado*. That was the younger, immature Naipaul: as he notes in *A Way in the World*,

> when I first read about Miranda and began to look at his papers, I too, but in my own way, thought of him as a precursor. I saw him as a very early colonial, someone with a feeling of incompleteness, with very little at home to fall back on, with an idea of a great world out there, someone who, when he was out in this world, had to reinvent himself. I saw in him some of my own early promptings (and the promptings of other people I knew). I feel now that I was carried away by a private idea of an ancestry. (252)

Again, the past tense shows the naïvety of the younger narrator, who, early in the book, works for the government copying colonial documents (22), rather than imagining anything outside of these documents (he also begins to write by writing descriptive landscapes: 28). The older writer can see Miranda for the mimic man of European thought that he was, and can distance himself from that position. This is a remarkable step for V.S. Naipaul, a new way in the world.

Like the author himself, V.S. Naipaul's writing has always kept moving, searching for new forms, structures and style to better represent the world. After he had seemingly settled on a journalistic, "objective" style during the late 1960s and 1970s, *A Way in the World* marks a significant departure from this brand of realism. This "sequence" revises much of Naipaul's earlier work, and points to a new orientation towards history, reality, and the artist's role in its representation. The poetics which Naipaul introduces in *A Way in the World* is the poetics of El Dorado, the poetics of mixture, hybridity, migration, and ultimately, globalization.

NOTES

1. R.C. Zaehner writes: "The Hindu mystical classics are not autobiographical and are not the record of actual experiences undergone by given individuals. They are either mystico-magical tracts [...] or the exposition of mystical doctrines in verse" (quoted in Cudjoe 44).
2. The realism of *A House for Mr Biswas* is contested by Homi Bhabha, who recognizes elements which realism cannot quite reconcile; on the other hand, Fawzia Mustafa finds the overwhelming "totality" of "Naipaul's major novels" (Mustafa 221) to be in keeping with the realist tradition.

3. See the glossary at the end of *Lionheart Gal* for this definition of "trace."
4. Belinda Edmondson's *Making Men* makes a similar argument. She points out that writers as disparate as Naipaul, C.L.R. James and George Lamming have all written in the style of nineteenth-century Victorian England, that is, the style of social realism.
5. Gordon Rohlehr mentions the photographic quality of Naipaul's style: "I think that what unifies the late and early Naipaul is that the eye of the writer functions as a very selective camera which severely chooses its images and what it is going to photograph" ("Space" 102).
6. We might juxtapose Naipaul's historical narrative with C.L.R. James' *The Black Jacobins*, as an alternative model of how West Indian history might be written if different discursive assumptions are made.
7. For a long discussion of Naipaul's faith in writing as a road to truth, see Lillian Feder's *Naipaul's Truth.*
8. For example, Foster Morris' criticisms of the young narrator are offered to explain the writer's shift from his early comic novels to the more serious *House for Mr Biswas.*

WORKS CITED

Auerbach, Erich. *Mimesis.* Trans. Willard Trask. Princeton, NJ: Princeton UP, 1953.

Bhabha, Homi. "Representation and the Colonial Text: A Critical Exploration of Some Forms of Mimeticism." *The Theory of Reading.* Ed. Joseph Graham. Brighton: Harvester Press, 1984. 93-122.

Brathwaite, Kamau. "MR." *Annals of Scholarship* 12.1/2 (1997): 1-28.

Burnett, Paula. "'Where else to row, but backward?' Addressing Caribbean Futures through Re-visions of the Past." *A Review of International English Literature* 30.1 (Jan. 1999): 11-37.

Cudjoe, Selwyn. *V.S. Naipaul: A Materialist Reading.* Amherst, MA: U of Massachusetts P, 1988.

Edmondson, Belinda. *Making Men: Gender, Literary Authority, and Women's Writing in Caribbean Narrative.* Durham, NC: Duke UP, 1999.

Mustafa, Fawzia. *V.S. Naipaul.* New York: Cambridge UP, 1995.

Naipaul, V.S. *The Mystic Masseur.* New York: Penguin Books, 1957.

——. *The Middle Passage.* New York: Vintage Books, 1962.

——. *The Loss of El Dorado.* New York: Penguin Books, 1969.

——. *India, A Wounded Civilization.* New York: Vintage Books, 1976.

——. *A Bend in the River.* New York: Vintage Books, 1979.

——. *The Return of Eva Perón with the Killings in Trinidad.* New York: Vintage Books, 1981.

——. *A Way in the World.* New York: Vintage Books, 1994.

——. *Reading and Writing.* New York: New York Review of Books, 2000.

Paquet, Sandra. "Documents of West Indian History: Telling a West Indian Story." *Callaloo* 20.4 (Fall 1997): 764-76.

Rohlehr, Gordon. "The Space Between Negations: Gordon Rohlehr Interviewed by Selwyn Cudjoe, 6 May 1980." *The Shape of That Hurt and Other Essays.* Port of Spain: Longman Trinidad, 1992. 97-128.

Sistren with Honor Ford Smith. *Lionheart Gal: Life Stories of Jamaican Women.* Toronto: Sister Vision Press, 1987.

2

A House for Mr Biswas: A Study in Cultural Predicament

N. SHARADA IYER

The central focus of much of modern writing is in its presentation of society as too remote from or even hostile to the individual for him to feel any sense of belonging. In such a situation where the individual is seen as culturally or sometimes linguistically estranged the whole question of social, cultural and individual identity becomes an unattainable ideal. The strength of the modern literary imagination lies in its evocation of the individual predicament in terms of alienation, or exile or quest for identity. Literature of the third world is no exception to this general tendency in modern writing in which the theme of individual's predicament in the form of rootlessness, crisis of identity mainly lying behind the desperate affirmation of traditional culture has been explicitly explored. Naipaul's fictional work is concerned with the complex fate of the individual, societies and culture. His recurring themes are the collision of cultures and the resultant ambiguities in human adjustment, the colonial situation that produces a special kind of human psychosis. The problem that he projects in his work is how an individual resists or overcomes the conditions in which he is placed and eventually succeeds or fails to survive and succeed. Naipaul's fictions thus acquire a three dimensional significance—historical, social and psychological, and understandably Naipaul is at once a chronicler, historian and biographer.

East Indian by descent, Trinidadian by birth English by virtue of his Oxford education, Naipaul has given credence to inheriting something of the insecurities of the transplanted colonial with an ambiguous identity. The Indian background has become part of a mixed culture whose other components are equally eroded and warped. The tradition inherited from the past is transmogrified in the 'Society of Societies' losing its capacity to provide an authentic drive or psychological direction. For Naipaul the West Indies consists of races that have been uprooted from their original societies and have not produced a new culture, to replace what was lost. They have been abandoned in Trinidad, with little in common and without the various resources needed to create an energetic new society. Naipaul is interested in what happens to individual, in colonial ethos in the psychology of circumscribed individuals. His concern is mainly with how men and women respond and react to their environment and how in doing so they project a sense of themselves. Naipaul's early fiction is centred on the Indian community, it is apparent from his non-fictions that he saw the other ethnic groups in similar situation.

The displaced Indian finds himself in a complicated colonial situation where the act of living is precarious and uncertain and the individual is assailed constantly by the worst fear of being left behind. Naipaul referring to the Indian in Trinidad writes in *Middle Passage*:

> [...] a peasant minded, money minded community spiritually static because cut off from its roots, its religion reduced to rites without philosophy, set in a materialistic society, a combination of historical accidents and national temperament has turned the Trinidad Indian into the complete colonial.

The loss of roots in Indian culture implies deritualisation and eventually loss of its content. The Hindu society in Trinidad and elsewhere in West Indies is reduced to caricature and is confined to the externals of social life. The cultural displacement of the West Indian East Indian implies his intellectual rejection of Indian ways and morals. The Indian, like the other groups in a colonial society becomes a 'mimic man,' who looks down upon his own community and aspires to achieve the glory and the glitter of colonial culture. But try as he might his persistence in the sub-conscious reflexes of personality cannot be eradicated by his Western way of thoughts. The resulting conflict leads on the one hand, to an ironic stance towards West Indian moral and manner, while on the other it takes one to the brink of terrifying perception as an unaccommodated East Indian. The Africans and Creole show a greater capacity for accommodation and adjustment in terms of their environment, whereas the Indian is incapable of the same resilience and spontaneity. The difference in origin and background results in conspicuous gaps between the two sub-cultures, the process of fusion and conflict between the two communities. When people speak of the race problem in Trinidad they do not mean Negro-white problem. They mean the Negro-Indian rivalry, stated Naipaul in his book *Middle Passage.*

In his novels he depicts societies and individuals as they are affected by the decay and disorder prevalent in their culture. The sense of being abandoned, makes dereliction become increasingly acute in the individual as he tries to achieve success and recognition and identity in a pluralistic, post-colonial ruthlessly competitive culture. Given the society which he inhabit he lives under great stress and tension, painfully aware of personal failures, and fearing the loss of status and identity. Mr Biswas is the saga of Indian life in the Caribbes, the career of Mr Biswas in roughing out the obstinate substance of life in the West Indies is a testimony to an inheritance which is lost but not overcome. One of the major works *A House for Mr Biswas* looks at the almost impossible task for Indian immigrants in the Caribbean of trying to integrate into society while keeping hold of their roots. Mr Biswas, a failed pundit, an accidental journalist, one of fictions enduring citizen is an idea personified with lots of ancestral inputs. The tragic-comic evolution who is genetically modelled after Naipaul's father, is an essay in the existential grammar of the colonial citizen with no eversized angst. The book traces a life from the isolated, totally rural community of the first decade of the 20th century through its gradual contact with a larger society, culminating for Mr Biswas in his rise to becoming a reporter and house owner in urban multi racial Port of Spain. The later part of the novel, is concerned with the education of children, which allows Mr Biswas's son to earn a scholarship to study in England. If the novel is a success story of immigrants' life and New World assimilation, it also records the failure of Hindu culture to survive in the West Indies. It is a study of the confusion in Hindu society in Trinidad, both the ossification of a culture into rituals and the loss of traditional culture within a multi-racial society. In Mr Biswas Naipaul explores the tension of an individual caught in such a situation through a series of powerful and evocative metaphors.

The story of Biswas's career from being a fatherless, homeless child of six to becoming a father of four, established in a house of his own at the time of his death, is a story not only of Trinidadian born Indian, Mohan Biswas, but also the social history of the Indian community in Trinidad and by extension in the West Indies.

A House for Mr Biswas subsumes the world already outlined in the preceding books and developed fully the themes developed in them. Mohan Biswas is a more complex version of Ganesh in *The Mystic Masseur*. The restlessness that plagues Biswas, his dissatisfaction with his lot and the undefined longing to make a dent in the world, to be acknowledged, to overcome the limitation imposed on him by his circumstances are qualities present in Ganesh too. Ganesh's way out of the problem of identity for the Indians in Trinidad is to turn his back completely on his Indian past-become, G. Ramsay Muir from Pandit Ganesh Ramsurmair. Biswas too moves away from Hindu past but he is unable to cut himself off completely without repudiating his name or his religion he concentrates on the task of making a place for himself in the Creole World.

In the background of the story of Mr Biswas's transition from the isolated rural India community of Parrot Trace, where he was born to 'Miguel Street world of Port of Spain Naipaul has recorded the slow but relentless erosion of the Hindu social order in Trinidad. In Parrot Trace the first indentured labourer seems to have established a community life that appears to be no different from that of an Indian village. In *The Middle Passage* Naipaul describes:

> Living by themselves in villages, the Indians were able to have a complete community life. It was a world eaten up with jealousies and family feuds and village feuds,

> but it was world of its own a community within the colonial society, without responsibility, with authority doubly and trebly removed. (88-89)

It was here that Mohan Biswas was born and grew. His birth and childhood are besieged by bad omens, and the local pundits shake their empty head over his prospects. His childhood unfolds a series of daydreams punctuated by sores, illness, occasional brief moments of glory when his Brahmin status makes him desirable to flesh out ceremony or ritual, moments which only serve to underline the unreal nature of caste and custom in this society. Referring to one such occasion Naipaul comments "[...] as soon as the ceremony was over and he had taken his gift of money and cloth and left, he became once more only a labourer's son [...]. And throughout life his position was like that" (97).

Naipaul, though born in orthodox Hindu family of immigrants, describes himself as a born unbeliever. Religious ceremonies within the family remained meaningless, as he was neither taught nor sought to know their significance while remaining ignorant, he seems to have absorbed a certain supporting philosophy. But his writing show his Hindu background has in subtle, subterranean way ingrained itself in his sensibility, it shocks him with its disregard for individual dignity, fatalism, mystical retreat from reality, its lack of energy and preference for myths.

Mohan Biswas, like his creator, grows up with little attachment to the Hindu way of life. When sent to be trained as a pundit at Jairam's he performs the ritual without feeling. The Hindu rituals have become disagreeable incomprehensible "he copied out Sanskrit verses he couldn't understand" (52) at Hanuman House the deities seem unsightly and the Hindi books ungainly. This is the predicament of a divided cultural heritage. Biswas's roots are in the Hindu culture, it is infused in his blood yet, later he is considered an atheist and rebel.

Mr Biswas's Brahmin status meeting the Tulsi needs, is quickly bullied into marriage with one of the daughters and joins the Tulsi circus at Hanuman House. Mr Biswas feels trapped when he falls into the clutches of Tulsidom, for Naipaul depicts Hanuman House as a symbol of traditionalism, rigidity, cultural infallibility ritual duty, hierarchy and communal life. Mr Biswas is aware in an undefined way that by becoming part of the Tulsi household he had sacrificed his life and his future. The great rambling Tulsi household, ill defined yet curiously hierarchical eclectic, in religious practice, yet noisily pious; generous within limits yet unrelenting in its demand, is a single comprehensive brilliantly evoked metaphor for the traditional Indian community. The entry of Mr Biswas into the Tulsi household creates a disturbance because his ideas are different. He had spent his childhood in an environment more liberal than the one which prevailed at Hanuman House. He was a descendant from hut dwelling peasants, there was no single family house to keep all the members to live together. Even that house had been sold after his grandparents' death, and he began his journey early in life. He had experienced comparative cosmopolitanism at school experienced the rigid discipline imposed on him by Pandit Jairam, becomes a sign painter through the contact of a christian friend Alec. He was taught by Mr Lal, a convert Christian and contact with Bhandat and his two sons who had been leading an un-Hindu sex life. Hence it is not surprising that Mr Biswas finds himself out of place in Hanuman House. He dealt a blow to the old Hindu culture at Hanuman House. Against this world Biswas hurls a stream of revolutionary ideas.

Described as ambitious in an undirected way, throughout Mr Biswas has vague ambition to rise in life. The Tulsis are proud of conformity among its members, Biswas finds pleasure in asserting his own individuality. He has an inherent love of independence. He cannot stand a future of subjection to the Tulsis, and of attendance at their emporium and on their estates. He differentiates himself by speaking Creole English at Hanuman House while other speak Hindi. He ridicules Hari, the symbol of religious reference, he mocks at the young Tulsi sons by calling them 'Gods.' To the utter disgust of the entire household he throws food upon the head of one of the Gods. He openly disapproves Tulsi and her policies, challenges their religious belief and openly preaches the progressive and reformist idea of Arya Samaj.

Mr Biswas does not revolt against established customs because of social or political beliefs. His revolt is against any value system which denies the intrinsic importance of man, denies freedom and dignity. Biswas's heroic struggle to attain dignity and fulfil his aspirations, as reflected in his desire to own a house becomes an allegory of the attempt to emancipate oneself from colonial, determinist dependence. To him a house, is not simply where one lives. It is one's identity—national, cultural and spiritual.

Slavery, colonialism and war, have contributed to make this century and the last a century of the homeless. The more endemic the experience, of deracination the more magical the word 'home' has become. It becomes a symbol of all that has been lost, of ancient certainties of faith of security. In the present century, the exile far from being a solitary figure has become the type of modern man. It is this world-wide crisis that Naipaul addresses to. He has no comforting message, only the bleak knowledge that in todays rapidly changing world the yearning for 'home' can never be more than an unfulfilled ache—but at least Mr Biswas towards the end of his life dies in possession if only a caricature of his dream of responsibility, and freedom, a house shamelessly and cumingly jerry-built foisted on him by deception, one remains deeply aware of the heroism and importance of his struggle and what it represents. Penniless, months of illness and despair, a wife and four children, dying at the age of 46 in his irretrievably mortgaged house, yet he is struck again and again "by the wonder of being in his own house, the audacity of it, to walk into his own front gate, to bar entry to whoever he wishes, to close his doors and windows every night, to hear no noise except those of his family [...]. How terrible it would have been, at this time, to be without it, to have died among the Tulsis, amid the squalor of that large, disintegrating and indifferent family, worse, to have lived without even attempting to lay claim to one's portion of the earth, to have lived and died as one who had been born, unnecessary and unaccommodated" (4). The substance of the novel has to do with the transformation of Mr Biswas, a slave to place, history and biography, into a free man, the sign and realisation of that emancipation being his House.

But the old Hindu culture as typified by the Tulsi clan is by no means sacrosanct or inviolable. In the course of the novel one see the way in which the Western-oriented Creole culture of Trinidad undermines and corrodes Hindu traditional customs and beliefs. The cultural confrontation between the Hindu ideals and Western impact leads to a change of attitudes on the part of the Indian settlers and also to a psychological bewilderment among them. Mr Biswas is not the only disruptive influence. The Tulsi clan would have been influenced by Western culture even if there had been no Mr Biswas. The two 'Gods' Shekhar and Owad rebel against the orthodox Hindu custom. Shekhar Educated at Roman Catholic college, refuses to marry the girl chosen by his family, instead marries a Christian girl, Owad decides to go abroad to study medicine, returns completely westernised. He too marries a Christian, who wears only European clothes and speaks Spanish. The Western culture sets in the disintegration of the Tulsi family. Naipaul account of the Tulsi clan at Short Hills depicts the cultural transplantation.

The Westernization becomes all the more apparent when children speak English at home instead of Hindi, later they say they can understand but cannot speak Hindi, 'Ma,' 'Mai,' 'Bap' have been substituted by 'Daddy' and 'Mummy.' Modern status symbols—car—are acquired. European food is preferred. Food baskets, picnics, seaside holidays become part of life. Mother India is still the sustaining dream of the old. Hindus who lay for cultural stability, the young are caught in strong cultural cross currents and cease to dream of returning home. The first generation settlers see themselves as the last defenders of the old, pure and noble Hindu culture.

Geographical uprooting and the result of culture contact is an important thing. Each uprooting brings a further weakening of traditional forces. Yet the old culture though invaded by a new and alien one is not quite swamped. Naipaul's vision of Trinidad Hindus seems to be balanced. If Mr Biswas vigorously claims independence and individuality and while he denounces the old Hindu Code which tends to destroy, Biswas does accept the positive ones—it provides security, ensures financial and psychological support at times of need. Mr Biswas remains tied to the Tulsi world, despite his wishes, he remains an offshoot of those values, aberrant, but still rooted in the same stock. In a way he is a representative figure caught between the security of the old world and the possibilities of a new, a man trapped in the transitional phase between two worlds. Naipaul whose family has been influential in Trinidadian politics and Indian cultural movements has often written of the lack of the future of East Indian community in the Caribbeans. Such despair is behind the social comedy of *The Mystic Masseur* (1951) and the *Suffrage of Elvira* (58). The life of Pandit Ganesh in *The Mystic Masseur* is a humorous success story during the social and political change, but it also illustrates a rapid deterioration of Hindu culture, which finds culminating in *A House for Mr Biswas.* Religious practices have become Creolised, a confused stew of various beliefs, symbols and practices.

WORKS CITED

Naipaul, V.S. *A House for Mr Biswas.* London: Andre Deutsch, 1961.

——. *The Middle Passage.* London: Andre Deutsch, 1962.

3

Search for Identity: Ideology and Social Conflict in V.S. Naipaul's *A House for Mr Biswas*

PRAKASH CHANDRA PRADHAN

I

Any literary piece, especially a fictional text, represents a world of reality. Hence a fictional text "can only be properly understood within a larger framework of social reality" (Forgacs 167). A society consists of a lot of contradictions. Different social groups/classes have different world-views and ideologies. The ideologies of the individuals and their social origins/backgrounds play significant roles in relation to different social institutions such as religion, marriage and family. The structure of a fiction either reflects such contradictions (Lukacs) or distorts such ideas and ideologies. The term 'ideology' "generally conveys the sense of a collective representation of ideas and experience as opposed to the material reality on which experience is based" (Forgacs 169). The different classes, according to Marxist critics, represent different ideologies and conflicting social relations. Due to difference in ideologies, there are conflicts between higher classes and working classes—the bosses and the workers (Lukacs). Machery's production model questions the values ascribed to literature in society (1978). By bringing out a contrast between ideology and theory, Machery says that fiction stands between ideology and theory. However Goldmann views that great literary works are the coherent expressions of world-views, which are privileged forms of ideology (1975). These are global rather than partial ones. Hence he is stressing on the coherence with which ideology can be given shape in literature. On the other hand, Machery "views an ideology as sufficient unto itself in the practical world but radically undermines when it enters a literary text, when it leaves gaps that the critic has to explain" (Forgacs 169). Raymond Williams rightly regards "literature as a specializing social and historical category" (Williams 53). Hence literary criticism is now regarded as "practices in which ideological norms and established value judgments about literature and the world are deeply ingrained" (Forgacs 200-01). In the above context, the study of a fictional text can be more fruitful in bringing out the socio-cultural conflicts of the fictional world. V.S. Naipaul's exploration of the colonial set-up in *A House for Mr Biswas* is an analysis of the social conflicts of the colonial Hindu society of Trinidad which is rotten by contradictions, myths and rituals. This paper, therefore, tries to establish how an individual, more specifically, the protagonist, Mr Mohan Biswas, struggles hard in search of an identity for himself in a malignant, dogmatic society of conservative ideas and ideologies.

A House for Mr Biswas delineates the colonial situation at Trinidad around the time of World War II. The colonial set-up has been analyzed quite comprehensively. Mr Biswas, the protagonist has been set against the conventional and customary conservative Hindu ideas and ideology. He is completely isolated in a crowd and the lone fighter against the conservative system filled with rotten myths, customs and rituals. The inherent power of these narrow ideas of the Hindu community has been instrumental for inciting the spirit of rebellion in Mr Biswas. This man stands lonely against these predominant forces of dogmatism and mechanical habits. This happens so because he wants to liberate himself from the cruel narrow ideas and ideologies of the so-called Brahmin socio-cultural system and tries to establish his own identity in the society.

Mr Biswas has progressive ideas in contrast to sterile, obsolete customs and conventions in the colonial Hindu society of Trinidad. He has a clear thinking against the defective systems of Hindu community. In order to go on with the crusade against the unreasonable thinking of the smug, rotten colonial Hindu society, V.S. Naipaul weaves such a plot in the novel that Mr Biswas is married to Shama, a gullible, little-educated, immature daughter of the Tulsis. The Tulsis represent the then existent, narrow, irrelevant, unreasonable, dogmatic beliefs, customs and rituals of Trinidad Hindu colonial society. They are, so to say, the devoted pious Brahmins who stick to the unfounded conventions of Hindu cultural system. They also belong to the landed aristocracy in the Hindu community. Mr Biswas, being married to a simpleton of such a community, is but to undergo a lot of suffering as there are so much cultural clashes and social conflicts. It happens so because he belongs to a labourers' class. He inherits the "stamp of labour" from his father, who leaves no property to his family at his death. His family becomes houseless and penniless after his death. That is why the shabby treatment to Mr Biswas from his in-laws due to his inconvenient circumstances of poverty and compulsions brings a lot of torture and agony in him. His suffering is that of a penniless individual struggling to possess a minimum basic necessity in the form of a house. As such Naipaul explores the struggle of a working class individual to have his own house at least before his death. "Possessing a house" is rather symbolic of having an identity of one's own in the society.

II

Mr Biswas was not naturally rebellious. Rebellion was rather thrust on him by the predominant forces of ritual, myth and custom. His rebellion was significantly crucial in the plot of the novel. At first he was destined to become a *Pundit* and he could not become so because he rejected the rituals, customs and false notions when he was learning the skills from Pundit Jairam to be a *Pundit* in his childhood. From the time of his birth, he was thought to be "inauspicious" for the family because he had "an unlucky sneeze," "a sixth finger" and "good but wide teeth" (Naipaul 16). Because of spaces between his teeth, he would be "a lecher, a spendthrift and a liar" (Naipaul 16). Since the boy was born with inauspicious signs, the father was not to see him "in the flesh" for twenty-one days. On the other hand, he was to see him through a brass plate filled with coconut oil. If the father was not allowed to see the boy for twenty-one days, "much evil will be mitigated" (Naipaul 16). In truth the boy would eat his family. Pundit Sitaram predicted not only these things; he also warned that the boy should have been kept away from "Tree and water." By the cruel design of destiny it so happened that Raghu, Mr Biswas's father died when he was diving in the water to search for Mr Biswas and Dhari's calf. After his death, the family split at "Parrot Traace" because Pratap and Prasad, his elder brothers were sent to work at "Felicity" in the sugarcane estate with some relations. Dehuti was sent to work as a maid at Tara's House; and Mr Biswas along with his mother was to live at "Tara's bounty [...] in a back trace far from Main Road" (40) at Pagotes. Dhari's conspiracy made Mr Biswas practically a houseless wanderer in search of a house throughout his life as Bipti, Mr Biswas's mother and widow, was to sell the "hut and the land" to Dhari at a very very unreasonably low price. The untold miseries of a poor labourer's son are obvious in the following description:

> And so Mr Biswas came to leave the only house to which he had some right. For the next thirty-five years, he was to be a wanderer with no place he could call his own with no family except that which he was to attempt to create out of the engulfing world of the Tulsis. For with his mother's parents dead, his father dead, his brothers on the estate at Felicity, Dehuti as a servant at Tara's house and himself rapidly growing away from Bipti, who broken, became increasingly useless and impenetrable, it seemed to him that he was really quite alone. (40)

So Mr Biswas was the lone fighter against the malignant forces of the society, against the cruelty and callousness of the rich class who possessed property. A houseless man had no privacy. He was destined to live as if he had no private life of his own. He was to live in barracks. His doors and windows could not be closed in the night because he had to share the place of his residence with others. After being a great failure to be a *Pundit* he returned home to his mother at Tara's house. He reentered his studies with Lal, the teacher and went on learning sign-painting. He was also engaged with Bhandat's rum shop where he was severely beaten and returned to his mother at Pagote. Now the fatherless child wandered "for a job, for a house." On his way he met Ramchand, Dehuti's husband who helped him and Mr Biswas went to Hanuman house at Arwacas where he was engaged in sign-painting at Tulsi Store and loved Shama, the youngest daughter of the Tulsis. The Tulsis were famous among the Hindus as a "Pious, conservative, landowning family' (81). Hanuman House, the dwelling unit of the Tulsis represented all these conservative, outdated, dogmatic beliefs and customs. After the death of Mr Tulsi, Mr Seth was representing the Tulsis in expanding their empire. The weakness of Mr Biswas for Shama was an opportunity for Mrs Tulsi and Mr Seth to trap him to include as a member of the Tulsi family. To Mr Biswas it seemed that "the world was too small, the Tulsi family too large. He felt trapped" (91). Mrs Tulsi and Mr Seth were successful in trapping Mr Biswas in marriage with Shama, with "no house, no money, no dowry" (96). Just after the notice of the Registrar for marriage, Mr Seth and Mrs Tulsi were simply unapproachable. Mr Biswas had thought of being helped by the Tulsis. But it was not the case. "Mr Biswas had no money or passion. He was expected to become a Tulsi [...]. At once he rebelled" (97). Mr Biswas was expected to live in the Tulsi House just like his other co-brothers-in-law who were married to other Tulsi daughters, namely Chinta, Sushila and so on.

It was rather strange that Mr Biswas remained lonely in the overcrowded Tulsi house and revolted against the system. There were a lot of conflicts between Mr Biswas and Shama, who represented her mother with narrow, conservative ideas and dogmatic beliefs of the Tulsi family. The daughters had no real position in the Tulsi family. They were to live there as second class citizens whereas Mrs Tulsi, Mr Seth and the "two gods," Mr Shekhar and Owad, Mr Tulsi's sons were to live very comfortably with privilege and luxury. Mrs Tulsi was to live at a special room, namely "The Rose Room" and the "two gods" were to live at "The Blue Room." For Mr Biswas's revolt, he was shunted to move to "The Chase" as he could not be fitted into the Tulsi set-up. Because of his ideas and ideology, there was a great disruption in the Tulsi family. That is why Seth remarked, "This was a nice united family before you come, you better go away before you do any more mischief and I have to lay my hand on you" (141).

This is the reason why Mr Biswas left Hanuman House for "The Chase," the shop by which time Shama was pregnant. They were to start their life afresh there. The Chase was a long, struggling settlement of mud huts in the heart of the sugarcane area, which was absolutely remote. Few people from outside went to "The Chase" as communication was completely worse. Since it was not a profitable place for the Tulsis, so Mr Biswas was shunted to this place. Mostly the workers "in the sugarcane estate" and "on the roads" were living there. Naipaul comments on this unattractive place: "The world beyond the sugarcane fields was remote and the village was linked to it only by villagers' carts and bicycles, wholesalers' vans and lorries and an occasional private motor bus that runs to no timetable and along no fixed route." The place, therefore, disappointed Mr Biswas. He felt very lonely and disgusted. Even though he wanted to comfort Shama, he needed to be comforted. It was a very "frightening place" for him. Life, here, was quite different from Hanuman House which was "noisy with activity." Here Naipaul writes: "[...] Hanuman House would be warm and noisy with activity. Here he was afraid to disturb the silence, afraid to open the door of the shop, to step into the light" (145).

To him life seemed unreal here. He thought of a different life. As such The Chase did not give him any comfort. It did not fulfil his wishes: "Real life was to begin for them soon. and elsewhere. The Chase was a pause, a preparation" (147). In this rural area, people lived in a "wife-beating society" though the wives felt glorified by being beaten by their husbands. Both of them tried to build a house very soon. Shama was quite unhappy in this new place. So she could persuade to arrange a "House Blessing Party" there at "The Chase" and all her relations of Hanuman House were invited. But Mr Biswas "found himself a stranger in his own yard. But was it his own?" It was rather the Tulsi shop and people never knew much about Mr Biswas. He had no identity. Shama, the representative of Mr Tulsi was aware of living like a Tulsi. To her the process of life should have the established emotions: "Joy at a birth or a marriage, distress during illness or hardship, grief at death" (160). Life must have this established sensations in order to be full. They had their first child born and Shama was to live at Hanuman House for that reason. Mr Biswas was to suffer a lot and felt himself alienated in the Tulsi organization. He now lived alone at The Chase. He therefore felt that "Hanuman House was a world more real than The Chase" although he lived at The Chase for six years.

Mr Biswas, being fed up at "The Chase" and without being able to cope with "The Tulsis at Hanuman House," was sent to Green Vale as a driver and supervisor of the workers of the Tulsi estate. He was given an end room. By now he had four children and Shama alongwith the children were living at Hanuman House. That is why he wanted to build a house of his own. Unless he "started his house now he never would. His children would stay at Hanuman House. He would remain in the barrack room, and nothing would arrest his descent into the void" (237). Hence he thought of borrowing money from Tara, but failed to get that. Finally he decided to start his house with immediate effect with a meagre amount of hundred dollars. The workers' grudge against Mr Seth was gradually turning towards Mr Biswas. By now his son, Anand, was living with him. Mr Biswas was suffering from mental agony as he was unable to build his own house. By this time the dog, Tarzan was dead. Surprisingly the house was under collapse due to heavy rain and storm. Lightning, thunder and rain helped the house to collapse fully:

> Lightning, thunder, the rain on the roof and walls; the loose iron sheet; the wind pushing against the house, pausing and pushing again [...]. But Mr Biswas was very muttered on the bed, and the rain and the wind swept through the room with unnecessary strength and forced open the door to the drawing room, wall-less, floorless of the house, Mr Biswas had built. (292)

After the collapse of Mr Biswas's house he was completely shaken. There was the breakdown of his mental state. Thus he was taken to the Hanuman House for treatment by a doctor. His revolt against the established order had brought for him a lot of sufferings. That is how he was now in a dilemma if he would surrender to this established order (299).

III

Mr Biswas's illness lasted for a longer period. That is why his brothers and brother-in-law, Ramchand came to see him. Lying in the room he was thinking of his past life and he was also thinking about his future. He felt as if he were dead. He was making an analysis about the world:

> He was going out into the world, to test it for its power to frighten. The past was counterfeit, a series of cheating accidents. Real life and its especial sweetness awaited, he was still beginning [...]. The spasm of terror did not come. The knots of fear were still in his stomach, but they were so subdued he knew he could ignore them. The world had been restored to him. (305)

Mr Biswas was thus gathering his internal resources and strength to meet the challenges of life in future. Through his distress, he was not completely swayed by disappointment. On the other hand, he was preparing himself to do his assignments stored for him in *The Sentinel.* He left Hanuman House for Port of Spain after his illness. He lived with his sister, Dehuti and searched for a job and was appointed as a sign-painter for *The Sentinel.* Mr Brunett was very much impressed with his writing, "Amazing Scenes." However before being paid any salary, he was to work without pay: "A chance encounter had led him to sign-writing. Sign-writing had taken him to Hanuman House and the Tulsis. Sign-writing found him a place on *The Sentinel.* And neither for the Tulsi Store signs nor for these at *The Sentinel* was he paid" (323).

In course of time Mr Biswas was regarded as the best reporter of *The Sentinel* for which he was appointed and his salary was fixed at 50 dollars a month. His name was published everyday on the paper for his writings. As a consequence the Tulsis were much more impressed. Thereafter a reconciliation was brought about and Mr Biswas had a victory for his struggle. Shama and Mr Biswas along with their children stayed with Mrs Tulsi for some days. After a few days Owad went abroad to study Medical Sciences and hence Mrs Tulsi returned to Arwaca as she had no further business in Port of Spain. By this time Mr Biswas was writing a column, namely "I am Trinidad's Most Evil Man." In the meanwhile there was a lot of disturbance at Hanuman House: "Relations between the sisters and Shekhar's wife (Dorothy) had never been easy" (365). Because of '*views-oriented*' news, there was change of guard in *The Sentinel* and Mr Brunett, the editor departed. Due to new regime, '*facts-oriented*' features were published in *The Sentinel* and Mr Biswas was shifted to '*Sunday Magazine.*' There was also serious misunderstanding of Mr Seth with the Tulsis. Now the Tulsis decided to move to Shorthills after the misunderstanding.

Mr Biswas was now in a better situation and he also moved to Shorthills because "for him Shorthills was an adventure, an interlude. His job made him independent of the Tulsis; and Shorthills was an insurance against the sack" (402). He was apprehensive of the sack in case of problems in the new regime in *The Sentinel.* Shorthills brought many new problems for the Tulsis. For Tulsi children's education, a car was bought to take the children to the Port of Spain for school. Mr Biswas had now shifted all his ambitions towards Anand, his son. The death of Hari as well as Padma was another great shock in the Tulsi family. Bipti, Mr Biswas's mother came to Mr Biswas even though he had not yet a house of his own. As too many people were living together at Hanuman House, there were quarrels: quarrels between Biswas and Govind, between children, between Anand and Owad. Now Mr Biswas was concentrating on "Anand's future, his career closed. Change had come over him without his knowing" (494). Mr Biswas had now much conflict in himself when he thought of the Tulsi family philosophy: "Catch and trap and throw him in a coal barrel." In the meanwhile Mrs Tulsi was ill and she suggested Mr Biswas to leave the house for Owad because it was his father's house. Because of continuous quarrel between Owad and Anand, Mr Biswas was to take a final decision to leave the house. The children also wanted to leave the Tulsi family.

That is why Mr Biswas decided to purchase a house by incurring a debt of five thousand and two hundred dollars. In the meanwhile, Anand went to England for higher studies after getting a scholarship. Savi, his daughter also went abroad to study after getting a scholarship. After some days, Mr Biswas was ill for a month. "After illness Mr Biswas came to his own house and lived quite satisfactorily" (587). The second illness lasted for more than three months. The children were informed about that. Notice was issued to him from *The Sentinel.* Savi came back from abroad, but Anand did not turn up. Mr Biswas, the journalist now died and Shama was to live with her children without a single thought of going back to the Tulsis. Thus Mr Biswas had a victory. First, his wife and children were liberated from the moorings of Tulsi conservative set-up. Secondly Shama gathered courage and strength to live all alone in a practical world. Thirdly Mr Biswas died in his own house with full of privacy and satisfaction.

IV

A House for Mr Biswas is, therefore, a fictional text which basically explores the conflicting ideologies and social contradictions of different classes and communities, more specifically the conflicts between the landed aristocracy and the working class. In this novel Mohan Biswas represents the 'consciousness of dignity of a man' despite his poverty. His great obsession with establishment of his own identity brings out a superb conflict with conservative ideas of Tulsi set-up. This conflict starts soon after Mohan's marriage with Shama, the youngest daughter of the Tulsis. Hence the origin of conflict is based on relationship and the existing contradictions in ideologies of the individuals and classes in the society. Althusser views that "Ideology is a Representation of the Imaginary Relationship of Individuals to their Real Conditions of Existence" (87). He further writes: "What is represented in ideology is therefore not the system of the real relations which govern the existence of individuals, but the imaginary relation of these individuals in which they live" (89). Bakhtin rightly argues that literature's relation to reading is both positive and coherent: Literature and reality are of the same order which is ideological. However, the special qualities of literature have a "distancing effect on the ideologies that it represents" (Jefferson 43).

As such literature allows the reader to become aware of them as ideologies. Although a literary piece, specifically a fictional text, contains social structures and ideologies in it, it does not represent absolute social reality. Often a fictional text not only reflects the social reality, it also distorts the existing systems and value patterns in the society and brings out new conflicts to the fictional world. In *A House for Mr Biswas,* Naipaul attempts a subtle and comprehensive analysis of the colonial situation in Trinidad through his fine imagination and sensibility. This marvellous prose epic finally attains a tragic grandeur despite the superb comic insight throughout. Mohan Biswas's love for natural human liberty and individuality inspire him to fight against the lifeless, rotten rituals, myths and customs of a degenerated Brahmin cultural system represented by The Tulsis in the novel. Despite his marriage into the Tulsi family through Shama, he remains an outsider and does not follow the family in their habitual devotions. He does not submit and remains grand in his stature in the different contexts and situations in the novel whenever he takes a solitary stand against the mechanical, stereotyped and obsolete Tulsi ideas and ideologies.

WORKS CITED

Abrams, M.H. "Modern Theories of Literature and Criticism." *A Glossary of Literary Terms.* 6th ed. Bangalore: Prism Books Pvt. Ltd., 1993, 223-86.

Althusser, Louis. "Ideology and Ideological State Apparatus." 1970. *Contemporary Critical Theory.* Ed. Dan Lartimer. Harcourt Brace Jovanvich, 1989, 60-102.

Berger, Peter and Thomas Luckman. *The Social Construction of Reality.* Harmondsworth: Penguin, 1972.

Forgacs, David. "Marxist Literary Theories." 1982. *Modern Literary Theory: A Comparative Introduction.* 2nd ed. Ed. Ann Jefferson and David Robey. London: B.T. Batsford Ltd., 1986, 166-203.

Goldmann, Lucien. *Towards a Sociology of the Novel.* London: 1975 (tr. From *pour une sociologic du roman,* Paris: 1964).

Jefferson, Ann and David Robey (eds.). *Modern Literary Theory: A Comparative Introduction.* 1982. London: B.T. Batsford Ltd., 1986.

Laitimer, Dan. *Contemporary Critical Theory.* Harcourt Brace: Jovanvich Inc., 1989.

Lukacs, Georg. *The Meaning of Contemporary Realism.* London: 1963 (tr. From *wider den missverstandenen Realismus,* Hamburg: 1958).

Machery, Pierre. *A Theory of Literary Production.* London: 1978 (tr. From *pour une thorie de la production literaire,* Paris: 1966).

Naipaul, V.S. *A House for Mr Biswas.* Penguin: 1969. Reprint 1992.

Williams, Raymond. *Marxism and Literature.* Oxford: 1977.

4

Identity Crisis in V.S. Naipaul's *A House for Mr Biswas*

AMAR NATH PRASAD

V.S. Naipaul's *A House for Mr Biswas* is a beautiful work which deals with the theme of isolation, frustration and negation in a colonized society—a society that turns cruel and callous to the aspiration of the protagonist, Mr Mohan Biswas. The book, as we shall see, also deals with a number of physical or spiritual maladies *e.g.*, the clash of cultures between the old and the new in a multi racial society; a quest for identity in a conservative framework and above all, the protagonist's dry and monotonous journey full of many jerks and jolts. In technique and style the novel seems to conform to the metaphoric structure, though a bit wanting in proper structural unification as we see in James Joyce's masterpiece, *The Portrait of an Artist as a Young Man*. Like any other great novelists he tries his best to weave his material through the colourful threads of art and beauty, symbols and images, irony and pathos. To him, ideas are more important than plot. He admits: "I preferred the natural way of describing how, at different stages as one's life capacities, one looked at one's place in the world. And one does this through the series of narratives and the linking of themes and emotions."[1]

The primary business of V.S. Naipaul as a novelist is to project carefully the complex fate of individuals, societies and cultures. To him, fiction is an instrument of analysis. Perhaps this is why most of his novels revolved round the recurring themes of colonial psychosis, individual's search for identity and clash of culture. Naipaul's fiction, as

Dr R.A. Singh thinks, acquires "three dimensional structure—historical, social and psychological."[2]

Almost all the works of V.S. Naipaul have a clear-cut influence on Indian life and culture. His union background gives him the multiple experience of a marginalised culture. He uses such words and phrases, and creates such a situation that easily take the reader back to Indian myths and tradition, culture and civilization. Naipaul takes a very keen interest in a colonial ethos. Sometimes he becomes autobiographical in his approach. The writer himself had to face many ups and downs in order to assert his identity in a disinherited tradition. He admits: "Living in a borrowed culture, the west Indian, more than most, needs writers to tell him who he is and where he stands."[3] It is this cultural disinheritance that made Naipaul a great writer of commonwealth literature. His anger, frustration and futility sprung from his sense of disinheritance. As a matter of fact Naipaul's secret of his secret art lies not in his personal attachment to the establishment—individual, tradition, culture, but in his creative detachment beyond geography, history and ethnicity. In this respect he is a bit different from his contemporary west Indian writers like Mill Moltzer, George Lamming and Wilson Harris. Naipaul has tried his best to project in his novels a sustaining course for all those who are rootless or homeless. Keith Garebian rightly holds the view: "Naipaul explores landscapes in order to provide characters with a real home, a true place of belonging so that they will not continue to be homeless wanderers, unsure of themselves and their fates. But the mythology of the land is tinged with embarrassment, nervousness, hysteria and pessimism, all products in some way of Naipaul's own history as a colonial with an ambiguous identity."[4]

It is to be noted that the theme of identity crisis rings the note of almost all the major works of Naipaul. The characters portrayed in his world are mostly rural and poor. They have to undergo a lot of trials and tribulations, ups and downs. They long for a free and fair existence but unfortunately they are not able to cross the boundary of the colonial society. *A House for Mr Biswas* gives such characters wings to fly freely in the open sky and assert their own existence. *The Middle Passage* records the author's impressions of colonial society in the West Indies and South Africa. *An Area of Darkness* is a reflective of semi-autobiographical account of a year in India. *India: a Wounded Civilization* is an extend studies of the author about the miseries and sufferings of the general mass of India. This account shows the author's sympathetic attitude towards the downtrodden. *The Mimic Men* is the story of Ralph Singh, a disgraced colonial minister exiled from the Caribbean island of his birth. When he comes to politics he finds himself cut up in the upheaval of empire. In other words, he was badly enmeshed in the turmoil of two large events.

A House for Mr Biswas is a well-known work by V.S. Naipaul. It deals with the story of Mr Mohun Biswas, who is born in the village of Trinidad at the hour of midnight, an auspicious hour in that country. He is predicted by the pundit to be a lecher, a spendthrift and a liar. But this does not happen. Just after the birth of the protagonist, the family is split by the circumstances. His two brothers are also sent to some remote places for earning bread. Mr Biswas, along with his mother, goes to his sister Dehuti. He is admitted to the mission school where he learns mathematics and other things. Alec is his intimate friend. He also devotes his time in painting.

The second phase of Mr Biswas's life can be seen as an apprentice. He is kept with Pundit Jayaram, a Hindu priest. He learns a lot of things from Jayaram but unfortunately this relation does not last long. Mr Biswas was accused of theft of gifts. He was badly pulled up by the Pundit. He leaves his Guru in disappointment and goes to his Aunt Tara to find out employment and monetary help. Tara is highly sympathized with Biswas. She gets him employed in a rum shop run by her husband's brother, Bhandat, a man who was addicted to wine-drinking, and forgery. He always cheats his customers by giving them unmeasured drinks. One day Mr Biswas is charged by Bhandat of stealing one dollar from his pocket. So he turns Mr Biswas out of his shop.

One day when Mr Biswas was walking along the main road, he came across with Ramchand with whom his sister Dehuti had run away. Ramchand escorts Biswas to his sister. There he gets the job of a painter. It is only during Christmas days that he gets plenty of work. Though his mother tells him to get married but he refused to do so as he was not employed permanently. He goes to Hanuman House at Arwacas where he happens to meet Shama, the sixteen years old daughter of Mrs Tulsi of Tulsi Store. He falls in love with Shama and so their love turns into a marriage. Now Mr Biswas begins to live with his wife in the Hanuman House with other son-in-laws of Mrs Tulsi. Very soon he finds the place just the otherwise of his taste and temperament. But his marriage life does not prove to be successful. He suffers from the unbearable taunts and mental complexes due to the uncongenial family atmosphere. Shama always flings irony on Biswas and treats him like a prisoner and time and again retorts him. By this time Shama is pregnant. Mr Biswas has to sell his goods on credit to his customers. As a result, the shop is paralyzed. Shama delivers a female child, Savi and three years later a male child, Anand. Tulsi House appoints Mr Biswas an overseer at Green Vale on a payment of twenty-five dollars a month. But here too Mr Biswas is not satisfied with his work. During Christmas days he presents a doll's house to his female child Savi. This presentation shows his inner desire to have a house of his own. The house also suggests the sense of his freedom and security full of love and sympathy. So he starts making a house there. After completing the house (though half-house), he goes to live there where he feels at ease and fully relieved of his depression. But this does not exist long. He suffers from strange fears. In a dark rainy night he receives a mental shock in his incomplete house and is carried to the Hanuman House. After treatment, he gets the job of a Newspaper reporter in Port of Spain and brings his family in one of the houses of Tulsi family. Once again his life is revitalized when he gets a new government job as a Community Welfare Officer. He takes some money from Ajodha to build a house. He now owns a house and thus his long cherished dream for a house is fulfilled. But very soon misfortune knocks at his door. Ajodha's loan begins to multiply. The community welfare department is also abolished. He begins to suffer from the mental shock and depression. He dies at the age of forty-six.

One of the dominant themes which emerge from the reading of *A House for Mr Biswas* is the theme of the cultural clash—the difficulty of adjustment of the protagonist in Tulsidom, his constant yearning for a life of liberty from the Hanuman House. The ideals of Hanuman House is, to some extent, very near to Ayemenem House in Arundhati Roy's *The God of Small Things* where the male characters always prevail over the female ones; where conservatism and patriarchal domination rule the roost; where outsiders are rarely adjusted in patriarchal framework. This house can also be compared to *Wuthering Heights* of Emile Bronte where Heathcliff, like Mr Biswas, has to undergo many undeserved miseries and sufferings. The opening of the novel very well expresses the inner conflict going on in the mind of the main character. Naipaul observes: "Mr Biswas was forty-six, and had four children. He had no money. His wife Shama had no money. On the house in Sikkim Street Mr Biswas owed, and had been owing for four years three thousand dollars. The interest on this, at eight per cent, came to twenty dollars a month, the ground rent was ten dollars."[5]

Mr Biswas was trapped in the clutches of Tulsidom. He had his dream of his own house. The house of his dream is highly symbolic. It is an archetypal symbol, which connotes stability and permanence, something solid in life. It represents also Mr Biswas's partially successful attempt to escape from the ancient matriarchal order and medieval norms into a more western, private and candid state of life. Moureen Warner Lewis is of the opinion that in spite of the clash of culture in Tulsidom, Mr Biswas struggled for asserting his identity: "Into this apparent monolith of conversions, prejudices and conservatism, then, Mr Biswas barges. He openly disapproved of many of the Tulsi practices and policies. He even challenges their religious belief and associates with Hindus of another sect with whom the Tulsis disagree [...]. The religious ambiguity and syncretism and, in some case, even neglect of traditional religion, is one of the earliest aspects of cultural confrontation with which Naipaul deals in his novel. And he progressively shows the sometimes subtle, sometimes obvious, in which the western oriented Creole culture of Trinidad corrodes Hindu traditional customs and beliefs, and the shifting of attitudes and psychological bewilderment this produces."[6]

In brief the spirit of selfishness and rivalry was deeply rooted in the Hanuman House. But due to a highly disciplined system it was suppressed. This is why the members of the family are always seen flinging sarcasm and irony on any matter related to the protagonist. Mr Biswas felt silent pangs of restlessness in the company of the house. The house was nothing but a slave house. Gordon Rohlehr rightly remarks: "Hanuman House reveals itself not as a coherent reconstruction of the clan, but as a slave society, erected by Mrs Tulsi and Seth who need workers to help rebuild their tottering empire. They therefore exploit the homelessness and poverty of their fellow Hindus and reconstruct a mockery of the clan which functions only because they have so completely grasped the psychology of a slave system."[7] In other words, "the Tulsi family was just like the West Indies 'constructed of a vast' number of disparate families, gratuitously brought together by the economic need of a 'high caste' minority."[8] In this house men are needed for two reasons—husbands for Tulsi's daughters as well as labourers for the Tulsi's estates.

The status of women in the Hanuman House was very miserable. They have little real say in the affairs of the house. The Tulsi daughters of two generations ago had to abide by the rhythms and rituals of life. It is only on occasional funeral or on seasonal wedding parties that they get relief from the tedium of daily lives. In *The God of Small Things* we get the same attitude in the big 'Ayemenem House' where Ammu, the main female character performs the role of a tragic figure humiliated and insulted by her father, ill-treated and misbehaved by her husband. Naipaul is undoubtedly a writer of great worth who very well knows the art of blending both truth and beauty. Naipaul's world is the world of loneliness and homelessness set against a dry, sterile landscape. It is a world of "homeless nomadic migrants, making middle passages from Africa or India to the West Indies thence to England and back again, for, after three hundred years, there is no society and no system of values in which they can take root."[9] Against this crucial and critical background, the characters of Naipaul are seen struggling for permanence and stability—Mr Biswas's desire for a house, Mr Stones scheme for the aged and Ganesh Ramsumair's desire for education and religion.

It is interesting to note that Naipaul has developed his own conception about fiction. His approach to novel is a bit different from that of Conrad who seeks only to explain, to theorize and moralize about an event rather than to allow a situation to describe the happenings. Conrad is so much preoccupied with facts that there is a little room for the readers to enter into the action. Naipaul observes: "Conrad's value to me is that he is someone who sixty to seventy years ago meditated on my world, a world I recognize today. His achievement derives from the honesty which is part of his difficulty."[10] Naipaul views novel as a form no longer carries conviction; "And so the world we inhabit [...] goes by unexamined, made ordinary by the camera, unmediated on; and there is no one to awaken the sense of true wonder. This is perhaps a fair definition of the novelist's purpose, in all ages."[11] Naipaul has a very poor opinion about ostensibly objective kind of literature, a documentary approach to reality. He accepts a balanced human expression, which is the heart of a true artist. He is of the opinion that in art there must be a form, a metaphoric structure and the thought must be expressed through the medium of art and beauty. He believes in the theory of a camera, which exactly mirrors the reality. But he is dead against obscene photograph. He opines: "The violence some of us are resisting is not the violence which is a counter of a story-telling. It is the violence, which is clinical and documentary in intention and makes no statement beyond that of bodily pain and degradation. It is like the obscene photograph. It deals anonymously with anonymous flesh, quickened only by pleasure or pain; and this anonymity is a denial of art."[12]

Judged on the above conceptions, *A House for Mr Biswas* seems to be fully conforming to the ideals of the novelist. It has some fine symbolism and images, which weave the theme into the garland of art and beauty. The language comes as naturally as a rivulet comes from the mountain. The miseries and sufferings faced by Mr Biswas have natural conformity with the general human being placed in an alien land dominated by a colonized society; it is not the untold sufferings and thwarted desires imposed by the powerful Fate or Providence which is a dominant note of Hardy's novels. Rather it is just a natural process of a man's life, which is a fusion of both happiness and sorrow, rough and sublime.

To sum up, Naipaul's *A House for Mr Biswas* culminates the early phase of Naipaul's artistic development. The story of Mr Biswas is the general story of man. Tortured by communal pressures and threatened by an unstructured society, the protagonist is in constant suspension ever ready to assert his identity but failed to do so in the long run.

REFERENCES

1. Naipaul, V.S., Quoted by Dr R.A. Singh in *V.S. Naipaul: A House of Mr Biswas*, Prakash Book Depot, Bareilly, 1999, 22.
2. Singh, R.A., *Ibid.*, 2.
3. Naipaul, V.S., *The Middle Passage* 73.
4. Garebian, Keith, "V.S. Naipaul's—Negative Sense of Place." *The Journal of Commonwealth Literature*, Vol. X, No. 1, Aug. 1975, 23-24.
5. Naipaul, V.S., *A House for Mr Biswas*. Penguin Books, 1969, 7.
6. Lewis, Maureen Warner, "Cultural Confrontation, Disintegration and Syncretism in *A House for Mr Biswas, Critical Perspectives on V.S. Naipaul,* edited by Robert Hamner, Heinemann Educational Books Ltd., London, 1977, 97.
7. Rohlehr, Gordon, "Character and Rebellion in *A House for Mr Biswas*, in Robert Hamner edited book, *op. cit.*, 87.
8. *Ibid.*, 87.
9. Ormerod, David, "In a Derelict Land; The novels of V.S. Naipaul," in *Critical Perspectives on V.S. Naipaul* 162.
10. Naipaul, V.S., "Conrad's Darkness." *New York Review of Books* (Oct. 17, 1974) 17.
11. *Ibid.*, 21.
12. Naipaul, V.S., "The Documentary Hereby," *Twentieth Century* 173 (Winter 1964). Quoted by Robert Hamner.

5

Alienation and Home: A Study of *A House for Mr Biswas*

SANTOSH CHAKRABARTI

Yes: in the sea of life enisl'd
With echoing straits between us thrown,
Dotting the shoreless watery wild,
We mortal millions live *alone*.

—*To Marguerite*/Matthew Arnold

The sense of alienation articulated in these lines is bred from that of detachment and division between man and man. What Matthew Arnold felt in the Victorian age has become more acute in the modern age with man's inner inconsistencies and existential incompatibilities exacerbating the schism. Katherine Mansfield's feeling of insecurity and urgency for security which prompted her to write in 1911: "It is centuries since I believed in you,/ But today my need of you has come back [...]/ O God, I want to sit on your knees/ On the all-too-big throne of Heaven,/ And fall asleep with my hands tangled in your grey beard" ("To God the Father," which "nicely balances theological doubt against psychological need"/Gurr 60) have assumed different forms of alienation and displacement in different writers of modern times.

The sense of isolation, alienation and loss that was born in sensitive writers of the twentieth century informs the literature of that age. "The theme of exile and alienation is so pervasive in twentieth century literature that it may be called the literature of exile. It reflects the general disillusionment that beset the two post-war generations and deep spiritual isolation felt by man in a universe in which he felt himself to be inconsequential and a stranger. Not surprisingly, many of the great literary names of this century are those of actual exiles. In fiction alone one thinks immediately of Conrad, Joyce, Beckett, Solzhenitsyn, Nobokov and of course, V.S. Naipaul" (Joshi ix).

Naipaul's feeling of alienation stems however from a spiritual crisis—basically the result of the twin problems of an aversion to the Trinidadian society in which he was born and an infractuous diaspora to London where he sought to launch his publishing career but felt isolated and alienated. Even after living in London for three decades he feels himself distanced from the cultural-spatial milieu of London. "London is my metropolitan centre; it is my commercial centre; and yet I know that it is a kind of limbo and that I am a refugee in the sense that I am always peripheral. One's concerns are not the concerns of local people" (V.S. Naipaul, interviewed by Ian Hamilton, Joshi 10). His isolated life in his Wiltshire cottage bred in him a kind of alienation which is characteristic of a self-imposed exile.

More important surely is his strong aversion to the Trinidadian milieu with a multi-racial demographic composition, each racial group vying with the other for mimicry of the colonial masters for pseudo-Westernization. The ground reality of Trinidad was quite enough for spawning aversion and disenchantment which resulted in the diaspora. "Naipaul grew up in the multiracial society of Trinidad, peopled by migrants from four continents. He was a part of a joint Hindu family with its rigid, clannish, and suffocating atmosphere. Naipaul was an alien in the midst of other aliens. He observed how the various migrant groups, including his own, attempted to maintain their own identity. They failed to do so, because they were uncertain about what constituted their identity. They were either unaware of their cultural background or had a romantic fantasy about their past. When they were unable to latch on to their ethnic identity, they often rejected their past and attempted to adapt the identity of their colonial masters, acquiring in the process a hodgepodge of pseudo-Westernization" (Rollyson and Magill 2338-39).

The centrifugal forces of the city life of London have prevented any assimilation with the broad spectrum of life in the city and his Trinidad experience was not at all ameliorative.

So the etiology of his alienation relates to the problem of home. In *The Overcrowded Barracoon and other Articles* (1972) he articulates his concern about the 'sterility' of his continued London stay (*ibid.*, 2338) and in order to circumvent this fear he undertook an extensive tour in different lands, first in his birthland Trinidad and then in India, to find his roots. But the tour was unproductive so far as his search for home was concerned. On the other hand, it exacerbated his feeling of displacement and hence alienation. It is said that Naipaul's "rootlessness and estrangement contribute to the widespread contemporary experience of 'alienation' even among those who in the old world may have once felt inheritors of a tradition in the sense that T.S. Eliot defined it" (Thorpe: Scott-Kilvert 384).

It is common knowledge that Mr Biswas in *A House for Mr Biswas* is moulded on the image of his father, Seepersad Naipaul whom he describes as a 'defeated' man and, with his struggling writing career he felt alienated from the hierarchy of the family and solaced himself with 'easy contempt' (*op. cit.*). He redeploys his father's story of alienation within the fold of his own family to describe the alienation of Mr Biswas in the Tulsi household. But at most this is partially true, for it is Naipaul's own feeling of alienation which is knitted into the texture of Mr Biswas's story. The sense of displacement and alienation as chalked out above clearly demonstrates that Mr Biswas's story is the fictional representation of Naipaul's own predicament. Mr Biswas's marriage into the Tulsi household—his marriage with a Tulsi girl, Shama—is not at all conducive to the development of an independent personality. The Tulsi structure is so powerful and imposing that it limits the manoeuvrability of an independent-minded individual. Once made a part of it, no one can find it easy to escape: "The world was too small, the Tulsi family too large. He felt trapped" (*House* 92). The Tulsi house is the microcosm of an authoritarian Hindu world with an efficient hierarchy of control. The Tulsi society is actually founded on a system of classic slavery: food and security are bartered with independence. Gordon Rohlehr calls this society 'pre-individualistic' taking the term from Ralph Ellison who has used it to describe the situation of the Southern Negroes who 'suppress impulses to individuality in order to adjust their children to the Southern milieu' (Rohlehr: *i, C.P.* 90). Any demonstration of individualism is treated with exemplary ruthlessness. The incident of the doll's house which Mr Biswas gives his daughter as a gift and the ruthlessness with which it is torn apart are clear enough indications of the authoritarian way individualism is crushed in the Tulsi household.

An unattractive and repulsive existentiality forces alienation in him from which there is no immediate escape. Not only the above incident but the other conditions of the Tulsi household make his humiliation 'total' (Thorpe: Scott-Kilvert 389). The sons-in-law of the Tulsi household are expected to work on the Tulsi land and look after the animals. The abject submissiveness is against the grain of Mr Biswas's independent nature. He cannot and does not fall in line and hence suffers. The Tulsi custom in respect of a married daughter is revolting enough: "according to Hindu practice, the new bride should join her husband's family and accept her mother-in-law's dominance; Biswas accepts the role of the Hindu *wife* in the Tulsi household" (*op. cit.*).

The doll's house episode has a stunning effect on Mr Biswas. For however inconsequential his rebellion against the Tulsi customs and ways of life may be and however unimportant his form of non-compliance is (his revolt follows no concrete line of action, but only finds sporadic expressions of anger like throwing food out of the window on to Owad's head, calling Mrs Tulsi names etc.), his individuality gets such a beating that he is stunned into silence. This incident gives him a psychological torture which cuts at the root of his self-esteem. Mrs Tulsi's arrogance and concept of dominance militate against the spirit of independence and notion of becoming of a sensitive soul like Mr Biswas. On the one hand he cannot mix and mingle with the Tulsis submerging his identity in the Tulsi culture and on the other he has not the right means and resources, except his skill in sign-painting, for coming out of the trap in which he finds himself enmeshed. It is a dilemma which is symptomatic of that of the East Indian who cannot assimilate with his social milieu and yet does not have the resources to get out of it. The novel depicts a metaphorical colonial society in which the colonizer (Mrs Tulsi) demands subservience in exchange for food and security and "Mr Biswas's personal battle with the stronghold of the Tulsi household, a symbol of the colonial, manichean world, is a quest for existential freedom and the struggle for personality" (Singh 126). On the other hand, the weapon for domination as wielded by the Tulsis is psychological emasculation as typified by the doll's house incident noted above. It is a kind of Eriksonian 'identity crisis' that Mr Biswas represents and metaphorically speaking, whenever "Biswas is attacked by the sense of life as meaningless void, he immediately turns to his paint brushes and tries to create something against the emptiness" (Rohlehr: *ii, C.P.* 191). We have said 'metaphorically' because as a matter of fact, whenever his malice or rebellion is frustrated, 'he retreats into his insulated weariness and shame' (Singh 130). The above-mentioned 'identity crisis' bred by his sense of alienation is best summed up by Mr Biswas himself, as pointed out by Rohlehr. "To his bewildered son who asks him, 'Who are you?' he replies, 'I am just somebody. Nobody at all. I am just a man you know'" (Rohlehr: *ii, C.P.* 191).

His alienation has at least three modes of expression. The total denial of freedom and individuality at the Hanuman House and his strong refusal to acquiesce in the so-called rule of customs result in the reflex of rebellion ('[...] he rebelled'). But, as already said, nothing substantial has come out of this rebellion: he grows cantankerous and earns Shama's description of a 'barking puppy dog.' His failure to assimilate with the conditions of life in the Hanuman House and the infructuous nature of his so-called rebellion induce only one thought in him—that of escape. "Though his running from the burden he has unpremeditatedly assumed in marriage is described by Naipaul in terms of rebellion, his reaction, at least at first, is more one of evasion. Romantic dissatisfaction evolves into a desperate need to escape" (Hamner: *C.P.* 227).

There is a Freudian psychoanalytic perspective to his condition at the Hanuman House. The sense of evasion referred to above is the result of his schizophrenic sense of angst from which he suffers as he feels trapped following his marriage with Shama. A sort of what R.D. Laing calls 'ontological uncertainty' meaning a deep-seated uncertainty as to whether or not one exists (Finney 29) develops which breeds in him the 'desperate need to escape' as Hamner says.

The relationship with Shama as a Tulsi girl is not placed on an even keel. It is a see-sawing love-hate relationship as is evident from his kicking pregnant Shama in the belly. The animosity towards his wife is born from his hatred of the Tulsi clan. Most significantly, he develops a schizoid personality *vis-a-vis* his wife when one morning he is lying in bed and Shama comes to give him her motherly nursing care. He is violently angry and wants to scream in disgust when she undoes his shirt and puts her large, dark and foreign hand on his pale, soft chest. His schizoid persona 'is in a state where he can neither give nor receive the love he needs' (Rohlehr: *i, C.P.* 85). He is full of concern for his wife and children when he finds his bearing in life after the purchase of the Sikkim Street house.

At The Chase following his failure to run a Tulsi shop successfully his escapist tendencies and sense of alienation drive him to paint scenes but in spite of the boredom and futility associated with his six-year stay at The Chase the scenes are not at all ugly or evil-motivated: "He painted cool, ordered forest scenes, with gracefully curving grass, cultivated trees ringed with friendly serpents, and floors bright with perfect flowers; not the rotting, mosquito-infested jungle he could find within an hour's walk" (*House* 189-90). He also delves into the world of books to gain knowledge of the outside world. At Green Vale where his sensitive soul revolts against book-keeping and the sordid condition of the life of the labourers he suffers a psycho-physical calamity. His incompetence in labour management exacerbates his feeling of alienation. "At Green Vale he becomes a recluse, locking himself in his room and refusing to let Shama touch him. This segment of his life is crucial to his development because it takes him into the depths of despair" (Hamner: *C.P.* 228). This self-ostracism is compounded by occasional insults and ridicules hurled by Shama and even his children. All these create a sort of estrangement which forces him inwards as he becomes increasingly aware of the dangers which his half-built house spells for him:

> He was rocking hard on the creaking board one night when he thought of the power of the rockers to grind and crush and inflict pain, on his hands and toes and the tenderer parts of his body. He rose at once in agony, covering his groin with his hands, sucking hard on his teeth, listening to the chair as, rocking, it moved sideways along the cambered plank. The chair fell silent. He looked away from it. On the wall he saw a nail that could puncture his eye. The window could trap and mangle. So could the door. (*House* 239)

His inward-turning and nervous breakdown following the Green Vale house disaster are significant because, after the Tulsi household experience home is the only thing which can save him from the stasis of alienation. Though the first house that he builds or half-builds ends in disaster, it is his resilience which props him up. What is remarkable in the history of this defeated man is his resilience, his determination to find his bearing in the wide world: "The past was counterfeit, a series of cheating accidents. Real life, and its especial sweetness, awaited; he was still beginning" (*House* 318).

It will be worth-while to explain his failure in terms of the Law of Psychological Compensation which states that life goes on by compensating for a surplus in one department by incurring deficit in another and *vice versa*. Thus the surplus of his failure in Hanuman House, The Chase and Green Vale is to be followed by success in Port of Spain and finally Sikkim Street. The tall square house on Sikkim Street is the synonym for Mr Biswas's success. For despite the debt burden and the defects of the house itself he is saved from the neurotic fear of the Tulsi dominance and his feeling of entrapment and hence alienation. The house cements the family bond and there he dies, secure in the thought that the family is no more without shelter. "[...] *A House for Mr Biswas* stands out as an amazing act of redemption. Biswas, for all his lifetime spent as a fantasy man, an escapist, finds, heroically, a home. And in recording that achievement Naipaul acquires his own identity" (Gurr 71).

WORKS CITED

1. Andrew Gurr. *Writers in Exile.* The Harvester Press, 1981.

2. Chandra B. Joshi. *V.S. Naipaul: The Voice of Exile*. Sterling Publishers, 1994.
3. Carl Rallyson & Frank N. Magill (eds.). *Critical Survey of Long Fiction*, Vol. 5. Salem Press, Inc., Pasadena, second revised edn., 2000.
4. Article on Naipaul written by Michael Thorpe in *British Authors*, Supplement I, Charles Scribner's Sons, N.Y., 1987, Gen. Ed., Ian Scott-Kilvert.
5. (i) Gorden Rohlehr. *Character and Rebellion in 'A House for Mr Biswas'* in *Critical Perspectives on V.S. Naipaul*. Ed. Robert D. Hamner. Heinemann, 1979.

   (ii) ——. *The Ironic Approach—The Novels of V.S. Naipaul* in *Critical Perspectives on V.S. Naipaul*, 1979.
6. Manjit Inder Singh. *The Poetics of Alienation and Identity*. Ajanta, 1998.
7. *Character and Setting* by Robert Hamner in *Critical Perspectives on V.S. Naipaul*, 1979.
8. V.S. Naipaul. *A House for Mr Biswas*. Picador India, 2002.
9. R.D. Laing. Cited by B. Finney in Penguin *Critical Studies on Sons & Lovers*, 1990.

6

V.S. NAIPAUL'S *A HOUSE FOR MR BISWAS*: AN AUTOBIOGRAPHICAL STUDY

BHAGABAT NAYAK

V.S. Naipaul, the master novelist and expatriate literary circumnavigator occupies a significant position between cultures and countries, defines his position in his internalized nostalgia by his observation of the disintegration and hypocrisy of the Third World. He is preoccupied with the varieties of dislocation, migration, exile, the idea of being unanchored and displaced and the enigma of a disorientating experience in the explosive and disconcerting realities of the post-colonial world anywhere, everywhere. "He is like a living university" with an urge to visit monuments, museums, landmarks, and libraries, without much joy has known like any colonial what Fielding, Dickens, Lamb and Thackeray have failed to help him find, personal or autobiographical correlatives. In his search for identity in his fictions he has the poignant recollection of his life and ancestry that evokes the slow dereliction of an unwanted one, betrayed and cheated into a contract of indenture, and further disowned by the communities. He is "eternally an outsider—an Indian in the West Indies, a West Indian in England, and as described by man [...] nomadic intellectual in the non-descript Third World" (Nagarajan 2002: 4). He has assured his position as the most polemical among the contemporary writers who has inherited the collective unconsciousness of the Indian ethos in the erstwhile colonies of British Imperialism with a zeal "to strive, to seek, to find and not to yield." Being a Brahmin gypsy and a nomad he acknowledges his "colonial Hindu self," and as a man and writer suffers from the pangs of alienation, hating the oppressor and fearing the oppressed, but tries to establish his identity by converting autobiographical materials into poignant fiction on the tradition and cultural affinities with Trinidad, England and India. With the Swiftean vision of the life-consuming aspects of all colonial and post-colonial societies he has characterised his posture as that "of whiteman's nigger" always "looking down."

With the decline of the British imperialism and the rise of the American power bloc in the second half of the twentieth century the world has seen mass migration, expatriation and varieties of exiles, which have given new shapes to individual and national cultural experiences. Naipaul was born in the country town of Chaguanas in Trinidad in 1932 in a large Brahmin family of Indian origin in the state of Uttar Pradesh, had his early education at the Port of Spain, and then went on Scholarship to Oxford with "a feeling of privilege." From his very childhood Naipaul had found his father to be a victim of the limited, poverty-ridden, backward Hindu World for his career in journalism and story writing in his diaspora identity. He had also realised the factors that had denied his father to be a potential writer. Yet he says in an interview with David Bates about his departure from Trinidad and his early struggles to be a writer which bear a correspondence with his father's last attempts:

> The writing that has mattered most to me is that of my father [...]. It taught me to look at things that had never been written about before, and seemed dull in life, yet when transformed to paper became very surprising. A great deal of my vision of Trinidad has come strait from my father. Other writers are aware that they are writing about rooted societies; his work showed me that one could write about another kind of society.
>
> (*The Sunday Times* May 26, 1963)

Naipaul does see in his own literary reminiscences of Trinidad his father's imprint, his abortive quest to transcend the limits of a rural, orthodox and ritual-ridden locality. He has never thought of his future except as a writer. Unlike most of the writers he presents his autobiographical materials in most of his novels, either consciously or unconsciously. His development, achievement and success rest mainly on his four novels—*A House for Mr Biswas* (1961), *The Mimic Men* (1967), *In a Free State* (1971) and *Guerrillas* (1975). "In the case of *A House for Mr Biswas,* the knowledge that the central figure is derived from Naipaul's father, a journalist and short-story writer, and that most of the important events in the novel actually took place is likely to lead the unwary reader into seeing the author as a 'realistic' novelist in the limiting sense" (Salgado 1983: 316). Naipaul's autobiographical narration in *A House for Mr Biswas* is a "private epic" and is to be taken as a literal version of his life. The hero of the novel, Mr Biswas, is not an accomplice or a passive participant in his own colonization but a victim of the manipulation and machinations of others who seek to keep violence or rebellion, away unlike Ganesh in *The Mystic Masseur* and Ralph Singh in *The Mimic Men.*

A House for Mr Biswas is Naipaul's most personal book that is shaped after his father's stories, a vital portion of his heritage to his son who considers them "a unique record of the life of the Indian or Hindu Community in Trinidad in the first fifty years of the twentieth century. Through his father's stories he was learning a great deal about the writer's craft as they gave him a way of looking, an example of labour, a knowledge of the literary process, a sense of the order and special reality. The novel is the fictional version of experiences Naipaul has recalled in later autobiographical surveys which he describes as "very much father's book [...] written out of his journalism and stories, out of his knowledge [...]" (Naipaul 1984: 72). Mr Biswas as Naipaul's autobiographical revelation appears not only as an over reaction to a specific concern, but more fundamentally as the "fear of extinction," the annihilation of the self that his father continued to endure and transmitted to his son. In reconstructing his father's life he has traced the inception of his own process of self-creation on different planes in both tone and intention, theme and breadth, alienation and identity. "Mr Biswas may be colonized in the physical, economic and political sense, but his emotional urge for freedom, his sensibility to humiliation and slavery are signs of a temperament that bristles with rebellion subversion" (Singh 1998: 114). Naipaul locates the circumstances, socio-cultural and historical in character, that go into the making of Biswas's experience of a community caught somewhere in the larger process. Mr Biswas makes humanly interesting and compelling the immediate existential and socio-cultural themes in a transparent and natural style.

The novel presents a three-fold meaning in its autobiographical technique; firstly we see how Seepersad's encircled life in extended Hindu clan eventually dwarfed his ambitions to be a writer; secondly, how Naipaul himself through a "cathartic moment attained through his father's life, internally feared a similar fate; and finally, Mr Biswas's being colonized under conditions which are specific to his setting and background. The novel portrays the tentative approaches and withdrawals of the early relationship between father and son. Naipaul reflects his father's and his own life in Mr Biswas and his son. Thus, the novel appears to be a double autobiography in which Mr Biswas is modelled on Seepersad Naipaul's life and career and Anand, his son whose life and career run parallel to V.S. Naipaul's. Mr Biswas is the prototype of Naipaul's father who had passed his ambition on to his eldest, brilliant son with a determination to prove himself. His sketching of Anand is not much different from his creator as his "fictitious progeny." In the novel the portrayal of Anand as a "separation of man from writer," and a most poignant recreation, evokes reactions to his father—longing, attachment, fear, rage and reconciliation on individual and historical past Naipaul says that *A House for Mr Biswas* was "created out of what I saw and felt as a child" (Naipaul 1969: 22). These perceptions and feelings emerge in Anand's gestures, in his silences and laconic responses, in his sudden exclamations of anger and oblique expressions of affection and loyalty. Episodes in the novel appear autobiographical in external detail elucidating his inner life and his internalization of his father's "fear of extinction" along with his vocation. Naipaul's aim in the novel is as much to recall a world of imaginative fullness on the lines of Dickens, George Eliot and Hardy to connect it with the void of unidentified and unqualified Carribbean experience.

Mr Biswas's story is largely an odyssey of restless questing where the shifting locales are metaphors or analogues for his soul states. He is Naipaul's compassionate version of the being condemned to wander the world in his own psyche. He appears before us as a "visible man" in truer light like in Dostoevsky's *Idiot.* Naipaul writes him from his own experience with "a new reality" that transcends distinctions between fiction and no-fiction and stakes a claim to permanence. It is interesting to note that the novel is modelled on Naipaul's father's short story "They named him Mohun." The novel is the most moving autobiographical work that draws upon an experience totally based on layered levels of alienation and exile. The birth and early life of Mr Biswas is ridiculous because he is born in the wrong way with unfavourable horoscopic signs, including a sixth finger and "an unlucky sneeze." At his birth the midwife warned: "Whatever you do this boy will eat up his mother and father" and the pundit interprets midnight, the time of Mr Biswas's birth, as "the inauspicious hour." The pundit urges that Mr Biswas be kept away from the tree and water—particularly water and prescribes his father Raghu, not to see his son for twenty-one days. He adds that the child will be a lecher and a spendthrift and possibly a liar as well as must be kept away from water. Mr Biswas's first name Mohun ironically means "the beloved, and was the name given by the milkmaids to Lord Krishna" (17-18), and he has a variety of absurd, clownish and grotesque experiences. John Thieme rightly comments "By giving Biswas a name accorded to one of the avatars of Vishnu, Naipaul ensures that his central character is viewed in an ironic light; he establishes him as a Hindu mock-heroic figure" (Thieme 1984: 507).

Like Mr Biswas Naipaul shows himself induced by 'Karma' and to be caught in a love-hate relationship with Hinduism, and estimates Mr Biswas's struggles to define himself by his tripartite vocation: to build his house, to succeed as a journalist and to prepare his son to leave home for study. Naipaul's realisation of fate is associated with the Hindu quest in a milieu where there is a strong belief that the individual is determined by forces beyond his control. Mr Biswas's pattern of subjugations and slave-like roles, is perhaps Naipaul's own fictional invention, while allowing himself considerable licence to alter the overall meanings. The disorder, hostilities and squalor that destroyed the inner peace of his father and resulted in Naipaul's bewilderment was "jumbled without sequence." Both Seepersad and Naipaul were deprived of father's presence in early childhood, and both were dependent on the arbitrary benevolence of their extended families. In the novel this similarity initiates an empathy that slowly develops between Mr Biswas and Anand. Mr Biswas taught Anand a lesson in self-assertion, a challenge he himself will not relinquish despite all obstacles. During Mr Biswas's visit to Arwacas, when he is living apart from his family at Green Vale, a sugarcane estate owned by Tulsis, Anand is generally shy with him, avoiding any physical contact. Mr Biswas feels the subjection of his son in the loneliness of his exile. Likewise, Mr Biswas's changing roles as a worker, labourer and an employee of the Tulsis are versions of his arrested growth in Green Vale, The Chase, Shorthills, and in Hanuman House itself. These perceptions and feelings he has presented in Anand's gestures, in his silences and laconic responses, in his sudden exclamations of anger and oblique expressions of affection and loyalty. On the other hand, Mr Biswas is tormented by the feelings of depersonalization, gets a hallucinatory visions, and struggles with his wife Shama and children to have a house. He tries to disguise his terrors and hostility to Shama, pretending that his strange behaviour is due to illness. When the father and son stay together their roles remain ambiguous in his distress and rare capacity; he makes toys for Anand and teaches him bits of religion and science. Different family episodes in Mr Biswas's life at different circumstances are however, fictional in chronology and setting and depicts the psychological condition that determines Naipaul's assimilation of his father's fear of the abyss, the "subsidiary gift" of his dual legacy. This appears similar in bringing a parity between Naipaul's and Biswas's family, as behind Naipaul's scattered memories of his father and the family disorder there lies interestingly his parallel struggle in London, away from Trinidad past, to fix a moment that would crystallize and make intelligible the mass of unorganised autobiographical materials at his disposal.

Naipaul's fictional portrayal of Anand's unconscious identification with his father reveals psychological affinities that he does not probe into in his autobiographical writings. Seepersad's wish to write an autobiographical novel too remained unfulfilled. The great amount of pain, suffering and humiliation that Seepersad went through is understandably part of the second generation post-indentured Indians in Trinidad. Naipaul describes this in his family relations when he describes Mrs Tulsi, Seth, Tara, Ajodha, Pundit Jairam, Owad and of course, Shama, a replica of his own mother and a rich family's daughter.

Naipaul has written *A House for Mr Biswas* at a different creative stage in his career, a stage when he did not have the later contemptuous and negative view of human experience. Anand's need to identify with the father is revealed in brief but important incidents. Naipaul's articulation of early life in his Caribbean experience is based on close observation and details that he presents in the novel. At the same time, the cultural and historical experience of colonialism and post-colonialism in different forms dominated the island that Mr Biswas left, a fictional transmutation of a variety of dominance under imperial arrangement in servitude. Mr Biswas's hunger for knowledge, his singularity and playfulness, shocking to the Tulsis, are attractive qualities to the child who had been deprived of a father's example. Biswas's remoteness grows through his fantasies and reading of the novels of Hall Caine and Marie Corelli. His literary heroes like in his countries where ambitions can be pursued and have meaning, but he is trapped in an absurd place without romance.

Beginning with *A House for Mr Biswas,* Naipaul transmits his father's legacy to many of his fictive characters. He expresses his view of the world in a structure at once naturalistic as "The substance of the novel has to do with the transformation of Mr Biswas, a slave to place, history and biography, into free man, the sign and realization of that emancipation being his house" (Walsh 1972: 29). The rising graph of Mr Biswas's life in a big joint family is led by his father, Raghu, who died by drowning in a village pond while searching for his son. So also Anand's danger of drowning is more decisive. For Anand the threat of drowning becomes the subject of his first original composition. "The threat of annihilation has demanded a truth to his actual experience that his education would deny" (Feder 2001: 40). Mohun's two brothers were sent away as sugarcane labourers and his sister Dehuti went to stay with her aunt, Tara. Mohun and his mother Bipti went to Pagotes and there they were accommodated by Tara. During his school days he became friendly with Alec who inspired him for the career of a sign-painter. His little education again inspired him to be a Pundit but later he was expelled by the Hindu priest Jairam from his house for greed and misconduct. Mohun went back to his mother and realised the predicament of a man without a house of his own in disappointment. Later, he was given a job in a wine shop by Ajodha's (Tara's husband) brother. It was a bad luck for him as he was accused by Bhandat of stealing a dollar from his pocket. He was sacked and later became a signboard painter coming in contact with his schoolmate, Alec. When he came to paint the signboard during his Hanuman House days he painted signs for Tulsi Store and came in contact with a rich, orthodox widow Mrs Tulsi who was running the house and store with her husband's brother, Mr Seth. This enabled him to come in contact with Shama, a young shop-assistant whom he married hastily in the tradition of the Hanuman House.

> Everybody lived at Hanuman House in a complex relationships and transient alliances, the purpose of which was to placate the authorities and to slide through life unnoticed. In this cruel, conic world, both crowded and solitary, bullying and servile, Mr Biswas kept alive a mere glint of independence and self by refusing to be either a suave or a mild victim. (Walsh 1972: 33-34)

Mohun was trapped among the Tulsis whom Naipaul describes a "totalitarian organisation family." The matriarchal dominance by Mrs Tulsi in every affair—politics, religion and occupation —indicates a feudalistic/totalitarian set up and its iron rule recoils on Mr Biswas's inner self-respect and desire for freedom. Thus, "Biswas is the first of his family to break with the feudal-capitalist hierarchy and forge an individual identity" (Walsh 1973: 30). He finds himself a complete misfit in Mrs Tulsi's household. Shama could not understand him till he purchased a house of his own and he found his marriage with her unsuccessful. He tells Shama that the Hanuman House was "a real zoo where all kinds of animals dwelt." Later Mr Seth saves him from a debt by paying the amount to an Insurance Company.

Mr Biswas's discovery of his vocation seems to be a redemption from his fear of extinction. Anand observes that his father's achievements impress even Mrs Tulsi, who suggests that he and his family share a house with her and one of her sons in Port of Spain. It is here that Mr Biswas like Seepersad Naipaul begins to supervise his son's education, to temper Anand's impatience so like his own. He was trapped by his obligations to his wife and four children. Mr Biswas never gives up his struggle against his own internalization of the historical forces that threaten his autonomy; he is part of the Trinidadian Indian community, yet he constantly questions its customs and values. As a reporter and later as a welfare officer, he adapts to the "widening world" into which he has ventured. But in his own house where he finally lives with Shama and his children remains as his monument. Naipaul begins Mr Biswas with himself as a centre that comprises his background, his education and his vocation. He often refers to the disadvantages of growing up in the colonial society of Trinidad overshadowed by a mysticized ancestral past from India. But in the composite portrait of the writer that emerges from the body of his work this point of departure seems a blessing. Mr Biswas's struggle against the Hindu fate, dramatised on more secular level as his quest for self-realization takes the form of his attempt to emancipate from the Old Hindu World of the Tulsis. Biswas's rebellion is less a revolt against Hinduism in favour of western individualism than a revolt against the Orthodox Sanatanist Hinduism of the Tulsis in favour of the reformed Hinduism of the Arya Samaj, whose missionaries greatly influence him when they visit Trinidad. On the evidence of his Indian travel books, one might expect Naipaul to adopt a more committed stance and to attack the inertia he feels lying at the heart of Hinduism, but in the novel his art remains one of detached ironic observation.

The autobiographical concerns of Naipaul heavily influence the story and structure of *A House for Mr Biswas*. The shaping of the story is conditioned by Seepersad's life and works but the immediate circumstances of Mr Biswas's life pattern among

Tulsi's household and estate are triggered by what Naipaul implies by saying that his father was "obsessed by circumstances of his birth." Mr Biswas's struggle against Fate looks initially as if it will be a battle against the version of his Karma provided by his horoscope, when he brings about the drowning first of Dhari's calf and then of his father as a result of having disobeyed the warning not to go near water and appears to be incapable of averting his predetermined destiny. However, as he gets older and becomes more self-conscious, he begins to rebel against the constraints placed on him by his immediate environment. He tries to choose for himself, but his choices are a negation rather than an affirmation. He appears to be condemned to repeat himself from situation to situation and every house he occupies is frustratingly alien to his special vision of his own house. Escaping the actual realities of slavery, Mr Biswas carries his colonized consciousness within him, in the way Naipaul had carried alienation and distancing within him from Trinidad landscape and through his knowledge of the present Third World realities. It appears that "Biswas's alienation is the consequence of his vivid imaginative life created and sustained by the alien influences of his education and his reading which channelise his ambitions unrealistically" (Karma 1990: 85). When he finally acquires the house on the Sikkim Street, St. James, Port of Spain, he discovers that the romance of the house is destroyed by the disappointing reality of despair. The house is an object and emblem of the loss of his El Dorado—the "golden dream" of his life. Houses becomes the places of his confinement as he moves "from one house of strangers to another" during and after his staying. He becomes constantly tired in his life and thinks all action is futile in his restless quest for the dream house. Time flies by "bringing disaster closer, devouring his life" (586). He runs down like an old, tired machine. We see death and darkness rising in him. During the last months of his life, his emotional states are marked as the consequences not only due to strokes but also to a lifetime struggle and unbearable tension made by his indomitable spirit and a few gratifying successes. His actual dramatic journey from society to social reality is based on Naipaul's rational and existential bias and unlike his existential struggle in his mental landscape for freedom from restraint.

Mr Biswas may be called a legendary figure from his infancy to death. No doubt Naipaul's feelings of rootedness, life of exile that results in personal insecurity and cultural instability are presented in the versions of Mr Biswas's experience. Being alienated from all walks of life and unable to belong either to England or Caribbean, Mr Biswas becomes a man without a side, surrounded by buffoons and impelled to be something of a tragic clown. On the whole Mr Biswas reflects Naipaul's struggle to assimilate his Indian past, his own complex and personal history, his continual self-evaluation and self-criticism, and sometimes his excessive reactions and the core of creative intelligence from his authorial vision. With a determination to express the truth of his experience, he exposes in his autobiographical references the identity of his pain and anger and his occasional churlishness, to consider his judgments and to correct his vision. Alienation characterises the affinity between the protagonist and the narrator as they are marginal men in whom body and soul are in conflict. Alienation or rooflessness is related to the loss of and quest for identity. It is the loss of identity that results in alienation. The house into which Mr Biswas and his family move near the end of the novel before his death and where he dies not long after, reflects the naïvete of his owner and the petty corruption of his society, but it remains standing. Naipaul's truth is that the self that speaks to the reader in the novel does not divulge details of his domestic or social affairs, but it is clear that his "innermost self" has, to some extent, been formed by his interaction with the worlds he has explored in Mr Biswas's exhausting fight against the Tulsis. On the other hand Naipaul makes a deconstruction of European colonialism in the novel for the reconstruction of the Caribbean culture, in its hybrid forms, in his imaginative revisioning of cultural history for a cultural transformation.

The very use of the title "Mr" for Mohun Biswas in the novel acknowledges the dignity and struggle for identity by owning a house is both existential and universal. Ultimately, the 'house' turns out to be the image of fulfilment, a release from years of slavery and tyranny of extended family. In the searching for a house "He plays at life because he is unable to live it" (Camus 1956: 52). In the colonized, pre-independence Trinidad society a White-Collar job and self-respect were rare things to achieve and in this kind of social milieu Mr Biswas is denied the honour or satisfaction of absorbing into the Hindu world or to represent it in the outside world. Mr Biswas's sense of belonging is a pre-requisite of assuming an identity. This is why "The 'House' in this novel is a symbol not for 'rootedness' but for freedom—freedom from slavery and oppression" (Das 1995: 102). Identity needs one's social and cultural base to be established which seems to be in crisis with his status as an outsider, a victim of denial, betrayal and tyranny. The fear of 'extinction' that haunted Seepersad and haunts Mr Biswas—is connected with the positive, inner vocation that can sustain a man. But Seepersad's fear which got transferred to Naipaul became quite real for the young and aspiring writer. He knew that fear could only be combated by the exercise of vocation.

Naipaul often refers to the disadvantage of growing up in the colonial society of Trinidad shadowed by a mysticized ancestral past in India. But in the composite portrait of the writer that emerges from the body of his work the point of departure at times seems blessing. The sort of fictional biography of his journalist father and father-son life history as presented in the novel seem quite autobiographical, and hailed as a three generation novel carries the responses on mixed, chaotic and disorderly Caribbean set up. In this regard Bruce King aptly remarks:

> In the case of V.S. Naipaul there is a tripple alienation since the author is dispossessed from several cultures and possible homes. Having rejected his Brahmin past, the small decaying world of Indian Trinidad, the lack of sophistication of Creole Trinidad, the provinciality of the West Indian Middle classes, Naipaul was unable to find in either England or India the high, purposeful culture he desired. Subsequently he has become the voice of the modern expatriate and of our time in feeling unattached, unillusioned, without purpose, an observer of the world follies, especially those problem which have resulted from the end of empire and the withdrawal of

> European rule from the Third World. Naipaul's work appeals to those who have felt the effect of rapid secularization, mobility and social change; the resulting world is large, overcrowded and yet an empty space. (King 1987: 6-7)

Mr Biswas is taken to be reprocessing a 'universalist' and a transcultural vision of man's rootlessness and a search for identity and place. "Naipaul is like Biswas, who having no tradition to turn to, must create his own. And this tradition has its roots in the rootlessness of West-Indian society rather than in the well-established European and Indian Societies" (Boxill 1983: 24). Unlike Naipaul Mr Biswas's life-long ambition is the ownership of a house to provide security and comfort. It is therefore appropriate that Naipaul should have made a 'house' the central and guiding symbol of the novel.

In the novel, the house becomes a kind of inverted fictional embodiment of Naipaul's own personal need for change and escape. While his father's experience becomes the story of any post-colonial man displaced from his origin by chance or choice, his Mr Biswas's 'unhoused' condition and alienation are the problems of every contemporary diaspora which is presented in the autobiographical design of the novel. The novel succeeds in transcending the individuals self by universalising the issue of alienation with a Naipaulean cry for identity in the post-colonial world. An autobiographical study of the novel reveals how the life history of Seepersad and his son, V.S. Naipaul is similar that of Mr Biswas and his son Anand who fails to absorb the Caribbean climate. Yet the novel is a tragic epic, densely populated, rich in variety and felt life, full of humour and beaming with vitality. It becomes visibly clear in *A House for Mr Biswas* that the fictional embodiment of Naipaul's own personal life is assimilated and absorbed into art.

WORKS CITED

Boxill, Anthony. *V.S. Naipaul's Fiction: In Quest of the Enemy.* Fredericton, New Brunswick: York Press, 1983.

Camus, Albert. *The Rebel: An Essay on Man in Revolt.* (Trans.) Anthony Bower. New York: Vintage, 1956.

Das, B.K. "From Slavery to Freedom: A Study of V.S. Naipaul's *A House for Mr Biswas*." *Aspects of Commonwealth Literature.* New Delhi Creative Books, 1995: 93-103.

Feder, Lillian. *Naipaul's Truth.* New Delhi: Indialog Publications, 2001.

Garebian, Keith. "The Grotesque Satire of *A House for Mr Biswas*." *Modern Fiction Studies.* 30:3 (Autumn 1984) 487-96.

Kamra, Shashi. *The Novels of V.S. Naipaul.* New Delhi: Prestige Books, 1990.

King, Bruce. "Protest, Alienation and Modernism in the New Literatures." *The Literary Half-Yearly.* 28: 1 (January 1987): 2-15.

Nagarajan, M.S. "Home and Exile." *The Hindu* May 5, 2002.

Naipaul, V.S. *A House for Mr Biswas.* Harmondsworth: Penguin, 1969. (All textual references are to this edition.)

____. "Prologue to an Autobiography." *Finding the Centre: Two Narratives.* London: Andre Deutsch, 1984.

____. *The Sunday Times* May 26, 1963.

Salgado, Gamini. "V.S. Naipual and the Politics of Fiction." *The New Pelican Guide to English Literature,* Vol. 8. (ed.) Boris Ford. London: Penguin Books, 1983: 314-27.

Singh, Manjit Inder. *V.S. Naipual.* Jaipur: Rawat Publications, 1998.

Thieme, John. "A Hindu Castaway: Ralph Singh's Journey in *The Mimic Men.*" *Modern Fiction Studies.* 30:3 (Autumn 1984): 505-18.

Walsh, William. "V.S. Naipaul: Mr Biswas." *Literary Criterion.* 10:2 (Summer 1972): 27-37.

____. *V.S. Naipaul.* London: Oliver and Boyd, 1973: 30.

7

Naipaul's *A House for Mr Biswas*, Arun Joshi's *The Strange Case of Billy Biswas* and Mordecai Richler's *Son of a Smaller Hero*: A Critique of Paradox of Life

S. KANAKARAJ and J. SAMUEL KIRUBAHAR

The West Indian, Indian, and Canadian novels, *A House for Mr Biswas* (1961), *The Strange Case of Billy Biswas* (1971), and *Son of a Smaller Hero* (1989) portray the demented world of their protagonists in which there is no way back as the only option left to them is to go forward for the virtual extinction of their soul in a kind of sophisticated barbarism without any purpose being a critique of paradox of life. These three novels, in fact, present a paradoxical drama of icy aloofness of their protagonists with a yearning for death—the virtual extinction of 'being' in favour of 'becoming.' Mr Biswas's retreat from the Tulsidom at Hanuman House, Billy Biswas's retreat from the systematized civilized life to the primitive world of Bilasia in SAAL forests of the Maikala Hills, a mystical force, primitive energy, libidinous and Lawrentian life force, and Noah's retreat from the Montreal Jewish Ghetto life and Miriam's libidinous illustrate, the yearning for the death of 'being' in favour of 'becoming' as the life becomes a paradox and a puzzle which may not be solved instantly.

Naipaul's *A House for Mr Biswas* is a West Indian novel of persuasion which is splendidly written with the Tolstoyan formula, portraying the everlasting quest of its protagonist, Mohun Biswas, a sacked journalist, dying at the age of forty-six in his irretrievable mortgaged house in Sikkim Street,

St. James Port of Spain and his efforts to have a house of his own to establish his own identity on the alien soil, the colonial Trinidad, West Indies. Right from birth he is branded 'unlucky' as it is predicted that he would eat his father. In the orthodox world of rituals, prayers, and customs, and the Hindu family, Biswas is ordained to be a priest. As he happens to defile Jairam's Oleander tree by his own excretion, it happens that he turns out to be a sign painter for Tulsi Store and falls in love with Shama of Tulsidom. Later fixed rules of Tulsidom make him feel submerged and smothered and makes him yearn to fly away. Later on he is offered a government job at a high start and builds a house in which he dies but has the satisfaction of dying in his own house in Sikkim Street.

Arun Joshi's *The Strange Case of Billy Biswas* (1971), which incidentally reminds one of D.H. Lawrence's *The Woman Who Rode Away* and Graham Greene's *A Burnt Out Case*, presents the odyssey of its protagonist, Mr Billy Biswas's, the son of a judge, educated in Britain and America and lecturer in Delhi University, from the systematised civilized world to the primitive world of Bilasia. He is a man of brilliant intellect, profound sensibility, and extraordinary obsessions. His father wants to make him an Engineer but he earns his Ph.D. degree in Anthropology as he is basically an Anthropologist. He has an obsession for the primitive consciousness. He affirms it saying:

> a strong woman keeps crossing my (his) dreams, I (he) have (has) seen her on the streets of Delhi buying bangles at a fair, shadow at a tribal dance. (*Strange Case* 97)

However, his marriage to Meena is not at all a successful one. On his visit to the SAAL forests, he mysteriously vanishes and falls in love with the young, tribal girl, Bilasia, whom he feels is the essence of that primitive force. Billy Biswas's union with Bilasia makes him discover that part of himself that he has been searching for all his life. Later, the searching police party hunts down Billy Biswas to his hidden lair and subsequently he is killed in the pursuit.

Mordecai Richler's *Son of a Smaller Hero* is a story of liberation from the slavish Montreal Jewish ghetto life through the long exodus to the longer understanding of self in existence. Noah Adler, the prodigal son of the bogus hero, Wolf Adler, deserts Adlers and falls in love with his professor's, Theo Hall's wife, Miriam. Later, realising that love making with Miriam is a responsibility of his own and understanding that his father, Wolf Adler, died in a futile Quest to save the money and his grandfather's, Melech Adler's, relation with the Polish girl, Helga Kowalski, he leaves the Jewish Ghetto. In fact, falling out of the family is the theme of the novel.

In these three novels, the protagonists are singularly individualistic and completely self-centred and their behaviour is incompatible with the natural laws of everyday life and reality as they indulge in actions which are instinctive and seem to be irrational to the rational world. Biswas's withdrawal from the Tulsidom at Hanuman House is an irrational attempt on the part of Tulsi clan, Billy Biswas's withdrawal from his family, and society and his sudden disappearance into the saal forests of the Maikala Hills seems to be an irrational primitive attempt on the part of the highly civilized people like Meena and Romi and Noah's withdrawal from the Montreal Jewish ghetto life controlled by his Grandfather, Melech Adler, seems to be an irrational attempt on the part of the ghetto life. They alienate themselves from the sinister and materialistic life and try to work out their destiny in their own way. Though successful in freeing themselves from the restraints of their external environment they remain subjected to the urges of their subconscious self—the very act of writing in the case of Biswas, the very act of subjecting himself to the primitive urge, the collective unconsciousness in an individual, in the case of Billy Biswas and protesting against the Jewish Montreal ghetto life in the case of Noah. The seemingly independent actions are in fact the results of the dictates of their 'Id.'

The structure of these novels vindicates the paradox of life at different layers as listed in the table on next page.

These three novels are basically divided into two parts: the so-called civilized world and the impingement of the civilized world on the primitive world of consciousness. The unconscious self of the protagonists drives them to renounce the monotonous respectability of their upper-middle class society. Biswas renounces the world of Tulsidom fearing that he would become a mere slave losing his identity being

A House for Mr Biswas	*The Strange Case of Billy Biswas*	*Son of a Smaller Hero*
Biswas's birth—ill omen that he would eat his father	Billy Biswas's education-interest in Anthropology	Noah's experience of the Jewish ghetto life.
Defiling the oleander tree at Jairam's house	Primitive urge and sex with Tuula	falling out of the ghetto life.
Love and marriage with Shama	Marriage with Meena	Love with Miriam
Retreat from Tulsidom—Hanuman House	retreat from the civilized world	retreat from Miriam
Builds a house and dies in it	falls in love with Bilasia —dies while Police Party hunts	voyages out from the ghetto

absorbed in that clan; Billy Biswas renounces the world of Meena and his father in favour of primitive calling within his self, and Noah renounces the world of Jewish Ghetto as he fears that he would become a mere non-entity in that circle without value. However, their attempts are not successful as they fail to understand the paradox of life—Biswas dies while writing, Billy Biswas is killed and Noah voyages out from the ghetto. They have been mysteriously taken by a phantom of their own desire to leave the so-called civilized world of creed, avarice, riches and hypocrisy. They forsake the meaningless existence in the civilized world because they feel choked by the phoney atmosphere of the modern, civilized world. They reject the artificiality, hollowness and snobbery of the modern sophisticated world with meaningless rituals and taboos. In fact, these novels established an aesthetic paradigm of withdrawal from the sterility of contemporary technological mechanics of human values.

These novelists present the struggle of a man, the protagonist, to establish an identity. In their fictional world, the individual is a victim of his own situations and that individual is neglected, abandoned, put in a world of desolation and humiliation. The protagonists in their fictional world belong to an unstable social order as the societies are on the verge of collapse. Their societies promote nothing except a vaguer sense of frustration and a sense of glory dead as life's expectations are nullified. Biswas's, Billy Biswas's and Noah's departure could have been averted if they had the rare feeling of empathy and a sufficient idea of human suffering but it is their lack of understanding this paradox of life that makes them drop outs and lands them on the edge of despair. One can even argue that sex is not an end in itself. It fails to release their tension as Shama, Meena, and Miriam stick to their world and are not willing to come out of their own conceptual world. Shama of *A House for Mr Biswas* belongs to the old Hindu, traditional, colonial, mimic world of Hanuman House, Meena of *The Strange Case of Billy Biswas* is an associate of the phoney society, a product of the sensate civilization and Miriam is a woman of both lust and love toward her husband, Theo Hall. They fail to satisfy the urges of the protagonists and as a result they have been neglected and abandoned. Naipaul writes:

> After a brief ceremony at the registrar's [...] Mr Biswas and Shama were given a part of a long room on the top floor of the wooden house. And now he became cautious. Now he thought of escape [...]. He didn't embrace or touch her. He wouldn't have known, besides, how to begin, with someone who had not spoken a word to him [...]. They had married Shama to him, simply because he was of the proper caste. (*House* 96-97)

Billy Biswas is fascinated by Tuula, the fellow student of Anthropology, because she has the primitive force and has an insight into the inner recesses of man's heart and has mastered hypnotism, auto suggestion, and intuition. But he states:

> The other side, you know what I mean, don't you. Most of us are aware only of the side on which we are born but there is always the other side, the valley beyond the hills; the hills beyond the valley. (*Strange Case* 18-19)

Even later with Meena, his wife, he feels intensely that no woman's body of this phoney society can satisfy him. On his own part, it is not a hunger for sensual satisfaction by mere sexual union; it is a quest for self-realisation for a union with the missing part of his soul. Noah's relation with Miriam is not at all a successful one. All the time Miriam raises a question related to racial identity. She inquires, "Noah, do you worry about being a Jew? You know what I mean" (*Smaller*

Hero 60). Moreover Miriam is ten years older than Noah. On having Miriam, Noah feels as Mordecai Richler vividly writes:

> A kind of lethargy came over him. That world, which was turbulent and chaotic; outside, where strangers had ambitions, needs, contests; where there was dying—no longer existed. All that remained was him, the woman in his bed. (*Smaller Hero* 98)

But later Miriam begins to slip away from both Theo and Noah. Richler writes:

> Such loves, such remedies are without truth. So, as he found her present circumstances sordid, Miriam suddenly turned against both Noah and Theo. They were ugly and unlovable. She wished them both away. (*Smaller Hero* 101)

Biswas is exposed from the order of enclosure in the house of the Tulsis to the order of exposure. Billy Biswas is also exposed from the enclosed society of America and India to that of the strange, remote, alien hills and forests. Noah is also exposed from the rigorous order of Montreal Jewish ghetto to the order of exposure outside the ghetto life with Miriam, the sensual world of existence which nullifies the expectation of the craving soul for truth and wisdom. Contrary to their effort, they have been exposed to physical and spiritual humiliation. With Biswas the humiliation starts with the horoscopic predicament, with Billy Biswas it starts with his interest in Anthropology and Tuula, and with Noah with the incidents at the coalyard and later with Miriam. In fact, their baracoon is a suffocating, a coarse-grained, chaotic, overcrowded, and a fading one. Their world is a world of illusion and they realise it as V.S. Naipaul in *A Bend in the River* writes:

> But home was hardly a place I (they) could return to. Home was something in my (their) head. It was something I (they) had lost. (117)

Biswas, Billy Biswas and Noah are marginal men for whom the status in a society is denied at an earlier stage. The societies they encounter fatalistically leave them orphans. And as a result they are flogged, duped, thwarted, cheated, maligned, robbed, humiliated, frustrated, disappointed, and frightened. They chart their odyssey of life with confrontation and their confrontation is a waste one as they succumb to the tragic culmination of their life. They wander from one place to the other without a permanent root as they portray their fearful future. They fear that they will be a curse and destroyers of their society. They care-little, do-nothing, fragmented, failure oriented societies of Biswas, Billy Biswas and Noah make them pathetic figures with the tragic culmination of their lives. In their cases, the call and the urge to enter a needs world are strange in their psyche. It is because of the novelists, Naipaul, Arun Joshi and Mordecai Richler who recognise a reality beyond the mere phenomenal world, a reality which the artist could imagine and capture by giving a constant form to the shapeless facts of human existence. Biswas, Billy Biswas and Noah are totally aware of the deeper layers of their personalities and feel totally alienated from the superficial reality of their life. Renouncing his past life in the Hanuman House, Biswas goes in search of a house of his own, Billy Biswas also goes in search of the meaning of life leaving back his own family, wife, father, and a child and Noah renouncing the life of Jewish Montreal ghetto goes in search of the meaning of life after having a love affair with his Professor's wife, Miriam. They turn introvert since they are not in harmony with their surroundings, their family, their ladies, and as a result their souls get hurt and estranged, they retire within themselves. Theirs is an enigmatic pilgrimage to the spiritual world of meaning and function. Their voyaging out on their journey to the inner world of their own is a journey from darkness to life. It is their renunciation in search of enlightenment.

Though Biswas, Billy Biswas and Noah are family members they are not able to feel integrated with their family members. Biswas is not able to find himself as a part of Tulsidom and remains an island, an alienated human being among the cobweb of Tulsidom. Billy Biswas, right from his sojourn in New York, is not able to unite himself with others and remains a mystery, a Strange Case. Noah, right from the incidents at the coal-yard up to the death of his father as a bogus hero, is not able to adjust himself to the ghetto life. They go out in search of bigger reality armed with truth alone. In fact, they remain alone, isolated, strangers, as they are extremely sensitive and theirs is a case of explosion of senses. The reasons for the flight can be categorised as below:

Biswas	*Billy Biswas*	*Noah*
Marriage with Shama	Marriage with Meena, had sex with Tuula	had sex with Miriam
No compromise with Tulsidom,	no compromise with the sophisticated world of Meena	no compromise with the Jewish ghetto life
Gap of communication with Shama & Tulsidom	gap of communication with Meena	gap of communication with Miriam
No sexual satisfaction with Shama	no sexual satisfaction with Tuula and Meena	no sexual satisfaction with Miriam
Escapes to construct a house	escapes to the primitive world	escapes to identify the meaning of ghetto life.
Capacity to turn vision into reality	capacity to respond to primitive impulses	capacity to respond to the question of the validity of the Jewish ghetto life
Flight	Flight	Flight

Human pettiness, moral pettiness, the triviality of many of the forms, titles, customs, preferences, and points of honour could well be seen in Biswas, Billy Biswas and Noah who renounce the world in favour of their own self. Biswas's journey from unsatisfactory households to the fatal end of his life, Billy Biswas's journey from Tuula to Meena and from Meena to Bilasia and Noah's journey from the Jewish Ghetto life to Miriam are not a mere trifling of sensual and sexual gratification but a development of the soul from sex to sympathy to sublimation. They have renounced the larger world in favour of the inner man and have engaged themselves in a search for the essence of human living. Their search is directed at the inscrutable region of human psyche and they enter into the mysterious region of uncertainty and inscrutability. Biswas realises that,

> His freedom was over, and it had been false. The past could be ignored: it was never counterfeit; he carried it within himself. If there was a place for him, it was one that had already been hollowed out by time, by

> everything he had lived through however imperfect, makeshift and cheating. (*House* 316)

Similarly Billy Biswas is not only sensitive to the past but also conscious of the identity of his being as he says:

> It seems [...], that we are swiftly losing what is known as one's grip in life. Why else this constant blurring of reality? Who am I? Who are my parents? My Wife? My Child? [...] I cannot decide who they are or what accidents of creation has brought us together. (*Strange Case* 97)

Noah in his voyaging out states:

> I am going and I'm not going. I can no more leave you; my mother, or my father's memory, than I can renounce myself. But I can refuse to take part in this [...]. (*Smaller Hero* 199)

True to the statement of Noah, the novelist writes:

> He had expected that by moving away from home something wonderful would happen whereby he would end up a bigger and freer man. Instead there was only this anguishing. (*Smaller Hero* 25)

In fact, theirs is comparatively a drama of spiritual stress and strain and they uniformly strive to be loners in the world of their own. They are the archetypal examples to prove that the modern world and its age is an age of alienation. The potential meaninglessness of human existence has corroded their lives from various quarters.

In short, the injuries inflicted upon them and the scars left on the psyche generate a cynical attitude towards the established social norms and values, and make them grope for life's relevance. They cherish an awareness that they are suffering from a gnawing sense of meaninglessness. Their departure is a prelude to an arduous quest for something beyond themselves. It is not an escape from life and its realities but an escape into what they consider to be the real life far from the madding crowd and the sordid meaninglessness of existence in the civilized world.

Even though they are defeated again and again in search of truth in life, they leave this world of the so-called civilized barbarians in search of a place where they are not treated as outcasts, not culturally uprooted, socially isolated, and self-estranged. They uniformly strive to be loners in the world of their own when the potential meaninglessness of life has corroded their lives from various quarters. Their departure is a prelude to an arduous quest for something beyond themselves—the excursion of the psyche.

In portraying such a paradoxical condition of life, the novelists become chroniclers of disaster as they present a world inherited by individuals without values and without a belief in the dignity and goodness of man, as man has tragic yearnings through his endless struggles to attain perfection. The undeviating employment of narration in these novels makes these novels a symbolical representation of man's unfulfilled desire, modified by the irony of the loss of the pursued object and the death of the hero in his hour of triumph, and by the paradox of victory in defeat, life in death, and true happiness in pursuit rather than in success. In fact, the assertion behind these novels is that man is an absolute victim of circumstances and incapable of choice.

This is all symptomatic of what we call the general debility of our time as the contemporary man, lacking the sense of the goodness of man and the meaning of life, labours under a curse to be an island—no house, no strange case, and not a son of a great hero.

BIBLIOGRAPHY

Joshi, Arun. *The Strange Case of Billy Biswas.* Delhi: Hind Pocket Book Ltd., 1971.

Naipaul, V.S. *A House for Mr Biswas.* 1961. U.S.A.: Vintage Books, 1983.

Richler, Mordecai. *Son of a Smaller Hero.* Toronto, Ontorio: McCelleland & Steward Inc., 1989.

8

Shock, Derision and Satire in V.S. Naipaul's *An Area of Darkness*

SABITA TRIPATHY

Postcolonial migrant literature is written by elites. Writing has become an integral part of self-definition for a postcolonial writer. The two great postcolonial fiction writers, V.S. Naipaul and R.K. Narayan, having published widely, give cusp utterance to their colonised experience. Whereas R.K. Narayan employs English language and literary conventions to chart the socio-cultural life of the south Indians in a series of novels beginning with *Swami and Friends,* cultural expatriation is the chief motif of Naipaul's postcolonial writing experience that establishes the bases of his reputation from national bonding to international wanderings. Naipaul's crusading literal zeal is reflected in the minute dissection of the cultural stasis and social hypocrisy of Indian society that was once colonized by the British for more than two hundred and fifty years. Naipaul's *An Area of Darkness,* a migrant text, shows evidently the impact of colonization along with the cultural metamorphosis the writer was imbued with, the diversification of taste that developed during the British Empire. In such an experiment Conrad is Naipaul's literary mentor. In this regard Elleke Boehmer makes a pertinent remark on Naipaul's postcolonial response to Indian situations: "As a writer enamoured of British culture, and scornful of formerly colonized societies, Naipaul is central to any discussion of assimilation and duality of postcolonial identity."[1]

Naipaul's objective of postcolonial writing is a quest for personal and racial/cultural identity. As a third generation immigrant, the pull for a visit to India is not out of love but out of curiosity. Like Sally Morgan's *My Place* (1987) Naipaul's *An Area of Darkness* is a quest for family roots. In his odyssey he employs the polemics of anti-colonial indictment and the rhetoric of nationalist introspection. All that he says about India cannot be truthfully accepted as his deliberate representations in the text referred above appear to be increasingly made up of "misconceptions and inappropriate enquiries." In the scholarly assessment of Fawzia Mustafa in *V.S. Naipaul*:

> For almost his entire career [...] Naipaul's writings and their idiomatic reflections have been simultaneously celebrated and castigated with descriptions that range between "objective" or "a historical," "unsentimental" or "culturally ignorant," "unafraid" or "hysterical."[2]

Cultural expatriation is the chief motif of Naipaul's postcolonial writing experience as his grandfather was brought to Trinidad as a boy from the Eastern Uttar Pradesh some time in 1880s trained as a *pundit.* This boy who grew up as a *pundit* was named Nypal or Naipaul, which later on became the name of his family. Though Vidyadhar was born and brought up in Trinidad, by self-choice he became an expatriate in Britain. Having established his reputation as a British author, he made his maiden visit to India in 1961. Of course, he had residual childhood memories of India as a land of myths and legends, which he had heard from his grandmother. As a traveller in the cultural spaces of India, he anatomises social mannerism, tradition and custom but his Western rational mind is unable to cope up with cultural shock. The ironic distance he tries to maintain is through the language of shock, satire and derision in the texts, which is reminiscent of Evelyn Waugh or George Orwell. India of his mythological conception, the residue of his childhood memories, is a land different from what he really sees in his peregrination:

> Yet a special joy had been with me throughout the pilgrimage and during all my time in Kashmir: It was the joy of being among mountains; it was the special joy of being among the Himalayas. I felt linked to them [...]. In so many of the brightly coloured religious pictures in my grandmother's house I had seen these mountains, cones of white against simple, cold blue.

> They had become part of the India of my fantasy [...]. The pictures I knew to be wrong; their message was no message to me; but in that corner of the mind, which continues child-like their truth remained a possibility.[3]

Once he is in India, Naipaul's attempt at orotund identification with the crowd in Bombay fails. That he is a writer and an outsider is even unnoticed by the surging crowd. He feels dejected with the feelings of an expatriate:

> Now in Bombay I entered a shop or a restaurant and awaited a special quality of response. And there was nothing. It was like being denied part of my reality. Again and again I was caught. I was faceless. I might sink without a trace into that Indian crowd. I had been made by Trinidad and England; recognition of my difference was necessary to me. I felt the need to impose myself, and didn't know how.[4]

Postcolonial theory downplays political liberation that fails to bring economic liberation because without economic liberation there cannot be any true political liberation. For the last three decades or so, the post-independent nations have been scourged by neo-colonial ills, economic disorders, social malaise, and corruption, etc. Naipaul in his colonial discourse orchestrates the conditions of the decolonised countries that ape the values of the former colonizer and their power hierarchy. He anatomises the doubling of white man's image in Indian society, the perpetuation of the surviving British Establishment and the ruin of many things. Colonial systems of education, law and administrative machinery have created waves of mental colonisation of the elitists, India to him "signifies strangeness, a painful absurdity, and a hopeless country progressively ravaged by moral and historical degeneration." Civilized and primitive retain here their customary meanings. He sees "Indian darkness" engulfing different facets of Indian life. Naipaul's bizarre vivisection lays bare that Indians are basically irrational and repose their blind faith in religion. The main flaw in their character is the "defect of vision." There is a note of derision in Naipaul's analysis of Indian interpretation of history:

> It is well that Indians are unable to look at their country directly, for the distress they would see would drive them mad. And it is well that they have no sense of history, for how then would they be able to continue to squat amid their ruins, and which Indian would be able to read the history of his country for the last thousand years without anger and pain?[5]

With such myopic vision, people have no go but to retreat to fantasy and fatalism. But in the same passage where Naipaul deplores the sense of people's historical blindness, he admires their unusual excellent achievements of ancient India unparalleled in the history of the world. He is shocked to observe how that supine spirit of the people has become congealed and blind to its glorious past so much so that they love to sit amid the ruins and learn nothing from their past:

> The aeroplane was known to ancient India, the telephone, and the atom bomb: there is evidence in the Indian epics. Surgery was highly developed in ancient India [...]. Indian shipbuilding was the wonder of the world. And democracy flourished in ancient India. Every village was a republic, self-sufficient, ordered, controlling its own affairs; the village council could hang an offending villager or chop off his hand.[6]

In a country hallowed by such glorious past, the writer painfully reiterates, the filth and mire of the colonial period remain unabated; and problems pile up due to recurrence of "disputes about language, religion, caste and region." The spiralling problems of India goad him to make a satirical prediction: "India, it seems, will never cease to require the arbitration of a conqueror." Does not Naipaul's apprehension sound correct in the present context as the Indian Government is dependent upon a superpower to stop the cross-border terrorism sponsored by the neighbouring country, Pakistan?

Decolonisation questions the very faith in Western rationality. A postcolonial text emerges out of the grit and specificity of local culture or history that may not be comprehensible to foreign tourists. Naipaul fails to study the implications of the untranslatable cultural ethos and the enigma of Indian social life, so he derides the attitude of Indians who are basically bounded by custom and tradition. In his scything criticism of the orthodox people, he does not even spare his grandparents. In his grandparent's house he finds to his dismay "something of darkness remains, in those attitudes, those ways of thinking and seeing" which are no longer to be found in the community in Trinidad. Many things in his grandmother's house were irreparable because they had no weavers, dyers, workers in brass and makers of string beds. Left to himself, Naipaul would disband such an establishment and give it a Western look:

> They were cherished because they came from India, but they continued to be used and no regret attached to their disintegration. It was an Indian attitude, as I was to recognise. Customs are to be maintained because they are felt to be ancient.[7]

Sir Vidyadhar's grandfather suffered from a deep sense of nostalgia for his village and community. Whenever he returned from his village, he took more of things from India. When he built his house he ignored all colonial style in Trinidad and constructed a typical Indian house prototype of which Vidyadhar saw in his first visit to Uttar Pradesh. It is obvious that the writer shows a supercilious way of paying scant regards for the sentiments of his grandparents and an attachment to his family roots and the reasons are not very far off to seek. Living in a multi-racial country, Naipaul admits, there was no cross-cultural relation or any process of aculturisation. His family had its distinctive mark: "We ate certain food, performed certain ceremonies and had certain taboos; we expected others to have their own. We did not wish to share theirs; we did not expect them to share ours."

It seems in those days Naipaul was not free from religious fanaticism even though he later on married to a Pakistani journalist, Nadira. He views the Muslims with deep suspicion. Although he employed a Muslim, Aziz, as his personal attendant, he confides his readers that he never trusted him. His childhood memory of a particular grey beard Muslim who embodied "every sort of threat prompted him to become mistrustful of Muslims." It went deep into his psyche, which probably is the root cause of his derisive suspicion. His disdainful attitude towards the loyalty of the Muslims is not only personal; as he confesses in *Among the Believers,* it comes out of a feeling of group animosity. This youthful bigotry probably sprang from group psychology that was nurtured among the Indian community of Trinidad:

> Muslims were part of the small Indian community of Trinidad into which I was born; it could be said that I had known Muslims all my life [...]. The difference was more of a matter of group feeling, and mysterious; the animosities our Hindu and Muslim grandfathers had brought from India softened into a kind of folk-wisdom about the unreliability and treachery of the other side.[8]

Academic disciplines have begun to cast serious doubts on the permeability of other cultures to Western understanding. Colonialism has brought some benefits from modernity, as its apologists continue to argue, and was singularly destructive with regard to the indigenous cultures with which it comes into contact. Being brought up in an Indian Brahmin family, he declares himself a "born unbeliever." He even refused to go through "the Janayu or thread ceremony" which ends with the head-shaver Brahmin boy in the garb of a "Hindu-mendicant scholar bound for Benares." As a born atheist, he is very sceptical of the Hindu ceremonies and rituals from his childhood days. The Katha ceremony was organised by his grandmother under a *peepal* tree in the Botanical Gardens, a few hundred yards from the governor's house. Naipaul feels shy of such a scene being put up by his grandmother as it attracted "the silent interest of a small mixed crowd of morning strollers and the proselytising attentions of a Seven Day Adventist." It implies that he is never proud of his grandmother's faith or religion. More so he used to derive no pleasure in those religious rituals even though he was fed and given money and clothes by some devout Hindus. His lack of interest may be due to his ignorance of the language and the symbolic significance of those ceremonies. He admits that in his case it is "a betrayal of heredity." His distaste for the ceremonies and ignorance of Hindu culture could only foster in him a vague sense of caste or religious rituals of the Hindus. In certain Hindu ceremonies food is given to birds and animals but he is horrified at such unhygienic practices. Moreover, he is shocked to observe that the people use the very plates on which food is put out for animals. He strongly disapproves the practice of "women sipping from ladles with which they stir their pots."

It has already been pointed out, Naipaul is opposed to the division of caste because it is based on the degradation of human beings: Mahatma Gandhi too advanced the same reason. For Naipaul no menial work is mean. On this basis the profession of a latrine-cleaner is not to be looked down upon. Even though the division of caste encourages expertise in particular profession, the practice of treating some people as untouchable should strongly be considered a crime and heinous practice. Caste occupation binds people to their own locality and checks migration in large scale. The duality of tradition and modernity has been inextricably mixed up in the life of some people in India. He is shocked to know that people in Bombay lit candles and electric bulbs in Diwali festivals and not the rustic clay lamps still used by the Hindu community in Trinidad.

Colonial rule developed in people's mind a false sense of vanity and a mania for social status that prompt them to behave hypocritically. A strong belief in their particular caste, community, creed or group is orchestrated through their dress code or appearance. It could be keeping or cutting the beard, a special hat or turban, or the caste mark on their body. It also developed in them no sense of dignity of labour that greatly hampers the general economic uplift of the people of India:

> The man who makes the dingy bed in the hotel room will be affronted if he is asked to sweep the gritty floor. The clerk will not bring you a glass of water even if you faint. The architecture student will consider it a degradation to make drawings, to be a mere draughtsman [...].[9]

This being a serious Indian lacuna it increases their sense of dependence and thereby prevents them to become self-sufficient. It has greatly contributed to the bourgeois mentality in which Indian society grovels under painful conditions. Frantz Fanon points out that no true bourgeoisie exist in an underdeveloped country: "There is only a little of greedy caste, arid and voracious with the mind of a huckster, only too glad to accept the dividends that former colonial power hands out to it."[10] The motto of the middle class too is get-rich-quick.

People in various offices lack abominably the sense of work culture: they would not do any piece of work assigned to anybody lower in rank than their own. Naipaul is shocked to find Ramnath audaciously giving a reply to his boss Malhotra: "I am a steno, sir, I am not a typist." When Malhotra issues the letter of suspension on the charge of insubordination, Ramnath comes to his senses and strikes his forehead on Malhotra's shoes. "Sobbing, embracing the shoes, polishing them with his palms." The behaviour of Ramnath represents the adamantine attitude of many subordinate servants who defy official responsibilities. In the postcolonial period top ranking people love to show themselves off as Western officials. Naipaul cites examples of an army officer who manages to look like British officers by his gait and bearing, mannerisms, taste in English drink, and use of slang in English. Instead of *babu*-mentality, Naipaul would use a word "mimicry" which has almost gripped all the educated people of India. In his opinion "no people, by their varied physical endowments, are as capable of mimicry as the Indian." Indian society is mimicry of "the fairy-tale land of Anglo-India, of clubs and sahibs and syces and bearers." Even amidst colonial mimicry, which is just like an outer garb, Naipaul notes that long colonial rule has not extirpated the inner life of people:

> The outer and inner worlds do not have the physical separateness, which they had for us in Trinidad. They coexist: the society only pretends to be colonial; and for this reason its absurdities are at once apparent. Its mimicry is both less and more than a colonial mimicry. It is the special mimicry of an old country which has been without a native aristocracy for a thousand years and has learned to make room for outsiders, but only at the top. The mimicry changes, the inner world remains constant: this is the secret of survival.[11]

The colonial mimicry has created *babu*-mentality and consequently a new aristocracy of various class and castes that craves for enjoyment of all privileges in post-Independent India.

The worsening condition of public health is another determinant factor of the aftermath of colonial rule. The coloniser paid scant attention to general public health. The exploiters' basic motive was to extract capital and convert India to a useful market for England's finished product. What the colonisers neglected most was the way in which people lived under utter unhygienic condition and poverty. Though Hindu tradition teaches a lot about sanitation, people do not try to learn with proper spirit. Naipaul takes a detestable note of people's awkward living condition:

> I had seen Indian villages: the narrow, broken lanes with green slime in the gutters, the chocked back-to-back mud houses, the jumble of filth and food and animals and people, the baby in the dust, swollen-bellied, black with flies, but wearing its good-luck amulet. I had seen the starved child defecating at the roadside while the mangy dog waited to eat the excrement.[12]

Naipaul satirises the unhygienic toilet habits of people who do not even spare the tourist spots. While describing Shankaracharya Hill, one of the beauty spots of Srinagar, he issues a note of caution to the tourists: "It has to be climbed with care, for large areas of its lower steps are used as latrines by Indian tourists." While defecating, women in groups giggle when they see a stranger as if the stranger has willingly exposed oneself to such a shameful scene. Invariably bus stops are the places for public lavatories. Travellers to pass their time raise their dhoti without any warning and defecate in the gutter. Out of sheer shame and disgust Naipaul makes a scything remark:

> Indians defecate everywhere. They defecate, mostly, beside the railway tracks. But they also defecate on the beaches; they defecate on the hills; they defecate on the river banks; they defecate on the streets; they never look for cover. Muslims, with their tradition of *purdah,* can at times be secretive.[13]

Naipaul blames Gandhism, which has become a common vogue in the post-independence era even though Gandhi produced a creative synthesis of various aspects of different religious thoughts. Rooted in Hinduism, Gandhi was open to all religious traditions and spiritual inheritance. Gandhian thoughts, in the opinion of Robert J.C. Young, have come under heavy scrutiny by the intellectuals in their postcolonial discourse:

> The Subaltern Studies historians are in many ways sympathetic to Gandhi's anti-elitist position, his espousal of the cause of the peasantry, his identification with the poor, the Dalits and all those pushed to the extreme margin of Indian society-subaltern-in a word.[14]

But Naipaul's assessment of Mahatma Gandhi's philosophy and achievement is bizarre and wholly unacceptable to Gandhian followers. In his opinion—symbolic action is the curse of the Indians. Gandhi utilised symbolic action: whether it is latrine cleaning or spinning wheel. So the great soul (*Mahatma*) remains a tragic paradox in India. His success and failure are put on the same scale as he is considered a great soul and profoundly revered and loved by his countrymen. But Naipaul daubs Gandhi as a revolutionary who became a god. The Gandhi legend is still active but his teaching and philosophy have receded.

As has been discussed above colonialism has persistently destroyed indigenous culture. The West has failed to understand adequately Hindu religion and social customs. The practice of veil (*purdah*) has its own merits. Women in India wear veil so that "men wouldn't get excited and think bad things." Naipaul is shocked at the sight of "ceremonial washing of the genitals in public before prayers." Religion is so much in the blood of the Indians that even scientists and physicians become religious fanatics.

Implementing the two-nation theory before handing over the country to the natives, the British sowed the seeds of communal disharmony. In the name of religion fanatics perpetrate bloodshed and massacre in Kashmir. It is the reason the region has remained a bone of contention between India and Pakistan in the postcolonial period. Many Kashmiri clans are still Hindus. But these Kashmiris retain no memory of their Hindu past. Naipaul deplores Aziz's attitude towards the

Hindu ruins which lay just at the side of the main road. In a satiric tone Naipaul points out that Aziz's history only began with his conquerors. The religion as practised in the valley was not pure: Islam is iconoclastic: "the Kashmiris went mad when they saw the hair from the prophet's beard." Equally Naipaul's assessment of Hindu Gods is a lopsided view. God in Amarnath Cave is worshipped as a massive ice phallus. As per the Hindu conception the world on one hand was thought of to be illusion; but on the other hand the symbol of phallus and female sexual organ are worshipped. The sight of a *sadhu* walking barefooted on Himalayan snow with a trident in his hand made Naipaul aghast. He was a young man of sinister beauty, having disquieting appearance with his languid genitals arrogantly exposed.

Instead of appreciating the infinite capacity of tolerance of the Indian society, Naipaul pooh-poohs the idea of India possessing an infinite capacity for being plundered by foreign powers. He receives a shock to find the monuments of the fanatic Muslim rulers: "Mosque on temple: ruin on ruin. This is the North."[15] In India, the endless mosques and rhetorical mausolea, the great palaces speak only of a personal plunder. Even the Taj Mahal is "only a despot's monument to a woman," not of India.

To Naipaul, the England of India remains an incongruous imposition. But the England of the Raj can be found in many ways. It lived in the division of the country into two cantonments: "civil lines" and "military cantonments." It lived in army officers' messes, in their uniforms and moustaches, swagger sticks, mannerisms and jargon. It lived in the collectorates. It lived in the clubs, the Sunday morning binga. It lived in the dance floors of city restaurants. The legacy of British Raj in India has not yet been shaken off: "in India everything is inherited: nothing is abolished; everything grows out of something else [...].[16] In Mrs Mahendra's house Naipaul finds a strong craze for foreign products. The chemistry teacher, Naipaul met in Kashmir, expressed his disappointment in this country where he feels he is trapped. Such educated Indians suffer from frustration and the reason of their dislike for India is to go abroad:

> Corruption and nepotism everywhere [...]. Everybody wanting to go out to United Nation's jobs, Doctors going abroad, scientist going to America. The future is totally black.[17]

During the colonial rule the natives bribed officials. The same corrupt practices became rampant in the postcolonial period. A traffic inspector receives monthly protection money from various lorry-drivers. There were outbursts in press and parliament about corruption. It seems as if corruption has become the rule of the day. It so happens that people who object to corruptive practices and collection of dishonest money are either suspended or transferred on various grounds. In civil construction departments the engineers from top to bottom level receive fixed percentage of profits charged on the bills.

Naipaul puts himself in the subject position when he encounters his relatives in his ancestral village. Being a foreigner he fails to understand the sentiments of his relatives. He remains unmoved amidst Jussodara's tears. He does not reciprocate the warm welcome given out to him by Ramachandra. Unconsciously Naipaul reveals his sense of racial superiority when he describes disdainfully the eating habits of the south Indians.

> Food was a pleasure to their hands, chewing, sighing with pleasure they squelched curds and rice between their fingers. They squelched and squelched; then, in one swift circular action, as though they wished to take their food by surprise, they gathered some of the mixture into a ball, brought their dripping palms close to their mouths and flick![18]

Naipaul does not outright condemn the British rule in India. He urges upon Indians to remain forever obliged to Europe even if India was mercilessly ruled over by the British because "it was Europe that revealed India's past to India and made its veneration part of Indian nationalism. It is still through European eyes that India looks at her ruins and her art. Nearly every Indian who writes on Indian art feels bound to quote from the writings of European admirers [...]. Where there has been no European administration there is neglect."[19] The British refused to be absorbed by India unlike the Moguls.

Like the Moguls, the British never considered India a paradise on earth. While exploiting and dominating over India, they never stepped back to express their contempt for our land. Even the psychological damage wrought by the continued use of English as the official language is irreparable. The British tried their best to manufacture native elites in their own making who aped their socio-official life. The basic motive of the British Government was to extract capital and convert India to a useful market for England's finished product: "The British pillaged the country thoroughly; during their rule manufacturers and crafts declined." Even if the British government established somewhere a biscuit factory, it was a poor exchange for gold embroidery. Naipaul holds England entirely responsible for the Indian artistic failure.

Naipaul's expatriate sensibilities spring out from his dissociation with the tradition of his forefathers. He is oblivious of the facts that the strongest part of Indian close-knit family and social life is the attachment to Indian custom and tradition. It is the custom and rich heritage that have enabled this ancient civilisation to survive ravages wrought by thousand of years of foreign rule.

REFERENCES

1. Elleke Boehmer, *Colonial & Postcolonial Literature.* OUP, 1995, 176.
2. Fawzia Mustafa, *V.S. Naipaul.* Cambridge University Press, 1995, 1-2.
3. V.S. Naipaul, *An Area of Darkness.* New Delhi: Penguin Books, India (P.) Ltd., 1968, 167.
4. *An Area of Darkness* 43.
5. *An Area of Darkness* 201.
6. *An Area of Darkness* 201-02.
7. *An Area of Darkness* 29-30.
8. V.S. Naipaul, *Among the Believers: An Islamic Journey.* 1981; rpt. New York: Vintage, 1982, 111.
9. *An Area of Darkness* 47.
10. Frantz Fanon, *The Wretched of the Earth.* Penguin Books, 1963, 14.
11. *An Area of Darkness* 56.
12. *An Area of Darkness* 45.
13. *An Area of Darkness* 70.
14. Robert J.C. Young, *Postcolonialism: An Historical Introduction.* Malden: Blackwell Publishers Inc., 2001, 352.

15. *An Area of Darkness* 201.
16. *An Area of Darkness* 194.
17. *An Area of Darkness* 94.
18. *An Area of Darkness* 223.
19. *An Area of Darkness* 206.

9

A Million Mutinies in the Domain of Darkness

JAGDISH V. DAVE

I

Man does not passively sense the world as formless phenomenal stuff like a-linguistic and half asleep animal sentience. He transforms existence into the world of names and forms in his critical understanding of it. Then he is not satisfied with the apprehension of reality. He is essentially a creature of culture who must reshape what he naturally finds. That is how he turns one globe into many countries and many individuals into one society. The society he tightens further into state and raises its history divided into ages from indivisible continuity of time. He must evolve into ever better shape—institutions of administration, justice, education, police, armed forces, hospitals and other means of realizing human welfare.

Man is man as long as he behaves in this fashion. But in the history of the Hindu-world we discern, to borrow a phrase from Naipaul, a 'downward evolution' from full-blooded humanity towards animal torpor. To an impartial observer it might appear very clearly that man has not been man enough in this country for long in humanistic sense of the term. Nirad Chaudhuri called it the 'Continent of Circe,' not to describe its denizens as animals, but to distinguish them from normal mankind. He is not the only author to use a rather irksome appellation to denote our reality. Tagore, too, called it in terms of fiction the 'Kingdom of Cards' in the short story of that title, and Swami Vivekanada said that "through centuries of slavery, we have become like a nation of women" (Vivekananda 300). Naipaul too, did the same when he described the land of his ancestors as 'An Area of Darkness' where nothing appears to be astir with life.

There was a time when the Hindu-man had been as dynamic as the Western. In the absence of recorded history it is difficult to say when exactly the decay set in. But by eleventh century our degradation becomes too obvious to be overlooked. Al-Biruni, the Muslim historian of Iranian origin, determined to understand the Hindus sympathetically "on the very basis of their civilization" (Al-Biruni 270) in true post-colonial spirit centuries before the world had heard of the theory, notes what he easily sees when he writes of Hindu complacency, the illness of mind "for which there is no medicine" (10), the folly which assumed that the good is what is Indian and all else is evil. The Hindus, he observes further, "are haughty, foolishly vain, self-conceited and stolid" (10). Their "so-called scientific theorems" are "in a state of utter confusion, devoid of any logical order, and in the last instance, always mixed up with the silly notions of the crowd" (11). They cannot write prose (which requires clearheadedness), do not know history and are "very careless in relating the chronological succession of their kings, and when they are pressed for information and are at a loss, not knowing what to say, they invariably take to tale-telling" (192). Al-Biruni notes besides how Hindu spirituality of loving-kindness which sees God everywhere, is at variance with the vertical order of caste-divisions held together by mutual hate. If a Sudra or Vaishya, he says to illustrate its iniquity, is discovered to have recited the Vedas, his tongue would be cut off as punishment according to the king's order. The Bhagavadgita, he says, treats all living beings as brothers and proposes the idea of the family of Life. But the Hindus in their practice of caste do not recognize even the family of man. It is curious but obvious that Hindu spirituality has never influenced the formation of Hindu society.

The darkness that looks dense enough to Al-Biruni in the eleventh century, reaches its extremity in the eighteenth. Hegel had to draw the attention of his contemporary Indologists who were fascinated by the philosophical wisdom of our past, to the sordid and repellent shape of our reality at the time. He, perhaps, is the first of Europeans who tried to discover peculiar nature of our evolutionary progress and succeeded in seeing instead a static pool of time where all past is simultaneous, where the humanity of humanistic notion seems to be absent. There are castes that are high and low, and they can never flow into one another.

> Duties and rights, therefore, are not recognized as pertaining to mankind generally, but as those of a particular caste. While we say, "Bravery is a virtue," the Hindus say, on the contrary, "Bravery is a virtue of the Kshatriyas" [...]. Everything is petrified into these distinctions, and over this petrifaction a capricious destiny holds sway. Morality and human dignity are unknown; evil passions have their full swing; the spirit wanders into the dream world, and the highest state is annihilation. (Hegel 235)

Many castes then cannot make one people. How can they have public spirit or communal code of conduct? We have survived as isolated individuals indifferent to one another. Hegel's language is too blunt to be bearable when he tells us that "Deceit and cunning are the fundamental characteristics of the Hindu," and that "cheating, stealing, robbing, murdering are with him habitual" (241). But our open-eyed observation of the sociopolitical life around will testify to the truth of Hegel's statement. And remember how the Rajput princes fought their own brothers as the vassals of the Muslim rulers, how even today the village-Thakur bullies other castes, particularly the dalits, before you resent Hegel's assertion that "Humbly crouching and abject before a victor and lord, he (the Hindu) is recklessly barbarous to the vanquished and subject" (241).

India, Hegel writes further, has rarely experienced a system of Government. The kings here looked like tyrants. No kingdom knew regular institutions of education, justice, administration, army. It is difficult to contradict him when he writes:

> Hindu political existence presents us with people, but *no state* [...]. In India, therefore, the most arbitrary, wicked, degrading despotism has its full swing [...] nothing approaching even a resentful protest against it is left,

> except the corporeal smart, and the pain of being deprived of absolute necessaries and of pleasure. (242)

He is absolutely right when he observes:

> The spread of Indian culture is prehistorical, for history is limited to that which makes an essential epoch in the development of spirit. On the whole, the diffusion of Indian culture is only a dumb, deedless expansion; that is, it presents no political action. The people of India have achieved no foreign conquests, but have been on every occasion vanquished themselves. (232)

Al-Biruni is a friendly foreigner in his criticism of Hinduism. Hegel, baffled by the spectacle of Indian inertia so thoroughly opposed to Western dynamism, is not unfriendly. Tagore, Vivekananda, Chaudhuri, are patriotic Indians self-critical in national sense of the term. They would not contradict Al-Biruni or Hegel, for the respected truth. And they had passion for lifting India up from its wretched state of degradation. Naipaul's distinction is that he is neither an Indian nor a foreigner to India, but a bit of both. "This India," he writes, "or this anxiety about, where we had come from," has been with him "like a neurosis" (Naipaul: 1990: 7).

> I was far enough away from it to cease to be of it. I knew the rituals but couldn't participate in them; I heard the language, but followed only the simpler words. But I was near enough to understand the passions; and near enough to feel that my own fate was bound up with the fate of the people of the country. (491)

Naipaul's criticism of India is both a foreigner's criticism and a Hindu patriot's. Anger is his expression of love in *An Area of Darkness* and *India: A Wounded Civilization*. The substance of these two books has little more to say than Al-Biruni or Hegel. But he is more elaborate than Hegel, and naturally the details he describes, unlike Al-Biruni's, are modern and immediately verifiable.

As Naipaul moves towards India from England, he finds in Egypt the beginning of the East which exhibits the "chaos of uneconomical movement, the self-stimulated din, the sudden feeling of insecurity, the conviction that all men were not brothers and that the luggage was in danger" (Naipaul: 1987).

This is prelude to India where you find in the streets "the children, the dirt, the disease, the undernourishment, the cries of *bakshish*, the hawkers, the touts, the glimpses of minarets" (11). And he finds as he moves further Eastward that

> The physique of Europe had melted away first into that of Africa and then, through Semitic Arabia, into Aryan Asia. Men had been diminished and deformed; they begged and whined. (13)

Foreigners often come to India with the expectations of seeing a land of true spirituality. A gentleman comments on them in *An Area of Darkness*:

> You make up your minds about India before coming to the country. You have been reading the wrong books. (22)

The *Upanishadas* and the *Bhagavadgita* are the wrong books to introduce the socio-political reality of India, the real cultural behaviour of its people. The correct books like Naipaul's or Chaudhuri's would not attract the foreigners. Naturally, those who come to see the greatness of ancient India here are disappointed to find instead its modern wretchedness. They cannot understand why the humans in this country deal with one another and foreigners with cold indifference and unnecessary rudeness, even hostility.

Like Al-Biruni and Hegel, Naipaul, too, feels that time in India is a static pool. It lacks dynamism of history. "It is a history whose only lesson is that life goes on" (202). For more than a millennium our people have lived like frogs in the well ignorant of the wider world without.

> No civilization was so little equipped to cope with the outside world; no country was so easily raided and plundered, and learned so little from its disasters. (Naipaul: 1981: 7)

Since the first Muslim invasion of it in the eighth century, India has shrunk not only in physical size; culturally, too, it has shrunken:

> India absorbs and outlasts its conquerors, Indians say. But at Vijaynagar, among the pilgrims, I wondered

> whether intellectually for a thousand years India hadn't always retreated before its conquerors and whether, in its periods of apparent revival, India hadn't only been making itself archaic again, intellectually smaller, always vulnerable. (18)

With a sense of sadness Naipaul writes that India perhaps "will never cease to require the arbitration of a conqueror. (Naipaul: 1987: 202).

The India that Naipaul sees in 1962 or 1977 is not different from the picture that Hegel paints. The independence seems to have made no change at all:

> [...] the narrow, broken lanes with green slime in gutters, the choked back-to-back mud houses, the jumble of food and filth and animals and people, the baby in the dust, swollen-bellied, black with flies, but wearing its good-luck amulet. I had seen the starved child defecating at the roadside while the mangy dog waited to eat the excrement. (48)

The torpor of Indian life is akin to animal insensitivity that knows not how to protest against the situation or to dream of changing it. It feels no pain and needs nobody's sympathy, "[...] it is your gaze that violates them, your sense of outrage that outrages them." (44) But Naipaul is disgusted:

> Fear was what I felt. Contempt was what I had to fight against; to give way to that was to abandon the self I had known. (45)

Hinduism "has given men no idea of a contract with other men, no idea of the state" (Naipaul: 1981: 53). Racialism is alien to Indian mind, it is true. But it is because the Indians have more cruel and irrational divisions of caste:

> Caste imprisons a man in his function. (Naipaul: 1987: 75)
>
> It isn't that Indians are especially cowardly or have no admiration for courage. It is that bravery, the willingness to risk one's life, is the function of the soldier and no one else [...]. Every man is an island; each man to his function, his private contract with God [...]. It is inefficient and destructive; it has created a psychology which will frustrate all improving plans. (78)

It is difficult to dispute Naipaul when he tells us that we Indians are unable to face reality clear-sightedly:

> How often in India—at every level—rational conversation about the country's problems trails away into talk of magic, of the successful prophecies of astrologers, of the wisdom of auspicious hours, of telepathic communications, and actions taken in response to some inner voice? (Naipaul: 1981: 112)

It is the dread of reality, the reluctance to face painful history in order to turn its current into desirable and well-planned channels of future, that drives Indians to

> retreat into fantasy and fatalism, to trust to the stars in which the fortunes of all are written—there are lectures in astrology in some universities—and to regard the progress of the rest of the world with the tired tolerance of one who has been through it all before. The aeroplane was known to ancient India, and the telephone, and the atom bomb: there is evidence in the Indian epics. Surgery was highly developed in ancient India; here, in an important national newspaper, is the text of a lecture proving it. Indian shipbuilding was the wonder of the world. And democracy flourished in ancient India. (Naipaul: 1987: 201)

The world's 'second most populous country' with "intellectual second-rateness, which is generally taken for granted" has now "little to offer the world except its Gandhian concept of holy poverty and the recurring crooked comedy of its holy men" which "while asserting the antiquity of its civilization (and usually simply asserting, without knowledge or scholarship), is now dependent in practical way on other, imperfectly understood civilization" (Naipaul: 1981: 104).

II

Naipaul is right when he says in the first, of his books on India that it is "the featureless area of darkness" (Naipaul: 1987: 35), and in the second that its true crisis is the crisis of "a wounded old civilization that has at last become aware of its inadequacies and is without the intellectual means to move ahead" (Naipaul: 1981: 18). Both the books can be placed in the tradition of honest and impartial albeit harsh and bitter criticism of Indian life. But the third one, *India: a Million Mutinies Now*, is a somersault. India appears to be awakened to hectic activities to his view now:

> India has changed; it was not the good and stable country it had once been. In the days of the freedom movement, political workers, honouring Gandhi, had worn homespun as an emblem of sacrifice and service, their oneness with the poor. Now the political homespun stood for power. With industrialization and economic growth people had forgotten old reverences. Men honoured only money now. The great investment in development over three or four decades had led only to this: to 'corruption,' to the 'criminalization of politics.' In seeking to rise, India had undone itself. No one could be sure of anything now; all was fluid. Policeman, thief, politician: the roles had become interchangeable. And with money—the money of which the crowded, ugly skyscraper towers of Bombay spoke—many long-buried particularities had been released. These disruptive, lesser loyalties—of region, caste, and clan—now played on the surface of Indian life. (Naipaul: 1990: 4)

Periyar, Thakare, Bhindranwale, Ambedkar—these and many others of the kind are the icons now, the leaders of clashing groups. Pakistan, Dravidistan, Dalitistan, Khalistan, and many similar '*stans*' are the slogans now:

> Independence had come to India like a kind of revolution; now there were many revolutions within that revolution [...]. All over India scores of particularities that had been frozen by foreign rule, or by poverty or lack of opportunity or abjectness had begun to flow again. (6)

All this, Naipaul now feels, had been there even in 1962 under the surface. Now it immediately strikes the eye:

> The British peace after the 1857 Mutiny can be seen as a kind of luck. It was a time of intellectual recruitment. India was set on the way of a new kind of intellectual life; it was given new ideas about its history and civilization. The freedom movement reflected all of this and turned out to be the truest kind of liberation.

> In the 130 years or so since the Mutiny—the last 90 years of the British Raj and the first 40 years of independence begin increasingly to appear as part of the same historical period—the ideal of freedom has gone everywhere in India. Independence was worked for by people more or less at the top; the freedom it brought has worked its way down. People everywhere have ideas now of who they are and what they owe themselves [...]. The liberation of spirit that has come to India could not come as release alone. In India, with its layer below layer of distress and cruelty, it had to come as disturbance. It had to come as rage and revolt. India was now a country of a million little mutinies. (517)

III

How we wish Naipaul were right in reading our fissiparous violence as an incipient movement towards some eventual unity and peace! But, it seems, in his last book on India he has abandoned reason in favour of optimism. Perhaps he is tired of his despair. But his hope looks hollow.

In *India: A Wounded Civilization* Naipaul describes the post-emergency electoral victory of the opposition parties united against the Congress of Indira Gandhi, as "a revolution without ideas. It was an emotional outburst, a wallow" (Naipaul: 1981: 141). He is right. But which of the million mutinies now has an ideal content? It was absent even from the Gandhian struggle for independence. None had a constructive vision of what he wanted to do if independence came. 'Quit India!' was a negative slogan. So was 'Indira-hatao!' (Remove Indira!) What is truly positive about modern rage and revolt is a dream of selfish gain which could only break and not make a community.

Al-Biruni, Hegel, early Naipaul—all see the caste as a curse on the Hindu society. Now castes are clashing with one another instead of coexisting in proper subordination as before. Each of them wants to occupy the top position. But none wants to undo the hierarchy. The Hindu psyche of "sniffing differences" in the vertical order of high and low, remains intact. The birth of horizontal humanity does not appear even on the horizon anywhere. Our pluralism still cannot make a people, much less a state. How shall we say then that India has changed?

Look at the row between red and saffron historians. Each alike studiously evades the facts of the past for the convenience of a political dogma. None has passion for truth, none wants to build future in the light of past experiences. Shall we still say that the motionless pool of our past has now at last turned into a regular stream of history?

Are we not still repeating Western theories of withdrawing into our archaisms in our academic deliberations, papers, speeches? Attendance at one seminar, conference, symposium somewhere in India would have been enough to disillusion Naipaul, enough to teach him that we have yet to realize truly critical and objective grasp of things, and that our "intellectual secondrateness," that he deplored earlier, has now perhaps degenerated into thirdrateness with the passage of time. Look at the non-universities known as universities that have mushroomed in the country where non-teachers and non-students abound. With all of them and with so much expense on the so-called higher education, our contribution to the world-culture still remains confined to the "crooked comedy' of our gurus and godmen. Do we not still retreat into fantasy and fatalism? Previously there used to be only occasional lectures on astrology in the universities. Now regular Departments with Professors, Readers, Lecturers, etc. are proposed. Our 'evolution downwards' in all spheres of life continues as before. Just compare our institutions of legislature, justice, administration, education as we have now with what they were fifty years ago, to realize the regress! And are we not still vulnerable to foreign invasions? Look at Pakistan's proxy-war that has been harassing us for last fifteen years or so, and the attacks on the Red-fort, Kashmir Legislative Assembly and the Indian Parliament!

For more than a millennium chaos has ruled our land. The British came and imposed humanist discipline on us. That indeed was our good luck. But Gandhiji did not see it as such. He dreamt, as an alternative of a chaos, in an idealized form. The *Hindu Swaraj* would have no railways and machines, no schools and colleges, no hospitals, no courts of law, no parliament, no police or military force. Sports, theatres, arts or entertainments of any other kind are unthinkable indeed in the villages of his vision where men and women should pass their leisure hours in ascetic practices and live, after a couple of children are born to them, as brothers and sisters even if they are wives and husbands.

What gradually followed after the British left, however, was not the Gandhian, but gross anarchy of the pre-British period. Nirad Chaudhuri writes:

> Any one who has eyes to see and ears to hear and has no sense of guilt to shut them to the reality, will find what the actual state of the Indian people is: there is today more maladministration, corruption and lawlessness than ever was seen at any time during British days; in some provinces there is no government to speak of, power being in the hands of gangs like the Mafia; there is more suppression of civil rights, and shooting for political reasons; more denial of freedom of expression and of information; more disparity of wealth between Indians; more intercommunal, intercaste, and inter-provincial hatred; more oppression and even murder of the members of the minority and depressed communities; more exploitation by a privileged order of the people of India. (Chaudhuri: 1987: 860-61)

Chaudhuri writes this in 1987, that is, some three years before *A Million Mutinies* was published. Naipaul's perception is not different. But Chaudhuri sees despair where Naipaul irrationally reads hope. He does not look different from Papu of the book, who says:

> 'I am sure there's going to be a revolution. In a generation or two. It cannot last, the inequalities of income. I shudder when I think of that. I am very sure that the Indian mind is religious, fatalistic. Even after all the education I've had, I still think that destiny will take me—I'll get there whatever I do. This is why we haven't had a revolution. Now, with the growing frustrations, even if people are religious there is going to be a revolution. The tolerance is being stretched too far.'
>
> 'What form do you think the revolution will take?'

> 'It won't be *anything*. It will be totally chaos.' (Naipaul: 1990: 15)

Chaos calls for revolution. But revolution will be "totally chaos." What surprises the reader is that Naipaul appears to be chiming in with Papu's confusion. In his first two books the author takes his stand on humanism when he criticizes Indian inertia. In the last one he seems to have no specific stand when he views Indian internecine violence as a waking up from sleep. It seems that, the Great Anarch that is India has reclaimed Naipaul the fugitive at last to praise the chaos that has been steadily growing from bad to worse here, as our ultimate salvation.

Every revolution has come from a wave of idealism. The French and Marxist revolutions are the instances in point. Renaissance and Reformation even like early Christianity had been powerful waves of idealism which have humanized and altered for the better the history of mankind. India, too, needs idealism. Al-Biruni implies in his heartfelt admiration of Hindu spirituality that it should have shaped a Hindu fraternity of equals, and that sadly it has not. When it did, he fails to note, the community came to be called Buddhism. Buddha taught his followers to look upon all creatures as the actors in the same cosmic tragedy and realized in practice the family of Life higher than humanism. Our great reformers emulated his example in the nineteenth century, the only period of awakening during a millennium old sleep, when they turned to our tradition of spirituality well-known to our people, in order to draw from it the idealism necessary for secular reform, and altruism. Look at the work of Ram Mohan Roy, Ranade, Dayananda, Tagore, Vivekananda, the moderate leaders of early Indian National Congress, and a host of other less known luminaries that appeared all over the country, during the period! Even today we need the spirit of altruism, the passion for self-sacrifice and intense intellectual and ethical culture similar to one we find in the West, to safeguard us against the threat of a million mutinies to our national unity and integrity. Who would inspire such altruism, such idealism now! There is no reason why some Odysseus should not appear in the land to restore humanity to Circe's animals. Let us hope, even if it means hoping against hope, he will. This hope is at least more reasonable than Naipaul's irrational reading of the post-independence turmoil as true liberation.

WORKS CITED

Al-Biruni. *India.* Ed. Ahmad Qeyamuddin. Delhi: Rupa & Co., 1983.

Chaudhari, Nirad. *Thy Hand Great Anarch*. Delhi: Time Book International, 1987.

Hegel, Georz Wilhelm Friedrich. "The Philosophy of History" in *Great Books of the Western World.* Vol. 43. Ed. Adler Mortimer F. *Encyclopaedia Britannica.* The Chicago, 1991.

Naipaul, V.S. *India: A Wounded Civilization.* Penguin, 1981.

____. *An Area of Darkness.* Penguin, 1987.

____. *India: A Million Mutinies Now.* Delhi: Rupa & Co., 1990.

Vivekananda, Swami. *The Complete Works of Swami Vivekananda.* Vol. III. Mayavati Memorial Edition: Advait Ashram, 1979.

10

"But why call it a novel?": Varieties of Transgression in V.S. Naipaul's *The Enigma of Arrival*

DAVID MALCOLM

"But why call it a novel?" asks a perplexed Gabriel Josipovici at the end of a laudatory review of V.S. Naipaul's *The Enigma of Arrival* (24). This unease about exactly what *The Enigma of Arrival* might be is reflected in other reviews by Peter Kemp: "it reads as something scarcely fictional" (838) and Pankaj Mishra: "[t]his autobiographical novel" (15). In the following essay I will argue that Naipaul designates *The Enigma of Arrival* as "A Novel" precisely because, in many senses, it is not a novel at all, or at least not a novel in terms of certain powerful traditions and conventions. The author draws attention to the highly transgressive nature of his text by naming it as something which by many standards it is not.[1]

It is clear that *The Enigma of Arrival* is, indeed, a liminal and hybrid text, full of tensions and dissonances, frequently breaching traditional norms.[2] Its disruptive and transgressive nature can be seen in four aspects of the text: its uncertain status as fiction and/or autobiography; its narrator and the context in which he observes and the position from which he observes his physical and human environment; the connected motifs of illusion and negation that pervade the work; and the text's organisation as a deviant novel through its deployment of a particular narrative strategy and its (for a novel) unusual linguistic configuration.

The reader's uncertainty as to whether he/she is reading fiction or autobiography is encoded in the text. The unnamed narrator of *The Enigma of Arrival* is a writer from Trinidad of Indian background, the descendant of indentured labourers brought by the British to work in the West Indies. He recounts winning a scholarship to go to university in Britain and of early years of confusion and displacement in that country. He is a novelist, historian and travel writer. He tells of his visits to the Caribbean and to Africa and India, and of his sceptical responses to the political changes that de-colonisation has wrought there. Most of the text centres on his experiences in Wiltshire in the south of England, where he rents a cottage on a large and slowly running-down estate, which over the years becomes more and more dilapidated. He observes the rural life around him, his neighbours, his landlord. He speculates on change, passing time and decay. He considers the ironies of history that have brought him, a man from a Caribbean island, the descendant of people shifted halfway round the globe by the British Empire, to this corner of agricultural England, to an estate whose past and now tawdry, crumbling glories were based on money made in the time of Empire.

This clearly echoes much of what the implied reader of the text can be expected to know about Naipaul's life. This life is ably summarised by Hilary Mantel in a recent number of *The New York Review of Books* (see 10-12). The outline of Naipaul's own life and that of the narrator in *The Enigma of Arrival* are remarkably similar. The origin among the descendants of indentured Indian labourers in Trinidad, the scholarship, the years of uneasy residence in England, the painstakingly developed literary career, the novels, the travel books, the dark vision of politics and society in India and Africa—these form Naipaul's own non-fictional biography. "All this sounds exactly like Naipaul's own biography," notes Kemp in the *Times Literary Supplement* of *The Enigma of Arrival* (838).

But the two biographies—the fictional and the factual—do not overlap entirely. For example, there is very little about Naipaul's travels in the USA in the fictional narrator's cv in *The Enigma of Arrival.* Further, many of the characters of *The Enigma of Arrival*—Jack, the narrator's landlord, the Philippses, Mr and Mrs Bray, Mr Pitton—are not known from Naipaul's biography, and its narrator is never named. In addition, the author clearly designates *The Enigma of Arrival* as a novel, thus declaring it not to be a strictly factual account of his experiences, but a reworking of them, a selection of them, a shaping of them, through art. This insistence on fictional reworking functions as a metatextual point about all autobiographies (and biographies), that is that they are textual shapings of biographical material and very similar to novels. It also, however, stresses the text's ambiguity, its enigmatic status. "What is it really?" the reader wants to know, and the answer is that it is a text on the borders of two kinds of writing, autobiography and fiction, one which teases the reader with contradictory signs. This is Naipaul speaking of himself. Or is it?

The figure of the narrator in *The Enigma of Arrival* disrupts certain traditional expectations in another way as well. He describes himself at one point as "an intruder, not from another village or county, but from another hemisphere" (285). He is someone of Indian background, from the Caribbean, in rural England. It is striking that the narrator's racial difference, his darkness, is almost never mentioned in the text, and never seems to be an issue in the small country towns and rural roads of Wiltshire either for the narrator himself or for his neighbours. However, the narrator is very conscious of himself as an outsider, as someone from another world, who is observing the lives and landscapes that surround him. "[T]here would have been no room for me" on the estate at the height of empire, he says of himself (52), and he constantly emphasises that he observes Wiltshire from the perspective of his origins in Trinidad. He is "a provincial, from a far corner of the empire" (120).

There is certainly a tradition within European literature in which an observer from outside Europe, from a colonised, formerly colonised, or simply exotic part of the world, travels to Europe and observes the customs of the country with enthusiasm, disdain or simple confusion. Montesquieu's *Lettres persanes* (1721), which is an important example of this kind of text, presents a fictional foreign observer of French customs, and is in no sense an account of a genuine foreigner's observations. The fiction of Jean Rhys (*Voyage in the Dark*), George Lamming (*The Emigrants*), Timothy Mo (*Sour Sweet*) and Salman Rushdie (*The Satanic Verses*), among others, present, however, a much more genuinely extraterritorial view of contemporary Britain. Nonetheless, within British literature the reverse perspective is much more common, that of the British observer in an exotic world, in India, in Africa, or in South-East Asia, for example. Naipaul himself calls this "that tradition of imperial-expatriate writing in which the metropolitan outsider is thrown into relief against an alien background" ("Without a Dog's Chance" 29). He alludes to it in *The Enigma of Arrival* when the narrator says of himself that he "was glamoured by the idea of the metropolitan traveller, the man starting from Europe" who travels through the colonial world and reports back to a metropolitan audience. "It was the only kind of model I had," he adds (140). This is a tradition that runs throughout British fiction (for example, in Conrad, Kipling, Graham Greene, Lawrence Durrell, John Fowles and William Boyd), and it is one that Naipaul is consciously reversing in *The Enigma of Arrival.* Instead of Trinidad seen from Wiltshire, the reader has rural England seen from the Caribbean.

Paulus Pimomo argues that the whole issue of who writes about whom is central in postcolonial literature and literary studies (43-47), while Emily Bauman emphasises the importance for recent literary studies of "forms of (post)colonised subjectivity which stood on their own and gazed back" (79). Vijay Mishra and Bob Hodge make it clear how central the assertion of "legitimate consciousness, I-ness or self-hood" is in the context of a colonial and post-colonial social (and literary) situation (277-78). Naipaul's narrator in *The Enigma of Arrival* exemplifies these commentators' concerns. He—a man from a colonised Caribbean island—speaks of England. He emphasises his outsider status and makes his Trinidad-Indian provenance explicit, indeed central, to his whole ethos and vision. Rural Wiltshire is constantly compared to the Caribbean or to other distant and formerly colonised parts of the world. For example, Jack's working in his garden recalls for the narrator his own father's work on a small patch of ground in Trinidad (31). He is delighted to note that the gladiolus flower flourishes both in England and in Trinidad (33), while the English snow takes the shape of the sand on a Trinidad beach (45). England constantly suggests memories of other parts of the world. While writing a book about Africa, the narrator transposes part of the menace of his African landscape onto rural Wiltshire (156). A dead hare recalls the skeletons of pelicans on a Caribbean island (169), a ruined boathouse suggests dwellings seen on the Orinoco, the Amazon or the Congo (188), the smell of Pitton's house reminds him of that of poor houses in Trinidad (227), and Pitton himself at one point stands as the narrator remembers once seeing a "forest Indian" in Guiana stand (232-33). The allotments in England echo those in Trinidad, although here the narrator realises that the model has been deliberately imported from England and imposed on the Trinidad landscape (204).[3]

Thus, the way in which the narrator of *The Enigma of Arrival* sees the English landscape and English people is disruptive of a long-standing tradition in British fiction. One could further note that the narrator's own self-scrutiny (and there is much of this), his own musings on his situation as a post-colonial outsider in the former imperial centre, also reverse the tradition of much British fiction from the late nineteenth century to the present, whereby the metropolitan white British traveller or colonist journeys to distant parts of the world to learn more about himself (usually himself) and to test himself against the other that is Africa or India or South America. This is clearly Marlowe's motive in his choice to go to Africa in *Heart of Darkness*, while in John Buchan's *Prester John* Davie Crawfurd becomes a hero and a mature man in the challenges of Southern Africa. This is a pattern echoed in more recent fiction too, for example in Candia McWilliam's austere Conradian novel *Debatable Land*. It is decisively reversed in *The Enigma of Arrival*, in which the Caribbean expatriate in England examines himself, his moods, his doubts, and his development as writer and human being, in the context of a largely alien, and for him exotic, world, surrounded by enigmatic (not to say, downright strange) foreigners. The voice that is subaltern and silenced in much British fiction set abroad speaks clearly from the centre of this novel.[4]

The disruptive and trangressive nature of *The Enigma of Arrival* is embodied in repeated motifs that run throughout the text. These are motifs connected with the enigmatic status of objects. Things are often—literally—not what they seem.

This "not-ness" of things is emphasised in the first few pages. "The river was called the Avon; not the one connected with Shakespeare," the narrator informs the reader on the first page of the text (11). "I saw a forest," he tells us later. "But it wasn't a forest really" (12). "There was no village to speak of," he continues (13). The narrator throughout the text is confronted with illusions, some of his own making. He initially misinterprets Jack's methods of gardening, seeing them as stemming from Jack's being "the remnant of an old peasantry"—"falsely, as I got to know soon enough" (22). He thinks the farm manager actually owns or leases the farmland that lies near his cottage, and gives him in his mind a "farmer's walk," only to discover that he is just an employee (29). Jack's beard makes the narrator think him young; only later does he see that the beard is grey and Jack is in his forties (32). The countryside the narrator walks through at first seems "an unchanging world." "But that idea of an unchanging world was wrong. Change was constant" (34). Near his cottage the narrator notes "a building that pretended to be a rough old farmhouse" (49). It is, in fact, "a fives-court or squash-court." The nearby church has been restored in the Victorian or Edwardian period "and architecturally was as artificial as the farmhouse" (49). Of the latter, he writes subsequently that it is "not farmhouse, not squash-court" (59). Later in the text, although the experience dates from an earlier point in his life, the narrator feels that the "grandeur" he had expected in London "belonged to the past," and that his "fantasy" had created something that is now no longer accessible (120). He acerbically notes the illusions, what he sees as the simplifications and sentimentalisations of the Caribbean past, in the politics and self-understanding of people in postcolonial Trinidad, St Kitts and Anguilla (146-48). His discoveries of the illusory nature of buildings near his Wiltshire home continue throughout the text. What he had thought an imitation forester's hut, part of a "play settlement or village around the lawn or manor 'green,'" turns out to be a stable (176). The narrator bemusedly sums up the stage props that surround him: "A stable like a forester's hut (I allowed my fantasy to persist); and across the lawn a squash-court built to look like a farmhouse, its apparently rough walls as carefully thought out as the walls of my own cottage" (177).

If the narrator's environment is consistently not quite what it seems, then the "novel" itself that he has written (it is revealed he is the writer of the text on the last page [318]) is also an enigmatic entity, also not quite what the reader might expect, not quite what the subtitle "A Novel" indicates. Four technical and linguistic aspects of *The Enigma of Arrival* render it a disruptive and transgressive piece of work. These are: the sequencing of its story material; the story material itself and its particular realisation; the foregrounding of metaphor and simile in the text; and certain features of its linguistic configuration, particularly lexical repetition and syntactic parallelism. Naipaul himself writes of his own sense of how important it is to develop and change the novel. "Every serious writer has to be original," he declares in his essay "On Being a Writer," "he cannot be content to do or offer a version of what has been done before. And every serious writer as a result becomes aware of this question of form" (7). This essay is also marked by Naipaul's sense of the conventions of the British novel tradition, and of the burden they place on writers, a burden he feels it necessary to cast off (7).

Narrative sequencing is certainly not what it is in one major strand in the British (or even European) tradition. It is clearly not linear, neither logical nor chronological over the text as a whole. The first part of the text ("Jack's Garden") covers the whole several years of the narrator's stay in his cottage in Wiltshire, from his arrival to his departure to a new home ("I was also, sadly, preparing to leave" [84]). Part 2, "The Journey," casts back to events and experiences that predate his arrival in Wiltshire, for example, the journey from the Caribbean in 1950 that takes him to Britain, and other journeys elsewhere in the world. At the end it returns to the Wiltshire cottage. Part 3 deals largely with the people that the narrator gets to know during the years in the cottage, his landlord, the Phillipses, Pitton, Bray, among others. Part 4 most closely follows a linear pattern, dealing, as it does, with the concluding years in the cottage on the estate after Pitton's departure, and detailing Bray's relationship with a chance-met woman, Mr Phillips's death and Mrs Phillips's remarriage. The final section, "The Ceremony of Farewell," provides an account of the narrator's attending the ceremonies connected with his sister's death in Trinidad, in the mid-1980s. At the end of this section, he reveals that he began writing *The Enigma of Arrival,* shortly thereafter, calling up his memories of Jack's garden which begin the novel.

Non-linear narrative is certainly not unknown in British fiction in the twentieth century, although the degree to which it is widespread before the 1980s is questionable. Conrad's *Heart of Darkness* stands out in the early twentieth century as being to some extent non-linear, but even radically experimental texts such as Woolf's *The Waves* and Joyce's *Ulysses* follow the convention of linear narrative. It is in the 1980s that one finds substantial disruptions of linear narrative sequencing in British fiction, in, for example, Alasdair Gray's *1982 Janine,* Graham Swift's *Waterland* and Kazuo Ishiguro's *An Artist of the Floating World.* Even what is, in many ways, an innovative text like Salman Rushdie's *Midnight's Children* does follow an overall linear sequence of events, for all that it is constantly casting back into the past. Naipaul's digressive, associative narrative technique in *The Enigma of Arrival* harks back to Sterne's *Tristram Shandy,* but is still in the late 1980s within British fiction quite disruptive of narrative convention. In Naipaul's case this is all the more so because the reader cannot always be certain when events occur. The text provides some dates, and certainly at times relates events to each other, but often one is rather at sea in establishing the exact sequencing of events. *The Enigma of Arrival* lacks in many places the convention of clear temporal signposting and linear sequencing that is so much part of the British novel tradition.[5]

This transgressive approach to tradition is even more apparent in terms of the text's story material and its realisation. The narrator draws attention to his strategy in this respect when he writes of the death of a famous racehorse that has been kept in a paddock near his cottage. "In a short time the horse ceased to be in the paddock. It had died. Like so many deaths here, in this small village, like so many big events, it seemed to happen off-stage" (41). Later he talks of the life of a one of the characters and her family that their past "had really been the absence of a great event" (74). The narrator's treatment of his story material is to ignore or allude fleetingly to the "big" and "great" events that are part of it, and to focus rather on events, occurrence and experiences that could be seen as trivial or peripheral to those larger occurrences. The narrator deliberately and self-advertisingly refuses to provide the material one might expect. As Josipovici notes, *The Enigma of Arrival* is "a book almost without incident," at least in most conventional senses (24). For example, an incident or an event the narrator does recount is an encounter with an ill-behaved and unhappy boy on a bus (36-37). This is a trivial incident, in comparison with the deaths, affairs and separations that underlie the narrator's accounts. It is also quite inconclusive. The "story" has no clear climax and no resolution either. Trivial words are exchanged and the protagonists do not meet each other again.

Jack's "death, his funeral—like the death and funeral of his father-in-law some years before—seemed to have happened secretly," the narrator informs the reader, off-stage, like his heroic, "poetical" trip to the pub when he is already dying (47-48). The narrator writes extensively about Jack's garden, but very little about Jack's death, and the one "big" event he does choose to write of is simply a sick man's drive to a pub. This strategy of skirting round what are self-evidently conventionally important actions and situations is clear in the narrator's treatment of the Les and Brenda material. Here a "story" of social ambitions and marital dislocation, adultery and murder is covered fragmentarily and allusively over a few pages (64, 67, 71), given not much more space than the configurations and suggestiveness of the English snow (45-46). The adjacent farm fails. The narrator learns about this considerably after the event and passes over it rapidly (79). There are constant hints of stories in the text, stories that are never developed—the man in the hangar in Puerto Rico (101), the woman with the child on the plane to whom the narrator offers a banana (102), Angela's life (129). "There was a story there—if it had occurred to me that there was," reflects the narrator about her experiences (129). The reader learns of the narrator's father's death in a brief aside (137). Alan's life and death is the most developed of all the "stories" that shine through the narrator's accounts of walks and views, but even it only covers seven pages (259-66), and Bray's relationship with his "fancy woman," its extent and its consequences are presented much more elliptically and enigmatically (276, 305), as is the decorator's unhappy marriage towards the text's end (295-96). The narrator writes extensively of Pitton's ritualistic movements at work, of the tie he always wears and the kind of clothes he buys (203-07). He also recounts the occasion when he finds Pitton drunk from the champagne his employer has given him (233), a moment entirely inconclusive and enigmatic. What does it mean for the employer or for the employee? Most strikingly of all, the narrator—one realises at the end of Part 1—hardly writes of Jack at all, Jack who gives his name to the title of the first part, and who is presented as the occasion for the whole book at the end of the text. He spends more space not just on walks, weather and views, but on the linguistic idiosyncrasies of those around him than he does on a character named in a chapter title (182-84, 195, 221, 238, 267). In *The Enigma of Arrival,* Naipaul is exemplifying his distaste for what he sees as now stale narrative conventions in fiction, "its simplifications and distortions, its artificial scenes, and its idea of experience as a crisis that has to be resolved before life assumes its even course" ("On Being" 7). He is also providing an escape from "the need for narrative and plot" that he feels sat on the shoulders of nineteenth-century novelists "like a burden" (loc. cit.).

The Enigma of Arrival rigorously eschews material that in other novels would be central. It tells few "stories" in a traditional sense. One can see this deviation from the conventions of narrative texts in one particular linguistic feature: the narrator's fondness for parentheses. There are many parentheses. For example, the following sentence contains two ("at once diminishing [...] of men" and the passage within dashes):

> So the idea of antiquity, at once diminishing and ennobling the current activities of me, as well as the ideas of literature enveloped this world which—surrounded by highways and army barracks though it was, and with the very clouds in the sky sometimes seeded by the vapour trails of busy military aeroplanes—came to me as a lucky find of the solitude in which on many afternoons I found myself. (24)

Here one can note not just parenthesis, but also what linguists call arrest, the delaying of the main verb of the sentence and its placement towards the end of the utterance.[6] Both these features, parenthesis and arrest, de-emphasise narrative, by slowing down the transmission of central information. On the same page there is yet another example of parenthesis: "One autumn day—the days shortening, filling me with thoughts of winter pleasures, fires and evening lights and books—one autumn day I felt something like a craving to read of winter in *Sir Gawain and the Green Knight*" (24-25). On a later page there are even more striking examples, both of parenthesis and arrest:

> One day, later in the summer, walking past the old farm buildings and what had been Jack's cottage and garden—the junk and ruins which had formed no part of Jack's vision of a world ever renewed, ruins to which now, across the droveway, was added the burning-pit in the chalk for industrial-looking rubbish, the fire of which occasionally singed the silver birches planted years before to screen the old patch of waste ground—one day walking past the farm and its spreading litter and on up to where the Swiss rolls of hay had been stacked and were already going black and brilliant green with new shoots of grass, I heard the sound of a great fire behind the young wood—and that wood was no longer so young [...].
>
> On the way back—the fire burnt away, finished, ashes in the field behind the wood—on the way back from my walk, then and afterwards, the thick patch of moss below the dormer window on the thatched roof of the empty house, a green that was shining, unnatural, that green, once part of the beauty of thatch, seemed to stand for more than vegetable matter. (76)

These examples must stand for many others (see, for example, 11, 15, 66). *The Enigma of Arrival*—"A Novel"—is a text that does anything but tell stories and that constantly de-emphasises narrative motion.[7]

It is also a novel that markedly foregrounds metaphor and simile, placing these over event and action. Once again, there are many examples of this. Many emerge from the appearance of the countryside round the narrator's cottage. The beehives left abandoned in the fields (16), the carefully cut hay that has been left to rot (17), old farm buildings and an empty barn (18)—over a few pages the reader is presented with motifs that are underscored as metaphors and similes of decay. This strategy is continued throughout the text. Fresh snow transforms the farm buildings and the roadway "like a great clean thing, like a remaking of the world" (46). A plastic covered hayrick embodies the decay the narrator sees all around, "its texture now rather like the skin of very old people, like a faded rose petal" (54). Les and Brenda, after the murder and the emptying of their house, are directly metaphorized as bees (71). The green moss presented in the passage from page 76 quoted above is explicitly seen as a metaphor (it "seemed to stand for something more than vegetable matter"). The narrator turns his own experiences into metaphors. The humiliations and uneasiness of the first visit to New York in 1950—being cheated by a taxi-driver, being unable to tip a porter, eating greasy chicken over a waste bin, and being scalded by hot water—are returned to as metaphors of the narrator's own provinciality, his unreadiness for the metropolitan world (150-51). The process of metaphorization is constant. The rooks that arrive in the Wiltshire valley are "settlers" engaged in "colonization" (269), in parallel to the processes the narrator has discussed in Trinidad and in post-war London and Europe. The fire described on page 76 is returned to later in the novel and is explicitly seen as a metaphor, "giving me the idea that all matter was one, and that all disturbances, whether of fire or water or air, were the same" (297).

Once again, *The Enigma of Arrival* is enigmatic and not a little transgressive. It presents itself as a novel, yet not only de-emphasises narrative, but also constantly metaphorizes experience. There is a density of figurative language that one associates with lyric poetry rather than with prose narrative. This association with lyric poetry is reinforced by other features of the text's language.[8] Naipaul's novel is full of lexical repetition. It is no coincidence that the name of the nearby village and the manor in whose grounds the narrator lives is called "Waldenshaw," a name he glosses as "wood-wood" (13). A casual glance at almost any page in the first part of the novel will show to what extent lexical items are repeated. Two representative examples must suffice. The lexical repetitions are marked in italics:

> The straw was *golden*, warm; *the grain* was *golden*; but *the dust that fell* all around—on the concrete yard, the rocky lane, the pines and young beeches of the windbreak—*the dust that fell* after *the grain* had poured into the trays of the trucks was *grey*. At the side of the *metal*-walled barn, and below the *metal* spout, there was a *conical mound* of *dust* that had been winnowed by some mechanical means from the bigger *conical mounds* of *grain* in the barn. *The dust*—the *mound* firm at the base, wonderfully soft at the top—was very fine and *grey*, without a speck of *gold*. (19; emphasis added)

A few paragraphs later we find the following passage. Once again lexical repetitions are marked in italics.

> Jack himself, however, I considered to be part of the view. *I saw* his life as genuine, rooted, *fitting*: man *fitting* the landscape. *I saw* him as a remnant of the past (the undoing of which my own presence portended). *It did not occur to me*, when I first went walking and saw only the view, took what I saw as *things* of that walk, *things* that one might see in the countryside near Salisbury, immemorial, appropriate *things*, *it did not occur to me that* Jack was living in the middle of junk, among the ruins of nearly a century; *that* the *past* round his cottage *might* not *have been* his *past*; *that* he might at some stage have been a newcomer to the valley; *that* his style of life *might have been* a matter of choice, a conscious act; *that* out of the little piece of earth which had come to him with his farm-worker's cottage (one of a row of three) he had created a special land for himself, a garden *where* (though surrounded by ruins, reminders of vanished lives) he was more content to live out his life and *where*, as in a version of a Book of Hours, he celebrated the seasons. (19-20; emphasis added)

The above passage also indicates another marked linguistic feature of *The Enigma of Arrival*—syntactic parallelism. In the above paragraph, all the "that" clauses and the two "where" clauses are syntactically equivalent, repeating the same structure with lexical variation. There are very many similar examples throughout the text. Consider the following paragraph. Here the principal syntactically parallel phrases are in italics.

> So *though the new asphalt layer was crushed here and there by the tractor wheels into dips*; and *though the rain,* running down the hill, *sought out every weakness and crack in the dips* and *then dug more deeply into the loosened surface,* and *the irregular edge of the surface was undermined by water running down in little channels* (miniatures of the larger channels of which our valley was a relic) between the hard black crust and the soft, grass-covered earth, *though there were these things that made me feel that the lane might be reduced again* to the rocky, uneven condition in which I had first found it, yet *the lane was made good,* and *then made good again,* and *withstood the winter,* which came fiercely that year. (44-45; emphasis added)

These few examples must represent many throughout the text. Both suggest that this novel is not a traditional novel, but rather, in part, something else. It is in places much nearer lyric poetry than prose. Both lexical repetition and syntactic parallelism are extensively discussed by Geoffrey Leech in his classic study of the language of poetry in English, *A Linguistic Guide to English Poetry.*[9] They are seen as among the distinguishing features of the discourse of poetry in English. They are not associated with prose or prose narrative to the same extent.

The lyric nature of *The Enigma of Arrival* is reinforced by one other linguistic feature of the text. The basic division of texts into epic (that is, narrative), dramatic and lyric is as old as Aristotle's *Poetics.* Texts in the epic mode have a narrator who recounts events; dramatic texts dispense with the narrator and present events directly; texts in the lyric mode involve the expression of the thoughts and feelings of a particular speaking voice. Obviously, few texts purely belong to one mode and most tend to be mixed to some degree, although usually one mode is dominant. *The Enigma of Arrival* is strikingly deviant from most novels in its extensive use of exclamations (and rhetorical questions). This kind of utterance is not narrative at all, but rather expressive. Once again, there are many examples throughout the text. For example:

> How sad it was to lose that sense of width and space! (26)
> Change! (54)
> Such refinement! (56)
> What immense views, what a memory of emptiness, down the vast droveway and over the flinty slopes of the downs! (58)
> Strange pilgrimage! (117)
> What mighty hind legs! (169)

One of the most forceful examples of this feature occurs when the narrator thinks of Brenda and Les, and their unhappy marriage:

> How often, to punish someone for her Italian failure, she must have "taunted" him! [...] And how, having started on the job of destruction—he had used a kitchen knife—having started on that, from which very quickly there was no turning back [...] how he must have struck, until the madness and the life was over! (71)

The use of exclamation marks is particularly important in this passage. It deals with "big" events that could supply the material for a whole novel. But even here, where events are given, it is notable that they are inferred by the narrator rather than presented as having actually happened, and by the use of exclamation marks, his feelings of shock and disturbance about them are emphasised over and above the events themselves. It is the narrator's response to the occurrences that matters, not the taunting and the murder.

At times, in certain passages, the novel that is *The Enigma of Arrival* takes on the features of a lyric poem—lexical repetition, syntactic parallelism, the embodiment of personal vision and expression. The following paragraph has all these, including phonological repetition (here, the repetition of /f/, and to a lesser extent /s/ and /b/)—again a linguistic feature associated with poetry rather than narrative prose. As Naipaul writes:

> I heard the sound behind the trees; saw the smoke and, between the black of the tree trunks the flames in the field beyond, the heatwaves distorting the view like a pane of old-fashioned glass; felt the heat; and then very quickly was engulfed by the noise, rising fast to an amazing crepitation. And I thought of another sound I had heard more than twenty-five years before in the highlands of north-eastern South America: the sound of a big waterfall. Water, fire—in great disturbance they made the same sound. And fleetingly to me, walking on the downs in that overpowering noise, it seemed that all matter was one. (76)

When one combines such linguistic elements with the text's references to Wordsworth (20, 26), Gray and Goldsmith (80), and Tennyson (98) (alongside frequent references to prose writers like Hardy and Maugham), one can see *The Enigma of Arrival* as a prose text that adopts a number of lyric features. The passages of the text where the narrator speaks of his own self-discovery and his sense of himself as the subject of his writing further reinforce this polarity. "Man and writer were the same person," he declares. "But that is a writer's greatest discovery. It took time—and how much writing!—to arrive at that synthesis" (102). The novel is ambiguous as ever on this subject. The narrator regrets missing the material, the stories that he encountered in London in 1950 (128-31). He insists that his true subject is not a smart world seen from a sophisticated point of view or, indeed, his own sensibility (128, 134). However, although he claims that his real subject "was not my sensibility, my inward development, but the worlds contained within myself, the worlds I lived in" (135), *The Enigma of Arrival* is a highly solipsistic text. The narrator's own musings about the landscape and about time and change dominate it. Like Wordsworth's persona in *The Prelude*, he gives the reader his moments of vision, his epiphanies, his insights into the nature of things. The aeroplane taking off from Trinidad and the spectacle of the landscape below (97-98), the moments of dark revelation then and later in New York (104-05), the revitalised vision of fever (298-99)—all these are like Wordsworth's "spots of time," moments of clear perception (*The Prelude* [1805-06] XI. 259/ [1850] XII.208). At times, it is difficult to shake off the sense that one is reading something like a short Wordsworthian lyric.[10] In the following passage, the repetitions, the parallelisms, the observation of nature and buildings by a single (and solitary) speaker, all surely echo Romantic lyric verse.

> I walked out between the stripped beeches and between the old, untrimmed yews, solid and dark green; and along the public road, past the cottages of flint and brick and thatch (but not yet seen clearly), and up the hill beside the windbreak to the barn at the top. I saw Stonehenge from a gap in the windbreak: a very wide view, the downs pimpled with tumuli and barrows. I walked down the hill to the farm buildings at the bottom. I asked a man the way to Stonehenge. He told me to go on past the farm buildings and then turn to the right, along the wide grassed way. Around the farm the ground was muddy, churned up by tractor tyres. Water, puddles, reflected the grey sky. The grass on the grassed way, up the slope to the barrows from which a closer view of Stonehenge was to be had, the grass was tall and wet and entangling. (155)

The Enigma of Arrival is a difficult, ambiguous and transgressive novel. While avoiding the more obvious means of disrupting convention in Indian fiction in English noted by Amit Chaudhuri (means of disruption both popular and commercially successful with publishers and public in Britain) (5-6), it embeds itself as a deviant and dissident text at the heart of British fiction. Naipaul takes English landscape, English characters and English fiction and appropriates them, moulding them into something new that breaches conventions and challenges traditions. Josipovici writes of *The Enigma of Arrival* that it is "unlike any other book I know" (24). It is certainly a disturbing, enigmatic and transgressive text.

NOTES

1. Naipaul has been widely criticised by writers and critics from outside Europe. Hilary Mantel discusses this in her review of Pankaj Mishra's collection of Naipaul's writings (10-11). See also the almost universally hostile comments about Naipaul in Darryl Cumber Dance's collection

of interviews with Caribbean writers. My essay argues that in *The Enigma of Arrival* Naipaul is offering a disruptive and transgressive engagement with British fiction, a postcolonial appropriation all the more interesting for its slyness.

2. Hybridity, discursive play and liminality are all seen (by Homi Bhabha and others) as important aspects of postcolonial writing and part of a rebellion against the norms and rules of the metropolitan coloniser. See Bauman 84, 87. Jean Franco discusses this in his essay on "The Nation as Imagined Community" (211). Amit Chaudhuri has a somewhat more balanced and reserved attitude towards the inherent value of hybridity (6).
3. Joy M. Lynch writes of the importance of who views a landscape and who has a right to name and describe it in the context of Mexican-American writing (see 119-44).
4. One could also suggest that *The Enigma of Arrival* reverses what Penelope Ingram calls "a captivity narrative, or a white 'going native' text" (159). The visitor from the Caribbean immerses himself in a native culture and seems in a large measure integrated into it, while being simultaneously and constantly aware of his difference from the aborigines around him. The centrality to a great deal of contemporary writing of the experience of exile and its complex shaping of identity is emphasised in the special issue of *MELUS* entitled "Confronting Exiles" (Fall 2001). See especially Leighton 3-30.
5. Anita Desai describes a cyclical and anti-linear sense of time as being important aspects of both traditional and current Indian narrative texts (210-11).
6. For a full discussion of this syntactic feature, see Sinclair 165-66.
7. The narrator's pronounced fondness for sentence fragments can be seen in this context too. The sentence without a main verb is a sentence that, in a sense, is static, not dynamic. Act is once again de-emphasised. See, for example, 16, 43, 45, 77, 80, 81, 123, among many others. These linguistic features are surely one of the roots of Kemp's sense of the text's "staidness and stillness" (839).
8. Naipaul's language is discussed by Chaudhuri (6) and by Mantel (12), in terms of "hybridity" and its unique configuration. However, neither commentator discusses it in the way suggested in this essay.
9. See particularly chapter 5, "Verbal Repetition" (73-88).
10. Josipovici compares *The Enigma of Arrival* to British Romantic nature writing and its psychological interests to those of *The Prelude.*

WORKS CITED

Bauman, Emily. "Postcolonial Theory and the Humanist Project." *Critical Quarterly* 40.3 (1998): 79-89.

Chaudhuri, Amit. "Lure of the Hybrid: What the Post-Colonial Indian Novel Means to the West." *Times Literary Supplement* 3 Sept. 1999: 5-6.

Dance, Darryl Cumber. *New World Adams: Conversations with Contemporary West Indian Writers*. Leeds: Peepal Tree Books, 1992.

Desai, Anita. "Indian Fiction Today." *Daedalus: Journal of the American Academy of Arts and Sciences* 118.4 (1989): 207-32.

Franco, Jean. "The Nation as Imagined Community." *The New Historicism*. Ed. H. Aram Veeser. London: Routledge, 1989. 204-12.

Ingram, Penelope. "Racialızing Babylon: Settler Whiteness and the 'New Racism.'" *New Literary History* 32 (2001): 157-76.

Josipovici, Gabriel. "A World in Flux." Rev. of *The Enigma of Arrival*, by V.S. Naipaul. *The Listener* 12 Mar. 1987. 24.

Kemp, Peter. "Severed from Rootlessness." Rev. of *The Enigma of Arrival*, by V.S. Naipaul. *Times Literary Supplement* 7 Aug. 1987. 838-39.

Leech, Geoffrey N. *A Linguistic Guide to English Poetry*. London: Longman, 1969.

Leighton, Joy M. "'A Chinese Ishmael': Sui Sin Far, Writing, and Exile." *MELUS* 26.3 (2001): 3-29.

Lynch, Joy M. "'A Distinct Place in America Where All *Mestizos* Reside': Landscape and Identity in Ana Castillo's *Sapogonia* and Diana Chang's *The Frontiers of Love*." *MELUS* 26.3 (2001): 119-44.

Mantel, Hilary. "Naipaul's Book of the World." Rev. of *The Writer and the World* by V.S. Naipaul. *The New York Review of Books* 24 Oct. 2002. 10-12.

Mishra, Pankaj. "The House of Mr Naipaul." Rev. of *Between Father and Son: Family Letters*, by V.S. Naipaul. *The New York Review of Books* 20 Jan. 2000. 14-17.

Mishra, Vijay, and Bob Hodge. "What is Post(-)colonialism?" *Colonial Discourse and Postcolonial Theory: A Reader*. Ed. Patrick Williams and Laura Chrisman. New York: Columbia UP, 1994. 276-90.

Naipaul, V.S. *The Enigma of Arrival: A Novel*. Harmondsworth: Penguin, 1987.

——. "On Being a Writer." *The New York Review of Books* 23 April 1987. 7.

——. "Without a Dog's Chance." Rev. of *After Leaving Mr Mackenzie*, by Jean Rhys. *The New York Review of Books* 18 May 1972. 29-31.

Pimono, Paulus. "The Centre Writes/Strikes Back?" *Critical Quarterly* 33.3 (1991): 43-47.

Sinclair, John. "Lines about Lines." *Language and Literature: An Introductory Reader in Stylistics*. Ed. Ronald Carter. London: George Allen and Unwin, 1982. 163-76.

11

V.S. Naipaul's Ironic Visions

EMILIENNE BANETH-NOUAILHETAS

Few modes of writing involve the author's subjective vision of the world with such immediacy as travel writing. The traveller himself, in many cases, projects the narrative of his adventures as a prospective horizon even while he is living through them: thus the experience of travel and discovery becomes a more or less self-conscious experiment in which the future author watches himself as actor, and weaves the material from which the narrative will proceed. This calculated rift within the traveller's persona, between the author watching the drama unfold and the actor involved in it, is particularly palpable in late twentieth century travel writings whose authors are 'professionals' of the genre, more or less seeking or provoking experiences worthy of being related. In the case of Naipaul, for instance, the travel experience is pre-tailored to fit the pedagogical and ideological aims of the author, and the narrative skilfully organises the apparently unexpected events or encounters around the axis of its demonstration. The traveller is thus constantly aware of the narrative to come, even in the midst of his experience; similarly, the narrator often maintains some critical distance *vis-à-vis* his own past actions as traveller, since the transcription of what has occurred inevitably acts as interpretation and dramatisation of it.

Such self-consciousness is particularly conducive to the practice of irony, understood both as a rhetorical form and as a vision of the world. Yet there are great differences between both forms: sustained irony is intimately connected with the questions of self-knowledge and self-expression, which are also the quasi-permanent companions of the travel writer. Of the ironist, in this sense, as of the travel writer, one could equally state that "life is for him a drama, and what engrosses him is the ingenious unfolding of this drama. He is himself a spectator even when performing some act."[1] Rhetorical irony is, however, a trope which can be used as a tool for the simple purpose of persuasion, and which refers more to the ironist's strong subjective sense of right and wrong. Between these two types of irony, there is often a blend, where the ironist occasionally asserts what he perceives as his truth through the use of rhetorical irony, and occasionally suspends his strong subjective stance in order to let an ironic vision flicker along the lines of his perception and discourse.

Naturally, the degree in which the traveller is aware in his actions of the future narrative varies considerably according to the writer and the context. Even in the case of Naipaul, the prospective self-awareness increases as he progresses in his career and as his projects aim at increasingly militant demonstrations. Thus in the later works it seems that the Naipaulian travel narrative is bound in two directions: first by the traveller's strong sceptical, critical stance, devoted to questioning or debunking appearances, and then by the narrative's demonstrative purpose.

This study will focus on the uses of irony in Naipaulian travel writings, and attempt to analyse how rhetorical irony is instrumentalised in an ideological vision of the world, and a "truth"-oriented or revelation-oriented narrative. It will also examine in what respect this tropological irony differs from a more deeply ontological form of irony (closer to self-questioning) which sometimes leads to the practice of humour.

Irony is the traveller's natural element and rhetorical mode as it is a rhetorical form of displacement, and of distancing. As travelling isolates the individual and puts his values and perceptions to the test through a confrontation with the unfamiliar, irony presents itself as a rhetorical refuge, a mode of expression that marks a strong presence of the enunciating subject, through his questioning of perceived realities. "The ironic standpoint is egotistical and self-sufficient"[2]: indeed, the distancing required by irony opposes the vision of the subject to more generally admitted interpretations of the world.

Thus it asserts the subject's freedom through his self-conscious questioning of the state of things; but it also brings into play the subject's own ideological frames of reference, and, occasionally, the traveller's subservience to prejudices or even clichés. In fact, irony as trope often relies on the simple substitution of one ideological frame of reference for another, which the ironist assumes to be shared by his interlocutor, and which is also inferred to be closer to the 'truth' of the matter.

In Naipaul's travel writing, the use of irony is constant and all-pervading, and often subtle, relying much on the reader's complicity (which reinforces its ideological inferences). Seldom does the narrator of *An Area of Darkness* resort to the simple artifice of antiphrasis: rather, understatement, enumeration and comic exaggeration are its vehicles, particularly in descriptions. This evocation, for instance, of the traveller's exasperation after a brush with Indian bureaucracy:

> I was shouting now almost as soon as I entered government offices. At times the sight of rows of young men sitting at long tables, buried among sheaves of paper, young men checking slips of one sort or another, young men counting banknotes and tying them into bundles of a hundred, all India's human futility, was more than I could bear. (*An Area of Darkness* 92)

The use of irony in this example illustrates Naipaul's mastery: at first, the target seems to be the travelling 'I' himself, with his frayed temper and grotesque, futile reactions. We can here recognise the theatricalisation typical of irony, at two levels: in the narrator's rendering of the scenes in which he was involved as an actor, but also at the first level of perception by the traveller. The young men he sees are no longer individuals but theatrical types to which he reacts like an automaton, on cue as if in a Punch and Judy show. These two levels of irony contribute to the reader's amusement and sympathy: sympathy for the apparently humble, exhausted narrator, but especially, in the end, for his caricature-like vision of the scenes. The emphatic repetition of "young men" in a slightly grandiloquent ternary rhythm reinforces this effect, as does the description of their activity, always linked to the handling of paper: this verges on caricature, with the use of a traditional comic device, the mechanisation of human beings.[3] But for all its comic quality, the scene remains ironic through the implied, symbolic, message: that paperwork is needlessly tapping all of India's strength, and even the visitor's. Thus irony, the narrator's ultimate intention, is supported by an instrumental comic scene. The comedy seems first directed against the narrator himself, but it is only used to showcase the absurdity of the situation he has to face, and enrol the sympathy of the (supposedly Western) reader, while exploiting an old Western cliché: that of State bureaucracy as necessarily inefficient and unproductive. There are many similar examples where Naipaul's keen sense of the comic is put to the service of his rhetorics of irony, which ultimately aim at making an ideological or political point.

Another frequent manifestation of Naipaulian irony comes with the lengthy quotations of local writings or of the utterances of interlocutors encountered during his travels, which the narrator more or less refrains from commenting on, as if out of restraint. But in fact the narratorial silence comes across as a very clear ironical subtext, for the purpose of the quote is not so much to support any articulate argument but to heap ridicule upon its writer or enunciator. Perhaps this is scorn, more than irony, transpiring in the way the very print of the writing is mimicked: "THIS TEMPLE HAS BEEN BUILT THROUGH THE CHARITY OF RAJA SETH BALDEO DASS BIRLA [...]" etc. (208), and so on for nine apparently pointless lines, until the narrator notes "The crudity of the language is matched by the crudity of the self-appraisal." Nothing can really support such a generalisation, but it relies on a common trick of irony: the superimposition of material details with the conceptual, general truths they seek to illustrate. Having simply demonstrated the incompetence of the sign-writer through this lengthy quotation, the narrator brings this flawed detail to bear on the vast reality of India, without further argument: "Self-appraisal, the crudity of the stonework and marblework, the imperfect use of the foreign language: they are all related" (208). The relationship, one is led to infer, is simply based on the one characteristic that provokes the ironic reaction: the discrepancy between things as they are, and things as they should be. Such a flimsy argument can be tenable only thanks to the seductive effectiveness of irony, that enrols the reader in the narrator's camp, and makes the anonymous writer of the text stand out as the pompous and illiterate culprit responsible for his country's loss of status.

Similar interpolated quotes are repeatedly used in *The Middle Passage*,[4] where frivolous articles from the *Trinidad Guardian* are supposed to amusingly illustrate the provincialism of Trinidad (49-56); the absence of any commentary is the most eloquent expression of the author's ironical intention, and of his reliance on the reader's complicity. For, indeed, it is fairly easy to find hollow articles in almost any newspaper: that Naipaul relies on these extracts to press his point without further explanation demonstrates his assertiveness as a narrator and the lack of any self-questioning, one might even say his prejudice, as a reader and traveller. Such prejudices do not bar rhetorical irony, on the contrary: the ironist's skill is precisely to invite the reader to share his ideological frame of reference by seducing him through the verbal attraction of rhetoric. The reader is implicitly invited to take sides with the narrator with whom he is supposed to identify in opposition with the incompetent writer.

In a similar vein, in *An Area of Darkness*,[5] the briefest of conversations is reported with hardly any added comment, as an illustration of what the traveller sees as India's unrealistic opinion of itself.

> At an official reception for the former governor of a state someone called across to me, as we sat silently in deep chairs set against the walls of the room, "How is Indian culture getting on in your part of the world?" The former governor, a heavily-stockinged veteran of the Independence struggle, leaned forward and noticed me. He was reported to be keen on Indian culture; I was later to read newspaper reports of his speeches on the subject. Wishing to show that I took the question seriously and was anxious to establish a basis for discussion, I shouted back across the large room: "What do you mean by Indian culture?" My IAS friend, under whose protection I was, closed his eyes in dismay. The former governor leaned back; silence returned to the room. (212)

Here again, the irony is very subtly introduced, as the traveller-narrator seems at first to be the primary target of a slightly comical scene: he is the initiator of a social "faux-pas" that provokes embarrassment and consternation. Shouting across a room, being the focus of attention, and putting one's foot in one's mouth: these are the basic ingredients of social comedy. As an apparent victim of his own naïvety, the character further engages the reader's sympathy. But in fact he is being cast in the role of the revealer of truths, much as Montesquieu's Persians. The disapproving silence that follows his apparently well-intended enquiry is enough to make his point and beyond: that this cultural consciousness is hollow and the ancient culture in fact inaccessible: "Spirituality and ancient culture, then, were as consciously possessed as Parson Adams and Tom Jones in Simpson's" (212).

The narrator's irony stands out in the delight of his description: the slight changes in posture, the smallest motions, all acquire a portentousness equal to what we are told is India's vanity. The narrative skilfully presents the entire scene in such a way that the reader can infer its demonstrative impact, and transform the traveller's apparent ridicule into the narrator's bitter triumph.

For truth, or truths, are at the centre of Naipaul's travel writings: the traveller seeks to "understand" and approach the truth of the countries he is visiting, and the narrative takes it upon itself to further that quest once the actual travelling is over. So irony, though it gives the narrative a lighter, more seductive touch, is truth-oriented here as it is in a more general way: as a trope, irony invites the reader to seek out the author's intent, and therefore to believe in the "truth" to be found behind the statement. In this respect, rhetorical irony points towards an assertion of the enunciative subject as a revelator; at the same time, the ironist as travel writer invites the reader to adopt his vision: and this vision is oriented towards the discovery of a certain "truth," revealed by the enunciating subject. On the other hand, sustained irony is much more a questioning of the world without reference to the subject's truth: but this is hardly practised by Naipaul, who consistently puts forward his opinions in his travel-writing. In fact he travels avowedly in order to make himself an opinion, which the narrative strives to construct as truth. This process is presented with clarity and lucidity at the end of *An Area of Darkness*, in a brief metaphorical reflection on the interaction between writing and experience:

> An oblong of stiff new cloth lay before me, and I had the knowledge that if only out of this I could cut a smaller oblong of specific measurements, a specific section of this cloth, then the cloth would begin to unravel of itself, and the unravelling would spread from the cloth to the table to the house to all matter, *until the whole trick was undone*. Those were the words that were with me as I flattened the cloth and studied it for the clues which I knew existed, which I desired above everything else to find, but which I knew I never would. (266)

This dream clearly translates the author's yearning for a single key towards that "something true which [he] could never adequately express" (267), but which he seeks through the narrative. Irony is a tool that Naipaul uses in his attempts at retranscribing this truth of experience: never does he seem to actually question its existence, although he acknowledges its evanescence.

In a later travel book, *Among the Believers: An Islamic Journey*,[6] this tendency is confirmed. Here rhetorical irony is used to subtly demonstrate what seems to be the traveller's starting point: a critique of Islam, identified with Arab imperialism. Once again, Naipaul as traveller often feigns helplessness or ignorance in order to get a point across, and subtly uses free indirect speech to convey his irony. In the following example, the narrative clearly capitalises on a minor incident in order to grind this axe:

> Behzad suggested that we should visit the shrine. If anyone asked, I was to say I was a Muslim. I said I wouldn't be able to carry it off. I wouldn't know how to behave. Was it with the right foot that one entered a mosque, and with the left, the lavatory? Or was it the other way round? Was it the Sunnis who, during their ablutions, let the water run down their arms to their fingers? Did the Shias, contrariwise, run the water down from their hands to their elbows? And what were the

> gestures of obeisance or reverence? There were too many traps. Even if I followed Behzad and did what he did, it wouldn't look convincing. (44)

Note that it isn't the deceit itself that discourages the traveller, but rather the lack of skill in deceit. The long list of questions is full of restrained irony, and though the free indirect speech means to give the impression that the questions were actually asked, they are more probably a narratorial artefact, a way of leading the reader down the road of the narrative's projected demonstration. The interchangeability of answers suggested by this mode of interrogation ("Wasit [...]? or [...]? was it [...]?") points out what the traveller perceives as the emptiness of these rituals, which become mere "traps" for the uninitiated. Thus the narrator exploits a minor incident in his trip—the debate around whether or not he could enter a mosque in Iran—in order to develop deeply critical reflections on the subject of religious practice. It is once again irony that makes this shift possible, and once again, the comical leads to the ironic: the enumeration has a distinct, accumulative, comical effect, and this serves the larger purpose of the narrative's ironic "revelation," which points towards the narrator's predetermined opinion. This bias is particularly clear in *Among the Believers*, where the narrator often camouflages his prejudices in a purported revelation, as if his vision were forced upon him by the painful confrontation with reality. This subtly cloaks a disparaging opinion in apparently naïve surprise, and enhances the effect of "truthfulness." So it goes for the description of Qom, in which the reader is slowly prepared for negative impressions through the initial disappointment orchestrated by the narrative:

> I had imagined that Qom, a holy city, would have been built on hills: it would have been full of cliff walls and shadows and narrow lanes cut into the rock, with cells or caves where pious men meditated. It was set flat in the desert, and the approach to it was like the approach to any other desert town: shacks, gas stations. (42)

The narrative here contrives the shift from expectation to disappointment: first a detailed fantasy vision ("I had imagined"), that tends to magnify and essentialise the supposed intrinsic qualities of sacredness of a holy city, then the (purported) frustration ("shacks, gas stations"). At first sight there is no irony here, but genuine disenchantment in the experience, reported in the narrative. Yet the anticlimactic effect is entirely induced by the narrator, who creates a sense of anticipation by developing the cliché image of his fantasy, after which the description of the real town is necessarily a comedown. What is implied in this contrived structure of reversal is that if Qom is an aesthetic disappointment, it is probably because its very holiness is questionable. Thus the narrator-traveller's "disappointment" is tinged with irony, for in fact, it is exactly what was expected: the irony is directed more against the fantasy of a "holiness" physically inscribed in a city or landscape than against the reality of an ordinary desert town. Thus the narrative translates the author's scepticism more convincingly than in direct statements of opinion.

Naipaulian irony therefore seems to just stop short of mockery, as it devolves upon the reader the responsibility of understanding the narrator's critical gesture, and of amplifying it in the process. The narrator feigns to be the mouthpiece of views that are in fact not his (for instance, the naïve aesthetic expectations concerning Qom), and in so doing invests the comic function of the gull, only to better enhance the ironic intention, directed against the discourse he is mimicking. This shift of voices is once again palpable in *Among the Believers* with the use of certain chapter headings, or indeed of the title itself, where the term "believers" is increasingly felt to be used ironically as one progresses in the book. The chapter entitled "Brave girls" (229) illustrates this ironic use of direct or indirect quotes. As part of the structure of the book, the chapter heading tends to be taken at face value, as an illustration or summary of the content of the chapter, and as the author's extra-narrative responsibility. Yet two pages into the chapter, it becomes apparent that this expression is to be taken with a pinch of salt, as it is directly quoted from one of the characters encountered by the traveller in Malaysia: "Shafi had promised to take me to the ABIM [Islamic Movement] school and even to find some 'brave girls' there who would talk to me. He had brought his friend to look me over. The friend apparently didn't disapprove; and early the next morning Shafi came for me in his car" (231). The phrase "brave girls" has been isolated here by the narrator, and is the only element of the exchange between Shafi and Naipaul, on this subject, that is directly quoted. Thus the quote itself, because of its isolation in the reported speech, becomes a sign of the narrator's distanced, and perhaps ironical stance as to the validity of its content. The choice of the same expression as chapter heading is therefore ironic, but is ambiguously so: it is uncertain whether the narrative means to cast doubt on the veracity of the assertion (that the girls in question are indeed "brave"), or on the common sense of the speaker who first utters the expression (Shafi). But the desired effect is potent: before the narrator has even begun to describe his encounter with the girls, the reader is inclined to believe that once again reality will contradict the promise of discourse (as in the case of the discovery of Qom), and, therefore, that the girls will somehow belie Shafi's brief characterisation of them.

Such a practice of irony tends to be less associated with comic effects than in the earlier narratives, which often relied on situation ridicule to justify the traveller's indignation or amazement. Instead, in Naipaul's later travel writings such as *Among the Believers*, irony is both more subdued and more effective, as in the case just quoted, for the traveller-narrator more regularly poses as an open-minded, unprejudiced interviewer, interlocutor, or even researcher, while the narrative on the contrary injects his conclusions or prejudices from the start. This process evinces the subtlety of ideological suggestion in travel writing, where the traveller—the author as actor—may feign a certain neutrality, which can at the same time be undermined by the narrative work itself—the author as narrator.

This transformation is probably the one referred to on the dust-jacket of *India: A Million Mutinies Now*, where Auberon Waugh is quoted for his review of the book in the *Sunday Telegraph*: "I loved the old Naipaul for his sardonic wit. The new one is to be loved for his sweetness of nature, amounting almost to sanctity."[7] However one attempts to interpret it, the notion of "sanctity" seems at odds with Naipaul's style and intentions, but one can assume that the reviewer is referring to the apparently empathetic project developed in *A Million Mutinies*. The style of the book is indeed quite distinct from that of *An Area of Darkness*, the account of Naipaul's first trip to India, which revealed a highly subjective, opinionated, and most of all, disappointed traveller, whose voice seemed directly linked to the narrative. But in his last account, Naipaul frequently seems to efface himself deliberately and to enhance the voices of his numerous interlocutors, in long, directly quoted speeches. This is a clear attempt to "understand" India by directly tapping the sources—the fantasy of a "truth" to be revealed is perhaps made more obvious by the accumulative and repetitive form of the numerous interviews reported. Yet the narrative remains the unifying thread and, with it, the narrator's voice emerges—his irony sometimes shining through certain cracks or pauses between interviews. For instance, in all the shifts to free indirect speech, the narrative suggests a note of amusement, or even, of irony, which the traveller-interviewer tried on the contrary to suppress. Such is the case in this exchange, translated for Naipaul from the Marathi, and in which the use of indirect speech is perhaps supposed to mimic the mediation of the interpreter. "How, growing up in that locality, had ambition come to Mr Patil? Had he been ambitious as a child? He had. He wanted to be famous. He didn't want to be famous for any particular thing; he just wanted to be famous" (19). The effect is slightly ironic: the choice of indirect speech creates a distance between the interviewer and the enunciated answers, a trace of scepticism, the equivalent of raised eyebrows in a conversation. Even more clearly, irony, which reflects the narrator's opinion on a subject, emerges forcefully when the narrative suddenly shifts from direct speech to indirect, thus attracting the reader's attention to a narratorial intervention, however slight:

> [Mr Patil is being quoted, on the power relations between Hindus and Muslims] "The Muslim shops have come back now, but they live in fear. The Shiv Sena is very powerful. I will tell you: the Muslims even give donations to the Shiv Sena."
>
> Nikil said on his own, "But isn't this extortion?"
>
> Mr Patil didn't think so. (23)

This brief answer in indirect speech is both slightly comical for its glibness, and clearly ironic, for it enables the narrator to mimic what he obviously perceives as the interlocutor's self-centredness, stubbornness, and ideological bias. Thus although the traveller's aim throughout his narrated journey is to collect as many "authentic" and diverse narratives as possible, while effacing his own voice, the presence of irony remains a unifying strain in the book. This is by no means a drawback, for the reading would be tedious without these slight narratorial interventions. Furthermore, the narrator never truly claims neutrality or even reliability: but this claim is implied in the presentation of long, directly quoted, autobiographical narratives. Within such a structure, the importance of narratorial silence, or of the smallest intervention through the choice of a mode of speech, is enhanced. Silence itself—the absence of comment after a long quote—intimates that the narrator believes that specific narrative (for example, Rajan's story, 121-35) has an emblematic value that the reader should reflect upon. Similarly, the briefest references to the traveller's role as an interviewer are loaded with meaning, and often irony, a reflection on the other speaker's discourse:

> [Deviah is recounting a mythological episode to Naipaul]
>
> Deviah said, "When he was wandering in the forest he came across a demon, and he killed the demon." There was a story attached to this demon. Deviah was quite ready to break off the main narrative and give the inset story. I asked him not to. (147)

In this instance, the author as actor-interviewer has had a direct influence on the narrative itself, through his plea for briefness. But beyond this anecdotal event, which naturally attracts the reader's attention and amusement (or perhaps even relief, in empathy with the author), it is in fact the narrator's intention that is translated. Indeed, it is the narrator who chooses to retranscribe the traveller's anxious petition, in a distanced, ironic, indirect speech: the mode is chosen for its quality of understatement, and suggests that if not controlled, the interlocutor keen on Indian mythology could go on forever, in a nightmare mise-en-abyme from one "inset" story to the next. Irony, therefore, interferes on the level of the narrative, as it translates the narrator's intention and ideology, and as such it can either support or modify the tonality of the traveller's own interventions in the course of his experience.

The striking point about *A Million Mutinies* is in fact that the traveller's sense of the comic seems to have all but deserted him, or so it would seem in all the narrative passages describing his reactions to the trip. "Bombay is a crowd" (1), or, in Calcutta, "I was overpowered this time by my own wretchedness" (346): these phrases insist on the immediacy of a body, identity shattering experience; irony, which is on the contrary all about mediation, seems to be reserved to the reception of other narratives, of other experiences. This confirms the initial impression of Naipaulian wit and irony: they have a mainly rhetorical function, and are part of the author's earnest argument for his vision, his truth. The immediacy with which any assault on the traveller's senses is described makes it clear that Naipaul lacks any such distance when it comes to his own identity, spiritual or physical. The integrity of his being, of his impressions, of his opinions, is still his priority, even if his approach to travel has changed: it certainly does not aim at "sanctity."

Thus, though Naipaul's narratives evince an undeniable ironic skill, it is an entirely rhetorical tool, manipulated at a narrative level for the purpose of persuasion. The more sustained, more profound form of irony that travellers ideally adopt as a self-critical mode of vision in their physical and ideological displacements is all but absent from Naipaulian writing. But V.S. Naipaul perfectly illustrates the seductive, quasi-totalitarian power of a rhetorical irony that relies on a strong figure of the writer as interpreter and revealer of truths: such ironic narratives act as confirmation of the writer's projected identity and assertive ideological vision.

NOTES AND REFERENCES

1. Soren Kierkegaard, *The Concept of Irony, with Constant Reference to Socrates,* trans. Lee M. Capel (Bloomington: Indiana UP, 1971) 300.
2. Candace D. Lang, *Irony / Humor: Critical Paradigms* (Baltimore: The Johns Hopkins UP, 1988) 29.
3. Henri Bergson, *Le rire: Essai sur la signification du Comique* (1940; Paris: PUF, 1999).
4. V.S. Naipaul, *The Middle Passage: A Caribbean Journey* (1962; London: Picador, 2001).

5. V.S. Naipaul, *An Area of Darkness* (1964; Harmondsworth: Penguin, 1968).
6. V.S. Naipaul, *Among the Believers: An Islamic Journey* (1981; London: Picador, 2001).
7. V.S. Naipaul, *India: A Million Mutinies Now* (1990; London: Picador, 2001).

12

The Post-Colonial Confusion and V.S. Naipaul

HIREN GOHAIN

The Times of India, the metropolitan English Newspaper with the largest circulation, published on July 16, 2002 an article by well-known Sociologist Dipankar Gupta with the title "An Academic Question." Gupta pointed out that today, half a century after independence, overseas recognition even for work done on Indian subjects had become an almost indispensable condition for domestic success of Indian academics. Further, he noted the anxiety of Indian scholars to gain a footing in Western campuses even though their foreign colleagues there might not show much interest in their field of study. Gupta expressed unhappiness at this state of affairs, but chose not to carry the analysis further. Post-colonial theorists consider such aspects of the post-colonial situation as beneath their notice. On the other hand, as I pointed out in an article published in an ordinary issue of *The Frontier* three or four years back (I don't have that issue with me), they theorise their expatriate situation and consciousness, their sense of being tolerated as honoured strangers in the Western academy with concepts that are at the same time convoluted and positivist.

Correspondingly there has been a wind of change blowing down the corridors of Indian universities, even those farther from metropolitan centres. No, I am not merely referring to the craze for technology—"bio-technology" and "information technology." The language and literature departments are awash with new intellectual currents like post-modernism and post-colonialism, and not by choice. Messengers from centres of higher learning in the West try to rally such departments to the support of the latest refinements of such theory. Seminars, visiting Fellowships, organisation of voluntary societies, are continually used to entice new recruits and converts the sceptics. An interesting aspect of such studies is the "post-colonial" approach to established European literary classics. When one can manipulate "post-colonial" readings of such classics, one has the delusive consolation that colonial hegemony over our culture and society has been overcome. This is not to deny intellectual brilliance to some of those exponents. But intellectual gifts are not sufficient insurance against ideological mesmerism.

Some of the concepts of post-colonial theory have undoubted heuristic and productive value. But since their concepts are themselves not supported by dialectics (*i.e.* by their grounding in reflexive analysis, and by rigorous empirical application), but are presented as axiomatic in *ad hoc* fashion, we are justified in postponing our assent.

We have already stated in a number of *earlier* articles (*e.g.*, "The Post-Colonial Hall of Mirrors," *The North-East Times*, 27-2-2000, "On Post-Colonial theory," *Journal of Literary Criticism*, Allahabad, September, 2000) etc., our reservations about post-colonial theory in the form of an external critique, and we have taken particular exception to the implied progress from colonial subjugation to post-colonial exchange and mutuality on the basis of equality. But an immanent critique is equally needed, as post-colonial theory is propped up by a prolific array of discursive concepts. As a post-modernist school, post-colonialism is committed to a vision of the world not as an order, but as a higgledy-piggledy ensemble of divergent discourses, and the truth-claims of each discourse becomes irrelevant. And once one gets sucked into such a black hole of theory, there is no escape from undesirable practical implications.

As was stated in our earlier articles discourse usually implies a course of action and action implies choice. Hence we cannot calmly contemplate the plural flowering of a hundred discourses, but are condemned to prefer a certain kind of discourses on the basis of its truth value. Of course, if we take the theoretical concepts for granted and concentrate on empirical research or ignore empirical investigation in pursuit a firmer logical and conceptual foundation for theory, the idea of truth will never impede our progress. However it is the intention of this article (never to be lost in uncontrolled "play" of meaning) to raise the question of truth.

A significant original contribution has been made by Tridib Sengupta in an article published in a Bengali little magazine, *Anushtup* (Winter 2002), where he deconstructs Homi Bhabha's discussion of colonial and post-colonial culture. Bhabha had differentiated them on the basis of two critical concepts "mimicry" and "hybridity." "Mimicry" occurs when the colonial native persistently and vainly tries to imitate the colonizing Sahib in the hope of totally identifying with him, but the very attempt negates by definition the identity between them. "Hybridity" on the other hand means mutual negotiations between co-existing but different cultures of the colonising Sahib and the native. Further, the two cultures are not different owing to some essential pre-given traits, but each exists as the "other" of its counterpart in a discursive space, which Bhabha calls the "Third Space."

Sengupta has rightly argued that Bhabha's notion of the post-colonial as somehow liberated from an unequal relationship cannot be sustained. The relationship at bottom still remains unequal and exploitative, leading to huge surplus-transfers from the third world to the first world. The only snag is the elusive character of the process which makes it impossible to identity directly the exploiting (colonising) agency. He points a "subjectless colonial process," perhaps failing to notice that with the development of monopoly capital and the booming of stock markets, organization of capital has itself undergone a change transcending its private and then its national boundaries. But the opposition between imperialist capital and exploited colony or neo-colony remains very much relevant even in this globalised world, and it is unnecessary to stop at the mere appearance of "subjectlessness."

Likewise the purely discursive treatment of "hybridity" by Bhabha and Sengupta also makes it *undialectical.* One ought to enquire into the concrete social modes and instruments of "hybridity" somewhat in the manner of Althusser's "Ideological

State Apparatuses." A trite commonsense question is enough to disturb the discursive security of the concept. Can "hybridity" form a tradition? Or does the culture of "hybrid" parents get relayed to the culture of their children? Do not the latter get more and more closely integrated with the culture of the dominant society, overcoming resistance? (Of course, there is also the possibility of increasing resistance leading again to a breakdown of negotiation.) Further a distinction ought to be made between "post-colonial" and "immigrant."

But the most significant and crucial contribution of Sengupta is a brilliant and lucid demonstration that the concept of "hybridity" applies to colonial as much as to post-colonial culture. Post-colonial theorists according to him assume that the agent and the target (=victim) of colonial "persuasion" remain distinct, heterogeneous entities making only a relationship of "mimicry" possible. (The methods of colonial hegemony are supposed to be "coercion" and "persuasion.") On the other hand in the case of post-colonial cultures, they consider the culture of the native as "homogeneous" while the culture of the Sahib is conceded to be "heterogeneous." The colonising Sahib constructs and presents the cultural space for the collaboration of the native in the process of persuasion. Because the language of the native is different from that of the colonizer, it is assumed rather too readily that discursive space for intimate collaboration cannot be constructed. Hence only "mimicry" and its predestined failure remain.

Sengupta conceives of a "synthetic hegemony" as distinct from "simple" subordination or "complex" co-existence. Where the persuading Sahib assimilates the principles of the native's own culture, and the distinct cultural identity of the native is retained, but in a displaced mode. The colonizer goes out of his way to conciliate in order to persuade, in a new ideological project following realization of the futility of "mimicry." The native becomes "reformed," "changed," even while retaining his identity in the new equation, and regards the reformed culture and displaced identity as the genuine article, his authentic culture and identity. But the basic equation still remains unchanged, and the native is fobbed off with "substitutes" and "surrogates." The full participation of the native in government is replaced by "recordation," the recording of reasons for all decisions of the colonial administration.

The concrete results are brilliantly presented by Sengupta. The intimate and humane cowherd-God of Indians is replaced by the terrible and forbidding God of Christianity in "reformed" Hinduism of Brahmoism. Bankim Chandra speculates on the basis and constituents of Indian "nationhood" while ignoring the question of self-determination. Vidyasagar and Ashutosh Mukherjee pass into legend for standing up to the browbeating Sahib, while overlooking the fact that the winning of courtesy from the ruler does not amount to the equality of citizens. At the same time the process is very different indeed from the "mimicry" posited by Bhabha, and is no different from "hybridity."

This is indeed a significant and original contribution. But since all scientific knowledge presupposes discussion we are compelled to raise a few queries. Had we all been bound inexorably by discourse, the struggle to overcome the colonial yoke politically and culturally for two hundred years would not have not taken place. If on the other hand the persistence of discourse in culture is insuperable, the struggle against colonialism itself must have been, and must remain, delusive. Since it is unlikely that Sengupta holds such an extreme position, he must make an effort to treat the question more dialectically, leaving the "pure" realm of discourse.

Indeed it is possible to trace in the course of the freedom movement of India various evolving responses of natives to the colonial hegemony. From Bankim's attempt to forge nationhood on the lines of European (capitalist) nationalism to Gandhi's endeavour to conceive a state as a continuum of village republics, there have been a variety of native responses to the persuasion of the colonizing Sahib. The history also reveals desperate, strenuous attempts to liberate the mind from hegemonic and enslaving thought-patterns. Sengupta's cast-iron model is too rigid for such dynamics. The pernicious notion that the subject is a minor epiphenomenon of structuration, discourse leads to this blindness.

But Sengupta's deconstructions of the colonial—post-colonial opposition, implying progress and emancipation through qualitative change while not abolishing traces of colony, remains a valuable contribution in cultural studies. It also raises the question if the colonial feature of mimicry also survives in some manner in the "liberated" post-colonial consciousness. We think it does. The colonial contempt for the native, the hidden fear, is mimicked in our opinion by the contempt of post-colonial spokesman against their own history and heritage. It is altogether a complex process. First it converts part of the native's heritage into an alien "other" of his emancipated, enlightened consciousness—in this case the Islamic becomes a surrogate ("metonym") for hated but unacknowledged imperialism. A simple rhetorical figure like metonymy cannot explain the process satisfactorily.

It has been noted by different commentators with some surprise that both Nirad C. Choudhuri and V.S. Naipaul, representing the free intellect of the educated, critical intelligence, had sprung to the defense of the barbarous act of destruction of the Babri mosque. Even their admirers were put off by this peculiar spectacle of the emancipated reason upholding an irrational savagery. But these reactions can be put down to the modified mode of mimicry surviving into the post-colonial culture. Both these masters of prose, where a magisterial judgment makes a wakeful assessment of empirical observation at the very moment of registering the observation, represent the post-colonial's unhappy relationship with his own history, of which he is ashamed. But the potent myth of decolonisation makes it hard to acknowledge the shame and gnawing sense of inferiority. Hence the attempt to overcome it by imagining a pure, pristine past polluted by an alien element or force. Like many other Indians both of them find that useful alien in Islam. The West's fear and contempt towards Islam, so ably documented by Edward Said and others, are mirrored in this perception, which mimics the Western consciousness. But the supreme Irony is that Islam also represents the more threatening other, the rarely acknowledged fact of colonial hegemony. As Homi Bhabha would perhaps have put it, Islam here becomes the displaced symbol—the metonym—of the colonial empire.

Here again there is a continuity linking the colonial past and the post-colonial present. We have a striking documentary or empirical evidence of this in Bankim Chandra's notorious revision of the original version of *Ananda Math,* the powerful patriotic novel that irrevocably turned the Muslim into the "Hindu nation's" other. Bankim Chandra first had a version where the so-called "Sannyasi Rebellion" was portrayed faithfully, keeping close to historical facts and showing the wandering ascetics rising in revolt against British. But Bankim developed cold feet at the time of publication, as the colonial power was ruthless against the slightest challenge. He brought out a revised version with the Muslims as the villain of the piece, and portrayed the British as the saviour of the "Hindu" nation, ordained by God to protect and nurture that nation. Thus Islam had been made a surrogate figure for the colonial empire already in the second half of the 19th Century.

V.S. Naipaul's *Beyond Belief* (Penguin Books, 1998) is a carryover from this tradition. Or if factual continuity is difficult to establish, it is at least evident that using Islam as a metonym for the colonial power is a typical and unconscious strategy of colonial native (and post-colonial) discourse. It is the native's facile identification with the viewpoint of the colonial rulers that turns Islam into a favourite whipping-boy.

The title of the book *Beyond Belief* has an unpleasant pun in it, putting the people he writes about at a vast distance from the reader, who enjoys the illusory privilege of watching from a great height herds of wild animals in a stampede. This book confirms the colonial (post-colonial) identity of Naipaul as he abandons all doubts and questions about the colonisers. A contrast with the much more humane and solid early novel, *A House for Mr Biswas* is quite in order of this point. The pun here is much more compassionate and penetrating. The word "house" in the title stands for shelter, refuge, security, roots, and of course, identity. And the character in reach for all these bears the slightly incongruous name "Mr Biswas." The novel presents in vivid details the tragic struggle of colonial man, uprooted from the past and his heritage by the violence of colonial power, to build not only his life but a meaningful world out of the constricted economic opportunities, cultural stagnation, and asthmatic modernity of the worst-type of colony, the colony with a plantation-economy. Naipaul captures the heart-rending pathos, absurdity and horror of the situation with a wonderful variety of tones ranging from clinical detachment to sardonic observation, hilarious lampooning to profound compassion. The searing loathing and contempt are kept under control by the author's inner struggle for balance and objectivity. He does not lose his sympathy for the hero/victim. In contrast, *Beyond Belief* is insufferably smug and patronising.

Beyond Belief is a travelogue with a theme—it is a study of countries that are late converts to Islam like Indonesia, with Hindu or Buddhist past, against the background of the rise of Islamic fundamentalism. The narrative presents deft portraits of a number of people caught in the great post-colonial search for identity following the removal of colonial power from the immediate scene.

It is interesting, and significant, that though Naipaul proposes to target Islamic fundamentalism, he frequently lapses into a blanket denunciation of Islam that comes across as intolerant, fanatical puritanical and impossibly blind and narrow. Consider the following quotations chosen at random from the section on Indonesia:

> Islam is not simply a matter of conscience or private belief. It makes imperial demands. A convert's world view alters. His holy places are in Arab lands; his sacred language is Arabic. His idea of history alters. He rejects his own, he becomes, whether he likes it or not, part of the Arab story. (*Prologue* 1)

> Converted peoples have to strip themselves of their past, of converted peoples nothing is required but the purest faith, submission, Islam. It is the most uncompromising kind of imperialism. (72)

Naipaul in his introductory remarks tries to guide the reader's responses to the narrative by claiming total objectivity for the stories. Consider for example the following:

> This is a book about people. It is not a book of opinions [...]. (*Prologue* 1) and again,

> It is less of a travel book; the writer is less present, less of an inquirer. He is in the background, trusting to his instinct, a discoverer of people, a finder-out of stories. (*Prologue* 2)

The canny reader cannot help feeling that Naipaul "discovers" what he himself puts in first. For example, talking about the immense "trauma" of conversion to Islam, Naipaul remarks:

> The disturbance for societies is immense, and even after a thousand years can remain unresolved [...]. People develop fantasies about who and what they are; and in the Islam of converted countries there is an element of neurosis and nihilism. (*Prologue* 1)

The person who represents most forcefully the "threat" from Islam to "the enlightened, civilized world," is Imaduddin, originally an electrical engineer who visits the West, (America to be specific) to acquire the scientific knowledge required for the conquest of the world. At Iowa state university he is visited by Pakistani fanatic and fundamentalist Fazul-ur-Rahman, who instills in him a vision of a grand revival of Islam under the leadership of Malay-speaking Muslims. The only thing Imaduddin cares to borrow from the Godless West is science and technology, and not the tolerant liberalism that provides shelter to people like him fleeing from persecution at home. Incidentally, Imaduddin once haunted by President Suharto's police, returns to befriend a trusted confidant of Suharto's Habibie, and becomes the pillar of Indonesian state that is clearly set on Islamisation (7-31, 52-54).

Naipaul clearly forgets that there are two other portraits in his section on Indonesia—the traditionalist stalwart Wahid and the imaginative, sensitive lady Dewi Fortuna Anwar. Both of them belonged to the old aristocracy, who had the benefit of modern colonial education as well as training in traditional learning and culture. Wahid stoutly maintains that faith in Islam should be a product of conscience, not fear and hence politics and Islam should be kept apart (35-38). And Dewi thought it might be possible to retain traces of pre-Islamic earth-cults and rituals of reverence for nature, as long as the central tenets of the Islamic creed are not jeopardized. She lived comfortably in several different worlds—Pre-Islamic and tribal, Islamic, modern and liberal—without any wrenching inner conflict (67-68).

It is true that both appear like figures from a receding and weakening past, while Imaduddin is the self-confessed "man of the moment." The question strenuously avoided by Naipaul is, why Islam should at this historical moment appear to be powerfully attractive to the awakening masses of Indonesia. Equally significant is the fact that Islam now in this new version seems keen to imitate on a world scale the earlier and triumphant campaign of Western colonialism/ imperialism. Is this not an example of "mimicry," though the model imitated has left its impression only on the sub-conscious? And is not Naipaul's horrified and scornful reaction to this kind of Islam (often simply called "Islam"), a repetition or mimicry of colonial powers' reaction to events like "The Great Mutiny" of 1857, or, to various kinds of nationalist upsurges in the colonies in the early 20th century? The cultural hegemony of the colonial powers clearly remains entrenched, and its symptoms are still to be found in unlikely places like the university campuses of India. The post-colonial mimicry imitates an image, an impression, of a campaign that has now assumed a different form with the label "Globalisation." To put the matter bluntly, Islamic fundamentalism is the mirror image of Western colonialism and neo-colonialism, provoked by the latter, though it will never admit its paternity.

It is time we now returned to V.S. Naipaul's claim to objectivity and detachment. There are in the book half-hearted attempts to qualify his rage against Islam here and there (*e.g.* on *Prologue* 3, 71). But what carries more conviction, like a cry from the heart, is Naipaul's dirge-like lament over the accident of his birth in the new world as made over by colonial power. Referring to his childhood in the Caribbeans, he recalls: "I began to feel when I was quite young that there was an incompleteness, an emptiness, about the place" (58). It was much later, in India, that he understood what had gone wrong. The place he was born and brought up in had lost its "sense of sacredness." Islam had nothing to do with it. Naipaul does not notice that in spite of several centuries of Muslim rule India had not been deprived of a sense of sacredness. Islam obviously lacked the ruthlessness of Western colonialism that had deprived Naipaul of his roots.

13

Trajectory of Displacement: Expatriate Sensibility of V.S. Naipaul

NANDA KISHORE MISHRA

In establishing a sturdy link between exile as a literary theme and his personal history, Sir Vidiadhar Surajprasad Naipaul has emerged as a rare individual writer with a self-autonomy as measure of his ostracism. He claims to possess a unique opportunity to have lived in three or four continents and developed a sense of cultural attachment with those races. Though he studied and lived in London, his *pundit* origin, his extended Indian heritage and lineage did not permit him to merge with London life. The account of his expatriate experience, his self-portraiture reveals the pain of his displacement; at the same time makes him cynical about other races and culture including that of India. But as an expatriate his life is less traumatic than Gao Xingjian, the noted Chinese author who won the most prestigious Nobel Prize for literature in 2000. For Naipaul, it is very difficult to break with his past. At the same time his disavowal of any national identity enables him to become a detached neutral writer.

In a way, Naipaul's is a case of self-exile and he had strong reasons for his expatriate life. To achieve literary fame and publish books, the Caribbean writers had to move abroad but for Naipaul the possibility to return home never existed. He was disengaged physically as well as emotionally from his homeland. He was born in Chagunas, Trinidad on August 17, 1932. His grandfather had slipped from Uttar Pradesh, India to Trinidad in the 1880s as an indentured labourer. Seepersad Naipaul, Vidiadhar's father, proved to be a source of inspiration for his son to adopt the vocation of a writer. He found no scope for the flowering out of his literary genius as the colonial Trinidad had stalled his ambition to become an established writer. He had seen his father who was trained to become a *pundit,* a total failure in his life. So Naipaul was determined to leave Trinidad as he thought that writers in that country were left to oblivion. Even as a child he felt Trinidad as an alien environment because he was meted out ill-treated of belonging to a minority community.

Another reason was his ecclesiastical origin, which could not allow him to identify his life with the Trinidadians. His expatriate sensibility is greatly affected by his marginalized existence. His sense of alienation is a compensatory measure for his cynicism and emotional adjustment. So his choice of terms is to be considered most seriously since he himself warns his readers: "When I talk about being an exile or a refugee, I'm not just using a metaphor, I'm speaking literally."[1] His self-portrayal at times verges on self-pathos.

Naipaul possesses all the advantages of portraying the cross-cultural relations in the post-colonial era. From a study of his writings one can gather that Naipaul never suffered from any anxiety of outside influence. He has no alternative community to identify himself. This unique position makes him a neutral observer. By venturing into travel writing he is treated as a mandarin possessing analytic understanding of the Third World countries. He is an avid interpreter of post-colonial societies in our times.

An expatriate writer is one who voluntarily moves to reside abroad. Expatriates leave their own land to taste life in other countries at the same time maintaining their national identity with a view to return to their native land when they get tired of life abroad. Thus, an expatriate is more privileged than a refugee. Naipaul's expatriate sensibility accounts for his "willed homelessness" with least possibility to return to Trinidad. Paul Theroux is one of the critics to endorse the persona Naipaul has fashioned for himself. Naipaul is wholly alienated and hence, a citizen of nowhere and everywhere. Theroux justifiably echoes Naipaul's rhetoric of displacement:

> (He ranks among) the former colonials, transplanted people who can claim no country as their own. They travel because they belong nowhere; they cannot settle, they are constantly moving—in a sense they never arrive—and much of their travel is flight. Rootlessness is their condition; it is opposite of those for whom being metropolitan is a condition. The homeless are not calm; their homelessness is a source of particular pain, for as with all travellers, they are asked, "Where are you from?" and no simple answer is possible: all landscapes are alien.[2]

Naipaul is the first of his line, without a tradition. He went into exile as a literary measure to gather vast experience and promote literary writings. He has a moral superiority over the British writers, as he is not prejudiced by the colonial powers; hence he acts as a counterweight to the third world. His is an authentic voice as an insider for the post-colonial societies whose views are unbiased and unaffected by politico-economical influence. Being a citizen of nowhere, he has no influence on any part of the globe; so his neutrality becomes a weapon of his writings to draw the attention of the people of the world. Mel Gussow rightly avers: "wherever he goes, it is a foreign country. For Naipaul home has lost its meaning [...] in Trinidad, wherever he has gone, he has been an outsider."[3] Therefore with Naipaul, a tradition begins with him.

Not only V.S. Naipaul is displaced from his homeland but also he has distanced himself from the mainstream of Anglo-American political and literary trend. The appropriation of travel as a genre of writing facilitates his rhetoric of displacement. He travelled from the Western Metropolis to Non-Western metropolitan culture with a wide ethnographic divergence. His travel writings become both an ethnographic and biographical account. Joseph Conrad is Naipaul's literary forbearer and mentor. The post-colonial writing of Conrad provides Naipaul sufficient inspiration and scope.

As a writer without roots, Naipaul has spared no one. He has said harsh things about Trinidad, India, America, Pakistan, Argentina etc. Along with his criticism of the post-colonial world he has enlisted some remarks on England and America even though he has stayed more than thirty years in England. His eulogy of the values of the English bourgeoisie smacks of colonial nostalgia and imperial glory. At one time he had declared his unequivocal attachment for "the few square miles, which make an international city, a great metropolis, London." Such an avowal gives him the vantage point of a metropolitan writer.

Naipaul was determined to leave his homeland, Trinidad as he saw that the writers of his country were lost in oblivion like his father. His non-fictional work *The Middle Passage* (1962) broadened the scope of his travel writings. The publication of *An Area of Darkness* (1964) and *India: A Wounded Civilization* (1977) recount his several ventures to India. His other travelogue, *Among the Believers: An Islamic Journey* (1981) records his journey through some Islamic countries such as, Pakistan, Iran, Malaysia and Indonesia. In *An Area of Darkness* he discharges the role of an observant outsider and portrays India as a hopeless land, enveloped by a moral darkness. One may not agree with him as his is a lopsided view. As a direct descendant of Indian origin, he fails to identify himself with Indian culture because his is the third generation removed from Indian soil. So he visits India totally as a stranger bearing only some childhood memories communicated to him by his grandmother. He came to India with a sense of belonging that was in reality belied. On embarking upon this country he found a great gulf between myth and reality. He gleans a defect of vision in Indians for which they are not able to see themselves objectively. It is due to this reason that political movements take upper hand in their national life. In tracking the myriad mutineers across India, he covers the entire range of cession's movements, from regional to religious including the caste chauvinism. He projects the various mutinies as prelude to a state of regenerative disintegration. Though his vision is critical yet it is not remedial. He finds India's moral darkness contradictory to his childhood memories.

Twenty years after his first journey, Naipaul again came to India in 1989 and visited most of the important cities. In his second visit to Kashmir he stayed in the same Hotel Lizard. By objectively analysing Indian culture he has the advantage of identifying himself both as an outsider and insider. Some critics view his rejection of India as an expression of his strong Indianness, which he is unable to cast aside from his racial memory. His rage against India revealed through his incisive criticism reflects his subdued love for his ancestral land. It is his inner faith and reverence that impelled him to pay a visit to the ancient shrine of Amarnath. One may not wholly concur with the views of Nissim Ezekiel's disapproval of Naipaulean criticism of India, which is "heavily flawed in detail." Ezekiel is unable to appreciate Naipaul's objective account of India, which in his opinion, is flawed by his partial and prejudice western view. In Ezekiel's opinion Naipaul's description of India is a consequence of his "temperamental alienation from his mixed background":

> My quarrel is that Mr Naipaul is so often uninvolved and unconcerned. He writes exclusively from the point of his own dilemma, his temperamental alienation from his mixed background, his choice and his escape. That temperament is not universal, not even widely distributed, that choice is not open to all, the escape from most is not from the community but into it.[4]

Actually a strong Hindu base in Naipaul's formative mind had continued in the diversified multi-cultural atmosphere of Trinidad. It is interesting to note that having inherited the sensibility of a Brahmin, he tries to view India objectively as a neutral observer. Such a set of mentality instead of being condemned by critics ought to be appreciated with a sort of reformative zeal. Are we not at times, in reality, vexed with some of our irrational beliefs and practice, which have lost their symbolic significance for our present-day mentality?

On his visit to his ancestral land, Naipaul finds his rational cast of mind aggrandised by the mystery surrounding India. The tension between his irrational memory and rational analysis results in his critical view of India. No doubt he fails to assess the profundity of India's philosophic thought and archaic belief as is succinctly revealed in his post introspection:

> It was only now, as my experience of India defined itself properly against my homelessness, that I saw how close in the past year I had been to the total Indian negation, how much it had become the basis of thought and feeling.

> And already, with his awareness, in a world where illusion could only be a concept and not something felt in the bones, it was slipping away from me. I felt it as something true which I could never adequately express and never seize again.[5]

In his second visit he reviews his former observation and admits that in asserting "the antiquity of its civilization" India still remains for him "an imperfectly understood civilization."[6] A strong Hindu base of his childhood memory continues hunting his mind. As a pilgrim to Amarnath, he experiences a special joy at the sight of Himalayan landscape. He was already acquainted with these pictures during his childhood in his grandmother's house. His hidden Hindu self marvels at the beautiful sight:

> Yet a special joy had been with me throughout the pilgrimage and during all my time in Kashmir. It was the joy of being among the mountains; it was the special joy of being among the Himalayas. They went together. In so many of the brightly coloured religious pictures in my grandmother's house I had seen these mountains, cones of white against simple cold blue. They had become part of India of my fantasy.[7]

There is a fundamental contradiction in Naipaul's identity as a travel writer. Once he reaches Bombay he feels as if he is one of the surging crowds. He tries to explore his psychological dependence on his difference in India but he does not succeed. Instead, he is forced to identify himself with the crowd. As he fails to assert his difference, he becomes faceless:

> There is nothing in my appearance or dress to distinguish me from the crowd eternally hurrying into Churchgate Station. In Trinidad to be Indian was to be distinctive [...] in Egypt it was more so. Now in Bombay I entered a shop or a restaurant and waited a special quality of response, and there was nothing. It was like being denied part of reality. Again I was caught. I was faceless. I might sink without a trace into that Indian crowd. I had been made by Trinidad and England; recognition of my difference was necessary for me. I felt the need to impose myself, but I did not how.[8]

He recoils from any type of belongingness to India because as a writer he has a tendency for self-imposition.

Naipaul's rage against India revealed through his incisive criticism is a mirror of his deep love for his ancestral land. It is his ingrained faith that impels him to visit the ancient shrine of Amarnath. Not only does he love India but also possesses a soft corner for poor Muslims. During his stay in Kashmir he develops a special liking for Mr Bhutt's Hotel Liwrad in Srinagar. He tips his *khansama* and distributed clothes to some attendants because he was moved by their poverty. He finds most of the illiterate Muslims in Kashmir quite unaware of the political ongoing in that state. In general he finds the Muslims romantic and passionate.

Despite his desire for privacy and loneliness, Naipaul found himself increasingly dependent on his personal attendant, Aziz, in the hotel as the latter was a sweet-tempered nurse. Service was the motto in Aziz's life in spite of his poverty. So Naipaul has no mental inhibition to openly acknowledge his gratitude to him:

> To possess a personal servant, whose skill is to please, who has no function beyond that of service, is painlessly to surrender part of oneself. It creates dependence where none existed; it requires requittal; and it can reduce one to infantilism [...] his glumness could spoil a morning for me. I was quick to see disloyalty and diminishing attentions [...] I wished, above all, to be sure of his loyalty.[9]

Naipaul finds both the Hindus and the Muslims superstitious and guided by canons of caste. On the other hand, he disapproves the way the upper class Hindus, the so-called Anglicized club going people, are called by their nick names such as Andy, Bunty, Freddy, Jimmy, Bunny yet leading a perfectly Hindu way of life. Naipaul mercilessly reveals hypocrisy of such people in the following passage:

> For among a certain class of Indians, usually more prosperous than their fellows, there is a passionate urge not to be considered part of the poor, dirty India that their values and standards are higher, and they live perpetually outraged by the country, which gives them

> their livelihood. For them the second-rage foreign product, either people or manufactures, is preferable to the Indian.[10]

It is precisely for this reason that Naipaul dislikes Mrs Mahindra who was his landlady in Delhi and he was a paying guest in her house. Mrs Mahindra's materialistic attitude towards life prompts her to go regularly shopping and at the same time to consult her astrologer and visit temples. But he shows strong disapproval of the life of such *sadhus* who possess "a fantastic capacity for inactivity," whose life is prone to "casualness and disorder."

Naipaul's incisive criticism of Americans proves that he does not alone denigrate the Indians. He records his cynical views about the Indo-American relation, which in his opinion hides under various guises "a cruel revenge joke." Compared to America his sympathy goes obviously to India, for her casual exploitation by the former.

> But I had grown tired of meeting young Americans in unlikely places. It was amusing, and charitable to think that some of them were hippies for CIA or whatever it was. But there were too many of them. It seemed more likely that they were new type of Americans whose privilege it was to go slumming about the world and sometimes scrounging, exacting a personal repayment for a national generosity.[11]

American women and girls are the butt of his sarcastic remark:

> It was these American girls now approaching who were inexplicable and outlandish; not content with the attention they would normally attract, they wore body-accentuating garments, which would have been outrageous in London.[12]

Rob Nixon critiques Naipaul's achievements as the most lionized literary mediator between "First" and "Third World" experience. Despite Naipaul's skeptical views, Nixon rates him as a unique authority on the subject of cross-cultural relations in the postcolonial world but raises a pertinent question:

> How has Naipaul acquired a reputation as an unconventional, extra-traditional writer while producing

> an oeuvre suffused with received notions about barbarism and dishonesty of Islam, cannibalism in Africa, the simpleminded irrationality of Indians, the self-destructiveness of Black Power, and the inability of the Caribbean and India to generate real history?[13]

Probably this is the reason Naipaul's travelogue stimulates disagreement. In recording his expatriate experience he resolves the tension between the ethnographic and autobiographical modes abrogating "Third World" experiences of historical change. Despite contradictory views on his experiences, both American and British writers have acclaimed him as the most brilliant interpreter in English of the Third World. As a novelist he remarkably demonstrates his analytical understanding of the postcolonial world.

NOTES

1. Adrian Rowe-Evans, V.S. Naipaul, (interview), *Transition.* 40 (1971) 59.
2. Paul Theroux, *V.S. Naipaul: An Introduction to His Work.* New York: Africana, 1972, 76.
3. Mel Gussow, "Writers Without Root's" *New York Times Magazine.* 26, Dec. 1976, 8, 9, 18, 19, 22.
4. Nissim Ezekiel, "Naipaul's India and Mine," *New Writing in English.* Ed. Adil Jussawalla. Baltimore: Penguin, 1974, 74.
5. V.S. Naipaul, *An Area of Darkness.* 1964; rpt. New York: Vintage, 1981, 266-67.
6. V.S. Naipaul, *India: A Wounded Civilization.* 1977; rpt. Harmondsworth, England: Penguin, 1979, 104.
7. *An Area of Darkness* 176.
8. *An Area of Darkness* 46.
9. *An Area of Darkness* 114-15.
10. V.S. Naipaul, *The Overcrowded Barracoon and Other Articles.* 1972; rpt. New York: Vintage, 1984, 49.
11. *An Area of Darkness* 161-62.
12. *An Area of Darkness* 127.
13. Rob Nixon, *London Calling: V.S. Naipaul, Postcolonial Mandarin.* New York: Oxford University Press, 1992, cover page.

14

A Journey of Rejection: V.S. Naipaul's *The Mimic Men*

VEENA SINGH

The Mimic Men is a parable of man's ship-wrecked existence. The Image of shipwreck dominates the novel conveying a sense of abandonment and dereliction. This sense comes in sharp contrast with the desire to achieve success and recognition. Naipaul presents a coherent view of human predicament in its paradoxes and contradictions. Once again his subject is the third world society, he examines its social, historical and political reality. At the same time he concerns himself with the psychic damage caused by historical upheaval. The emptiness and hollowness of colonial set up compel people to pose as the Mimic Men. These men live in the memory of the past or in the fantasies of the future, and cultivate an ambivalent personality. The annihilating forces of dark tradition and dead past threaten the very existence of human beings and offer nothing but escape from reality, a journey of rejection. These mimic men are caught in the conflict between order and destruction, corruption and truth, the old and the new. They look down upon their own community, and also, try to achieve the glory of the colonial culture. Naipaul explains this dilemma in an interview with Shankar Israel:

> The people I saw were little people who were mimicking upper-class respectability. They had been slaves, and you can't write about that in the way that Tolstoy wrote about, even his backward society—for his society was whole and the one I knew was not.[1]

The novel *The Mimic Men* written in the first person narrative describes the plight of a colonial politician, Ralph Singh, shipwrecked first on his native island, and then in England. His is a backward journey, a journey without direction, a journey of rejection. "I knew that my own journey, scarcely begun, had ended in the shipwreck which all my life I had sought to avoid," says Ralph Singh.[2] He is the *mimic man* but he is conscious of mimicry, and its negative aspects. Alienated from his ancestral roots, he seeks psychological defences in status, power and sex. He is like Willy Chandran of Naipaul's latest novel *Half a Life*, moving from one place to the other in search of meaning.

Once Singh has destroyed the old order, he is incapable of creating a new one. All his life, he attempts to find order, and to fight corruption. In the process his self is falsified. In an individual the mimicry is caused by loss of sense of belonging, and in the society it is caused by loss of culture. Naipaul like other commonwealth writers considers this cultural loss a threat to identity. The constantly shifting character of life is the cause of rootlessness. There are no place associations, as a result the individual becomes impotent rendering all values meaningless. Naipaul depicts the metaphysical alienation of man which is a significant aspect of the modern sensibility in literature. Like the absurd and displaced people of Albert Camus, Saul Bellow and other modern writers Naipaul's characters live life at different levels of identity. The vulgarity, brutality, sordidness and irrationality of the modern world create a stereo-typed man, a picture of impersonality. Jagdish Chander remarks: "The modern man cut off from sources of vitality, leads a rootless and disintegrated life: his existence is nightmarish."[3]

In the *Mimic Men* Naipaul presents his diagnosis of the circumscribed individual caught in cultural ethos. Singh feels himself to be "spectral, disintegrating, pointless, fluid."[4] He tries to impose his romanticized vision on the reality of the things. The protagonist is the narrator as well as the participant in the action, and his disillusionment colours the tone of the book. He recounts his story, the story of a man adrift in the world. The book is not just the political memoirs. It is, "more than autobiographical work, the exposition of the malaise of our times pointed and illuminated by personal experience and that knowledge of the possible which can come only from a closeness to power."[5] Singh, the exiled politician describes his journey backward and forward between Isabella and England linking past and present, colonial life and London, childhood and adult life, illusion and reality and, success and failure. Through creative activity of writing the narrator tries to impose order on the world. The disorder, emptiness and forlornness become part of his existence right from the beginning. He knows: "To be born on an island like Isabella, an obscure New World transplantation, second-hand and barbarous, was to be born to disorder."[6] Singh knows that in Isabella, to be poor is a disgrace. Son of a poor school teacher, he prefers to lay claim to his mother's family who owns the Bella Bottling Works. For him childhood is a period of "incompetence, bewilderment, solitude and shameful fancies."[7] He reacts to this incompetence by changing his identity from Ranjit Singh to Ralph Singh. His romantic dissatisfaction with his longings finds place in his fantasies. He sees himself as a chieftain shipwrecked on an unknown island awaiting rescue, "here the island was like a place still awaiting Columbus and discovery."[8] Robinson Crusoe is an aspect of the same fantasy. Singh lives in a world of Rajputs, Aryanas, Knights, horsemen and wanderers; a world of endless plains and tall bare mountains. His preference for mountains and snow is opposed to his native elements of sand and sea. The ugly reality of Isabella brings Singh down from snow covered mountains to desolate beach. There is a paradox in his fantasies. He dreams that he is being carried hopelessly down a swiftly flowing river. The new world transplantation offers only the ills of alienation and chaos. In his character Naipaul depicts a sense of the missing world. For Singh Isabella is a place of futile aspiration. He is compelled to mask this chaos by his mimicry and takes up the role of a dandy youth. He performs different roles for different people. He assumes the role of an actor who is safe behind the mask. He dramatizes his relationship with his father, his friends and his women. He identifies himself with Brownie, who lives in a world of bad movies, with Hok—the Chinese boy in whom Naipaul discovers the racial wounds, with Cecil—his cousin and with

Deschpsneufs who are the makers of the slave colony. Naipaul's mimic men are partly rooted. They are the inhabitants of the world corrupted by fantasies. The name R.K. Singh is not just an expansion of his ego, it serves as a mask for his private self. In school he comes to be known as the son of a leader, thus his personality is divided "bewilderingly into compartments." For him all action is betrayal of truth. Naipaul's Mr Biswas and Richard Stone act by accident in the midst of anxious lassitudes and live in the comic availability of fate; Singh is more intellectually aware of his Indian ancestry than Biswas, and more deeply involved in his roles than Mr Stone. He is also more acutely conscious of his abandonment than the inhabitants of the Miguel street, and is more acutely aware of his predicament than Ganesh. Naipaul's characters like Singh face defeats, distortions and violations in their journey to find their true identity. The journey often proves to be the journey of rejection. Nonetheless they find their moment of truth.

The outside world which Singh has denied so long, begins to invade his private hemisphere. Outside school, he is faced with a chaos created by racial, religious and cultural traditions. He feels a deep desire for withdrawal:

> Before it had been part of fantasy, part of the urge to escape shipwreck and to return to lands I had fashioned in my imagination, lands of horsemen, high plains, mountains and snow; and time had been as unreal as place. Now I felt that need only to get away, to a place unknown, among people whose lives and even language I need never enter.[9]

Singh seeks escape in London, but soon learns that it is a flight to greater disorder and final emptiness. At times the identities of the narrator and the author seem to merge. Singh appears Naipaul's alter ego. Like the author himself, the narrator feels that this world is all we have to live in. London fails Singh in the same way it disappointed Naipaul. Here the author often hears people deploring the disappearance of character. In his essay "London" Naipaul writes: "The privacy of the big city depresses. There are no communal pleasures in London. Between the activity and the response there is always the barrier of self-consciousness."[10] The disappointment of a colonial migrant student, recorded in London scenes is author's own disappointment. Naipaul maintains double presence of the narrator and the novelist. Victor Ramraj writes that "it is easier to distinguish Naipaul from the Ralph of whom the story is about than from the recluse Ralph who narrates the story. The former is a supercilious figure, a poseur and a libertine. The latter, detached from his former life and writing with restraint and coolness, is closer to Naipaul."[11] London only heightens the sense of narrowness, emptiness and forlornness. The protagonist's rootless isolation is merely transplanted to another city. The city where he has hoped to find the beginning of order offers nothing but empty and fraudulent life, and, the feeling of rejection returns to him with greater force. He describes: "Shipwreck: I have used this word before. With my island background, it was the world that always came to me." He encounters again in the great city "this feeling of being adrift, a cell of perception, little more, that might be altered, if only fleetingly, by any encounter."[12]

Singh lives with a group of people and each encounter pushes him deeper into emptiness. His non-entity is mirrored in the nameless English society. He pretends to be what people expect him to be. "As with his secret name the personality of the dandy allows for the protection of the secret self," writes James R. Lindroth.[13] He finds the people two dimensional and becomes one like them; with Leini, a son-lover brother; and with Beatrice, a sensitive young man. But he fails to fashion order out of these unrelated adventures and encounters. He cannot reciprocate their affection. He indulges in promiscuity. His various relationships only bring a sense of failure, deficiency and distortion. Finding himself on the fringe of society, Singh is unable to distinguish between reality and unreality. He suffers a nervous breakdown like Biswas in *A House of Mr Biswas.* Like him, Singh moves from house to house; Mrs Shylock's boarding house in Kenningston, Brownie's house a racial prison, the Roman house, the beach house, the Scandanavian house and finally the hotel room in London. But for Singh the houses are no homes, no centres of light. He prefers the feeling of impermanence and the absence of responsibility. "I had no feeling for the house as home, as personal creation."[14] Singh has the Prufrockian sensibility preferring the impersonal and impermanent character of a hotel room to a home. This sense of meaninglessness and nothingness is similar to that of Eliot's protagonist.

In Sandra, Singh looks for an anchor. The feelings of isolation and anonymity are suspended for a while. He shares with Sandra, a sense of self-violation. She fills him with a new hope; "To me, drifting about the big city that had reduced me to futility, she was all that was positive."[15] His marriage provides an occasion to return to the island of Isabella. It is followed by his success in business with the money acquired from Bella plantation. It leads to an alignment with a group of professional men who have studied abroad and have foreign wives. He describes the society in Isabella as "haphazard, disordered and mixed." "It was a group to whom the island was a setting; its activities and interests were no more than they seemed. There were no complicating loyalties or depths; for everyone the past had been cut away."[16]

The relationship which started as an act of drama collapses and the two drift apart. Sandra becomes a girl from the East End of London. Her confidence and ambition admired once, are now pitied by him. She is no longer like an oasis for him. The failure of marriage results in the awakening of Singh's fear of the unreality, "it was the fear of the man who feels the veils coming down one by one, muffling his deepest responses [...]."[17] In *A House for Mr Biswas* the metaphor of the house brings the family together but in *The Mimic Men* the Roman House of Singh and Sandra cannot hold them together. Writers like Anita Desai and Manohar Malgonkar also deal with the problems of the inter-racial marriage. Desai's Adit in *Bye Bye Black Bird,* like Naipaul's Singh, is disillusioned with the expressionless British face. Nevertheless his marriage with Sarah, though without love, is a success, because the two are without any strong racial and cultural identities of their own. On the other hand, in Malgonkar's novel *Combat of Shadows,* the racial and cultural prejudices are too strong for any lasting relationship. In *The Mimic Men* Sandra and Singh cannot obliterate the feeling of failure.

The memoirs of Singh are written in flashbacks, the action moves backward and forward. The events are not narrated chronologically. Naipaul's method of story-telling demands the reader to analyse not only the character and his actions but also his deeper self. The novel covers a wide range of episodes depicting its protagonist in his childhood fantasies and his relationships with different people. He is depicted as a dandy youth, a lover, a husband, a businessman, a politician and a writer, who finally rejects everything and withdraws to his hotel room. In addition, the novel has a political perspective. Like Ralph Ellison's protagonist in *The Invisible Man* Singh assumes a false role in his journey to self-discovery in the context of historical and racial patterns. Singh like Ganesh in *The Mystic Masseur* anglicizes his name and, like him he achieves political success. As a politician he looks at himself as a kind of messiah. His political ideas are based on the dictum of "Hate oppression, fear the oppressed." Like his father Ralph has the qualities of a performer and of creating dramatic moments. His destiny for all his unwillingness, is to be linked with his father's. Ralph's political lessons come from his father who broke four cases of coca-cola bottles and established himself as a leader. His rebellion was an act of drama. Similarly the son brings drama to the island which otherwise is incapable of any larger events. For him politics remained a little more than a game, "a heightening of life, an extension of the celebrity mood." He joins as an ally to oratorical Brownie and is elected to power. Brownie's government is established. The Bauxite contract marks Ralph Singh's political success. Naipaul gives an ironical description of Brownie who tries to obliterate all traditions and values which remind the people of Isabella their colonial bondage. Brownie initiates Singh into politics by urging him to write for the paper *The Socialist,* he is editing. Singh now finds himself in the role of a Chieftain.

After the success the descent is rapid. Singh finds himself at the centre of events which he cannot control. There are demonstrations of racial violence. For Naipaul, as it is for Graham Greene, violence is the symptom of the malady of times. In Greene's novels *The Heart of the Matter* and *The Power and the Glory* the external violence mirrors the internal disorganization. In fact the chaos outside is the embodiment of the moral confusion. Naipaul also thinks: "The chaos lies all within." Power brings problems. William Golding too, in *Lord of the Flies* shows that disaster comes not so much through the exploitation of one class by another as by the brutish nature of man. He believes that correct structure of society can produce goodwill and all social ills can be removed by reorganization of society. In Naipaul's Isabella the leaders are no better than the imperialists. Like *The Suffrage of Elvira, The Mimic Man* is a study in political corruption which produces the mimic men in a colony emerging into independence. Peter Nazareth calls it "political novel." According to him the novel is "relevant to everybody in an ex-colony going through a period of rapid political change."[18] In the novel, the narrator awakens reader's consciousness to corruption, but it is not correct to call it a political satire. The narrator does display a moral consciousness. Unlike Ganesh in The *Mystic Masseur* or Harbans in *The Suffrage of Elvira* Ralph Singh imparts a moral significance to what he has seen. William Walsh's description of the novel is quite appropriate:

> *The Mimic Men* a very much more substantial novel, is the dramatized reminiscences of an exiled politician. The framing effect of the reminiscences, the distancing of exile and the sieve of memory, give form to the novel and enable us to grasp the quality of detachment in the protagonist and the weariness sapping a soul corrupted by power.[19]

Singh's sense of abandonment becomes acute when he fails as a politician. He is divided between the fear of black domination and the fear of civilization. He is the betrayed, the violate and the entrapped individual. His realization of the unreality of political power brings a moment of total helplessness. He is condemned as a racialist, a radical, and is considered a dangerous man. He suffers indignity in London when he takes there a delegation on nationalization. He tries to negate this sense of failure in his love-making to Lady Stella, and an unnamed woman on the way-side station before he comes back to London finally to settle down as a writer. He passes through extreme moments of negation and despair while journeying from one place to another. The scene at the unknown country station is the climax of his desolation and homelessness. He feels that he has no past. He seems at the end of the world. The scene of Garbage's eating reflects his own disintegrated lifestyle. Singh's flight from active life is occasioned by his failure to cope with the chaos he finds in the world around him. He is left as much a Hindu castaway as ever. Neither his physical nor his mental journeys have brought him any real fulfilment.

Like Gurudeva, his father, Singh becomes a recluse. He sees himself a true Hindu who has fulfilled the Hindu division of life in four periods—the period of student life, the period of life as a householder, as a man of affairs and as a recluse. It is another act of self-dramatization. His Hindu self proves inescapable, he has affinity with Ganesh. He finds Hinduism attractive as long as it is confined to his fantasies but feels betrayed in its rituals, and is disillusioned in the horse sacrifice, an ancient Hindu ritual of Ashavmedha. He seeks security in racial purity. He is ultimately saved from despair by prospects of escape into writing. In the act of writing he tries to undo the effects of imperialism and to reestablish a rooted coherence. "So writing, for all its initial distortion, clarifies, and even becomes a process of life." [20] But Clark Blaise considers Singh's act of writing a pose. He finds *The Mimic Men* "least successful of island novels." Blaise writes: "Ralph Singh does not fully convince, either as an ex-politician, or an exile, or land-developer, his banishment to London to write his memoirs at forty is something of a pose, a convenient way of gathering up several selves into a single narrative."[21] It may be a pose, but as Blaise himself says that writing is also a means to gather up "several selves." The writing of his memoirs releases Singh from a sense of homelessness. Singh comes to terms with reality. A new pattern emerges, through the creative activity he learns to master his self-hood.

Ironically, Singh like Naipaul himself has to go back to London. London becomes a pivot of his memoirs of organising the facts and a means of distilling order out of chaos. Naipaul himself had to leave Trinidad and go to London: "to become a writer, that noble thing I had thought it necessary to leave. Actually to write, it was necessary to go back. It was the beginning of self-knowledge."[22] Singh also, who has earlier rejected London as a place of greater disorder and final emptiness, finds, "that this present residence in London, which I suppose can be called exile, has turned out to be the most fruitful."[23] Critics like Landeng White feel optimistic that Singh finds a release from his frustration in his writing. White writes: "For Kirpal Singh's discovery of himself as a writer marks his personal salvation. In act of writing, he finds at last that order and coherence which has eluded him in every other activity."[24]

Singh frees himself from one cycle of events. Though this freedom cannot be called his achievement, nonetheless he assembles the fragments of his shattered experience and records the disorientation of a colonial. Whether he is really able to create the order in the world or not, he at least, recreates himself as a free man. Singh expresses hope: "Yet I feel that in this time I have cleared the decks, as it were, and prepared myself for fresh action. It will be the action of a free man."[25] Naipaul ends the novel on a positive note. James Lindroth rightly comments that Ralph Singh passes from "the mimicry of the fraudulent pretence to the mimesis of authentic creative performance."[26] Naipaul's protagonists like Ralph Singh, Jimmy Ahmed, Ganesh Ramasumair, Mohun Biswas and Richard Stone are the self-centred people. They are the prisoners of their egos. Creative detachment imparts wider dimensions to their experiences and life, beyond their nostalgic memories and unreal aspirations. Naipaul like the modern writers of the age mirrors the tortured and twisted psyche of man, and also his ambiguous and irrational self. Like Ellison's *The Invisible Man, The Mimic Men* is not about politics or about a particular race or society but about the dissociation of sensibility, about the displacement, isolation and identity crisis.

REFERENCES

1. Israel Shankar, "V.S. Naipaul: Man Without Society" in *Critical Perspectives on V.S. Naipaul.* Ed. Robert D. Hamner. Washington, D.C.: Three Continents Press, 1977, 49.
2. V.S. Naipaul, *The Mimic Men.* Harmondsworth: Penguin, 1973, 7.
3. Jagdish Chander, *Modernity in Contemporary Indian Literature* (A collection of papers). Shimla: Indian Institute of Advanced Studies, 1968, 107.
4. *The Mimic Men* 52.

5. *The Mimic Men* 8.
6. *The Mimic Men* 118.
7. *The Mimic Men* 90.
8. *The Mimic Men* 111.
9. *The Mimic Men* 145.
10. V.S. Naipaul, *The Overcrowded Barracoon.* Harmondsworth: Penguin, 1976, 15-16.
11. Ram Raj Victor, "The All-Embracing Christ like Vision: Tone and Attitude in *The Mimic Men, Critical Perspectives* 135.
12. *The Mimic Men* 27.
13. James R. Lindroth, "The Figure of Performance in Naipaul's *The Mimic Men, Modern Fiction Studies,* 50.3 (1984): 421.
14. *The Mimic Men* 27.
15. *The Mimic Men* 45.
16. *The Mimic Men* 55
17. *The Mimic Men* 72.
18. Peter Nazareth, "Out of Darkness: Conrad and Other Third World Countries" (*Conradiana*), 4.3 (1982): 138.
19. William Walsh, *Commonwealth Literature.* London: OUP, 1973, 60.
20. *The Mimic Men* 251.
21. Clark Blaise, "The Commonwealth Writer and His Material." In *Awakened Conscience: Studies in Commonwealth Literature.* Ed. C.D. Narasimhiah. New Delhi: Sterling Publishers, 1978, 124.
22. V.S. Naipaul, *Finding The Centre.* Harmondsworth: Penguin, 1985, 40.
23. *The Mimic Men* 248.
24. Landing White, *V.S. Naipaul: A Critical Introduction.*
25. *The Mimic Men* 251.
26. Lindroth 529.

15

V.S. NAIPAUL'S *HALF A LIFE*: MEMORY AND THE MYTH OF ORIGIN

AIDA LUZ RODRÍGUEZ COLÓN

In the "Introduction" to *East Indians in the Caribbean: Colonialism and the Struggle for Identity: Papers presented to a Symposium on East Indians in the Caribbean,* V.S. Naipaul said that ignorance of the Indian community permeates inside as well as outside of itself. Indians must learn more about themselves. They must learn about the constituents of their community and of their culture. He added that the people tend to forget the past, and from such loss, self-awareness should develop. To him, beyond the grandfathers there is nothing, and that break with the past has not been understood. For that reason, "people can flounder and can become irrational" (4). Thus, to reach self-knowledge, people should pursue more scholarship to gain some understanding of their upbringing, and, along with intelligent inquiry, an understanding of the past and the culture of the grandfathers. In view of that, he adds:

> I begin with myself: this man, this language, this island, this background, this school time. I begin from all that and I try to investigate it, I try to understand it. I try to arrive at some degree of self-knowledge, and it is the kind of knowledge that cannot deny any aspect of the truth. (7)

The point becomes clearer in his essay, *Reading and Writing: A Personal Account*, which traces his development as a writer. To illustrate the process, he included in his works material from his childhood, from his father's doings, and from his experiences at school. For instance, in order to write a novel about India, he felt necessary to create a character like himself, "someone of my ancestry and background [...] to duplicate the original experience [...] to render it as faithfully as I could" (*Reading and Writing* 50). He built from memory until he discovered his literary voice, the tone, and the language. After that, he writes in different forms or genres, and to represent his experiences accurately, he creates a myth of origin to construct life in his works drawing from his memory, from his past. Aware of the strategy, Ian Buruma states that in Naipaul's writings "there is a kind of myth [...] an echo of older stories: the son leaving the village, breaking free from tribal beliefs." In this manner, the recent novel *Half a Life* (2001) exemplifies Naipaul's use of memory to create a myth of origin through an Indian character, William Somerset Chandran.

Willie, who is born and raised in India, attains self-awareness of his past, and by drawing from that past he reconstructs a background on which he can set his new life. What Willie does is to create a myth of origin to control the dynamics of the stage on which he moves in London and Africa. He believes that "[h]e could, within reason, remake himself and his past and his ancestry" (57). From his memory, he draws information of former times, but he attunes that information according to what he believes is appropriate to his new life. His doings reiterate the definition of memory in the essay "Between Memory and History: *Les Lieux de Mémoire*" by Piérre Nora, who says that "[m]emory is [...] open to the dialectic of remembering and forgetting, unconscious of its successive deformations, vulnerable to manipulation and appropriation, susceptible to being long dormant and periodically revived" (8). This also brings to mind the essay "Windows of Focalization: Deconstructing and Reconstructing a Narratological Concept" by Manfred Jan, who affirms that "[m]emory does no more than to set a stage." Therefore, within such a stage, Willie can only establish a foundation based on his "manipulation and appropriation" of memory. He cannot have control of the performers, of the surroundings, nor of the past from which he obtained the basic information for his scheme through his father's memoirs.

As the book opens, Willie wants to know why his middle name is Somerset. He asks his father about the name because the other children at school were making fun of him. The event provokes the recounting of a past and Naipaul's display of his skills as "manager of narrative" (xii), a diacritical phrase used by himself in the "Prologue" to his book, *Beyond Belief: Islamic Excursions among the Converted Peoples.* Using his skills, Naipaul manipulates the narrative to dramatize the act of recalling from the memory banks the source of Willie's middle name by developing a narrative technique of telling a story within a story. Therefore, the father becomes the narrator and tells his life story to Willie. Through the father's life story, Willie learns about the grandfathers, and Naipaul juxtaposes the present time when Willie asks the question with the story that the father is telling. This passage, in addition, reveals Naipaul's manipulation of the third-person narrator at the beginning of the book, switching to the first person when the father, as narrator, acquaints Willie with his ancestral background. In this regard, Miguel Gorra, in his essay, "*Half a Life*: Postcolonial Studies," says that "*Half a Life* is built like a sandwich, with the first-person narrations of the Chandrans, father and son, serving to hold a third-person filling in place." The third-person omniscient narrator also creates doubts about the father's story by mentioning that "[t]he story changed as Willie grew up" (3). That means that the father has developed into a "manager of narrative," just like Willie, and adjusted the past to fit the moment of recollection, although he says that "[t]his was what my grandfather told me" (7), which could also means that the grandfathers, too, adjusted the facts.

The father, continuing his account, even tells Willie how he had created the role he has lived, by turning his back on an excellent career, by marrying a woman of lower caste, and by becoming the "mendicant on the alms of the poorest of the poor" (5). Afterwards, Willie will remember and will carry the burden of those memories originated because of his father's decision. Willie, too, will learn about his father turning to the past to relieve his apprehension of the mess he had made of his life. Deploring what he had done, he tells Willie the necessity he felt to "go back. We come from a line of priests" (7). Concurrently, the expression "go back" reminds the reader of Naipaul's earlier pronouncement concerning the use of memory to identify the links to previous times. In addition, the passage gives the impression that by reaching out to yesteryear one may be able to find solace for the uneasiness suffered by many Caribbean individuals.

Legitimately, the father believed that at such moment what remained for him was "to make a life of sacrifice" (10). Together with this, the father tells Willie his decision to turn his "back on our ancestry, the foolish, foreign-ruled starveling priests my grandfather had told me about" (12). With regret, the father, lamenting how he had entrapped himself, felt that he could not escape the role he had created as husband, father, and mendicant. Remembering, Willie's father concludes that he "had fallen into ancestral ways" (31). Up to now, he regrets and bears in mind his actions. Memory, then, has represented a burden for him because, as he says, "[t]his shame was always with me, the little unhappiness at the back of my mind, like an incurable illness, corrupting all my moments" (32). The father suffers such mental state because, according to Simon Gikandi, "[t]he voice from the past contains both joy and pain; it ensnares and liberates at the same time" (192). For the father, memory brings pain, giving Naipaul the opportunity to illustrate through him how burdensome memory can be; and, simultaneously, the path to search through the memory banks for the data which is still in the mind of our fathers and grandfathers. Once the section of the father ends, Naipaul turns to the recourse of the third-person narrator, again. To do the switching, Naipaul introduces into the narrative a dialogue between Willie and his father. The conversion of the narrative perspective is to create the effect of a story within a story, and the sensation of travelling to the past. Through the dialogue, the reader learns how acquaintance with the past and the father's position brings about Willie's disdain of his father. Taking possession of his father's account, Willie began constructing his history, which later on he changes out of shame.

The act of learning all this about his father, and the fact that his father was a mendicant, caused Willie's embarrassment. In relation to the assumption of embarrassment, Gikandi explains that "the past [...] instead of functioning as a source of certainty and true understanding [...] often generates fear and shame" (172). Willie exemplifies the assumption because his past, his ancestor, ignited the shame he was experimenting. His humiliation grows bigger when he goes to the mission school and the teacher asks him about his father's employment. Instead of answering, because of his memory, and because he remembers the degraded names used to refer to his parents, Willie says, "'[y]ou all know what my father does'" (36). The statement provokes everybody's laughter, and the pang of his memory, inflicts him with greater force. As expected, Willie, just like his father, has to live with the burden of memory. To overcome the situation, Willie becomes successful at school, and he writes excellent compositions mixing the knowledge he has gathered from magazines with local details. For one of the stories, he records and adjusts the notions about his father and his ancestors. This signifies that in order to manage his world, he writes stories centred on his father's history. When his father reads one of the stories, he sees that Willie had titled it "'A Life of Sacrifice'" (45), a phrase that the father had used to refer to his own life. Two aspects are involved in this passage: Willie's recalling of the past to revenge himself on his father while achieving an outstanding merit at school, and Naipaul's narrative dexterity. This technique of inserting Willie's story within the main narration helps the narrative to gain significance because it enlarges the theme of memory as a source to create a myth of origin, and, equally, it shows how, in a similar manner to Willie, the writer can draw material from memory to include in his stories making them recordings of history.

Particularly interesting is the way in which the twenty-year-old Willie receives a scholarship to go to London, just like Naipaul, and in the same way as Ralph Singh, the central character in *The Mimic Men*. Unlike what happens with Singh, the crossing by ship for Willie constitutes an important source of information to nourish his memory. Amazed, he discovers that it was possible for a person "to recall everything [...] to find that he had stored up all the details of that stupendous first crossing" (49). Once he gets to London, he searches through his memory to verify the information he had obtained back home, and he realizes that everything was different. He recalls "the maharaja's palace" (50) as a more impressive place than Buckingham Palace. He also recalls his knowledge of Speakers' Corner acquired at the mission school, which did not correspond to what he was seeing. So, "remembering his own home life" (50), he infers that the family of these people must be happy to have them out of their homes. The words, then, imply that his own family was happy that he had left. Depressed and disappointed, "[h]e walked without seeing, thinking of the hopelessness of home and his own nebulous present. All at once, in the most magical way, he was lifted out of himself" (50). The burden of his memory has caused him to walk "without seeing," and the phrase, "lifted out of himself," promotes the belief that for him, he had to forget about himself, who he was because he has been "lifted" from the framework in which he had lived. The episode, without doubt, implies that he will forget his past, and that he will construct a myth of origin.

To do so, Willie must gather the information to put together a new self to help him overcome his lack of knowledge. The fact brings Willie to recognize that his ignorance comes from the "habit of non-seeing" (52), which he had inherited from his father, and from the "blankness" (53) he had gotten from his mother's side. He has had to learn new manners and ways to do the things he knew from home. This is a developing world, all new to him, and it is a world that turns out to be one of "make-believe" (56). Yet, he examines the customs of his college by going to the library to find out about the black gown they use for formal occasions. Unable to identify the origin, he presumes that the gown, probably, had been copied from the Islamic style. He decides that the gown was not a descendant from the Roman toga, but just another "piece of make-believe" (57). Through the vision of this developing new world, Willie comprehends that the rules he had left at home, which are still in his memory, "were themselves a kind of make-believe, self-imposed" (57). The passage helps Willie to see his capacity to reconstruct his life, to redesign a myth of origin according to the scenario in which he is performing, "within reason [to] remake himself and his past and his ancestry" (57).

To fulfil his intention, Willie draws information from his past, and adapts the facts to the role that he is playing now, that of a college student in London. The first thing he changes is his mother's background. Seeing the newspapers full of news about trade unions, and remembering that his mother's uncle had been "the fire-brand of the backwards" (57), he transforms that to "a kind of trade-union leader, a pioneer of workers' rights" (58). Because of his mother's education at the mission school, he sees her as "half a Christian," so he alters that by speaking of his mother as "a full Christian" (58). In addition, to disengage himself from the mission school, and interpreting from memory what he has read, he adjusts his behaviour to certain things suited to the manners of a Christian. He adds that his mother belongs "to an ancient Christian community of the subcontinent [...] almost as old as Christianity itself" (58). He also claims that his father is a Brahmin, and that "his father's father [was] a 'courtier'" (58). This is how, "playing with words, he began to re-make himself. It excited him, and began to give him a feeling of power" (58). By re-making himself intentionally, Willie invents or re-creates a myth of origin centred on his family's history in an attempt to gain acceptability and to manage his developing new world.

With his new background, Willie joins the immigrant-bohemian life of London, alongside people from the Caribbean, white African colonists and Asians. The bohemian parties give Willie an opportunity to enter another stage, that of the writer. He meets someone from the BBC (just like Naipaul), who asks him to write a sketch based on the history that Willie had created from memory, and which he had centred on the lies he told about his family, his past, and his ancestors. The act of writing these sketches brings him back to his past, to his mission school days; but, submerged in his play-acting, he enjoys the frenzy of playing the role of writer and reporter. Nevertheless, his past comes forth, and the pangs of memory inflict themselves on him again.

Full of joy, and happy with the life he is constructing, Willie tells his friend Roger, a lawyer, that he wants to be a writer. In view of that, Willie types up the stories he had written at the mission school, and shows them to Roger for evaluation. Roger discards the stories, telling Willie: "you don't want to write about real things [...] I feel about these stories that the writer has secrets. He is hiding" (79). Without knowing Willie's adjustment of fact to meet his own performance, Roger identifies the stories as "real," and, concurrently, unmasks Willie, although only Willie knows what is going on. The fact is that, ingeniously, Naipaul has developed a complicated situation to confront Willie with his past and with the myth which his life has become. The act could be sustained as ironic, a reversal of life. When Willie gives the stories to Roger, he thinks about the esteem he has for Roger's friendship, and considers his stories too unimportant to come between two friends. After Roger gives his opinion, Willie leaves thinking that he "will never see Roger again" (79). Willie regrets his decision to show the stories to Roger, and, depressed and disappointed, concludes: "He is right. That is the worst part" (79). This phrase confirms Willie's acceptance that "[h]e is hiding" information from his memorial past. Overwhelmingly, the burden of his memory and the data from his yesteryears have come into the world, the myth he has molded, to hit him with great force: "It was like the time at home—long ago, as it now seemed—when he had begun to hate the mission school and had given up his old dream of becoming a missionary, someone of authority, and travelling the world" (80).

Significantly, the mission school, his father, his family, and his past keep popping back along with his memories. For instance, when Willie meets Roger's editor at a party, the editor brings to Willie's mind the image of Willie's father. The next day, Willie writes a story about the editor, places him in the Indian town where the story is set, and makes him a holy man. The novel says that the story he wrote is a peculiar one: "[i]n substance it was like the story Willie had heard over many years from his father" (96). In a way, what Willie has done is to take the knowledge stored in his mind and use it to re-create the image of his own father through the figure of the editor. The story stimulates Willie's writing, and, coincidentally, shows him a new way to view his family. Out of this story-writing section comes his book, but although it gets published, race riots surge up and plunge Willie back into his own memorial misery. He feels so ashamed and scared that he hides in the college, remembering that "[i]t was what they used to do at home, when there was serious religious or caste trouble" (103). The passage shows how, to cope with the world, Willie, just like his father, goes back in time to find solace and a way to handle the situation. He is still feeling ashamed when a letter from home pulls him back into the framework from which he has been "lifted." With the new vision he has developed of his family, he feels sorrow for his father, and becomes depressed remembering the children who must have made the envelopes. The vision appears to remind him of the hopelessness of his home if he were still there.

A menace to the myth he has put together arises when Willie receives another letter, this time from his sister. Her letter denotes the conscientious self she has turned out to be, as she tells Willie not to become an idler like his father. She feels that he is wasting his life in London doing unimportant things unconscious of what he is doing. Unknowingly, she has sensed Willie's doings, which are transforming him into an idler. Her ability to see beyond is only part of the menace; the other part is her visit to London in a few days. Her presence constitutes the utmost point of vulnerability that Willie must face. As it threatens the myth of origin, which has enabled him to face the world, Willy is shown to be afraid that "in five minutes she would have babbled away all Willie's careful little stories about their family and background" (109). In addition, her presence makes him realize that he is like his poor father, even sexually.

Then, searching through his memories he realizes that the "philosophical-practical way of dealing with sex belongs to our past" (111). Once more, the burden of his memorial past inflicts him. Whenever he wants to make love, the old ideas overcome him and he becomes frightened and ashamed making him unable to perform. In that manner, his ancient history affects the role, which he has played all this time in London. To handle this situation, he fantasizes with the idea that something might come up someday. That chain of reasoning brings him closer to his idle father because that is the way an idler thinks.

Little by little, along with the role of college student, Naipaul has given Willie the qualities of the father. That is why, inserted in his myth of origin, Naipaul ingrains through the letters, and through other characters, the tools for the reader to perceive Willie as an equal to his father. To some extent, the situation involves some dramatic irony since Willie is unaware of the information rendered by the narrator controlled by Naipaul. Efficiently, Naipaul has embodied Willie in two ways, through the myth of origin created by Willie himself, and by making Willie resemble his father. Unaware of this, Willie thinks about his accomplishments as a London student: he "had made an active and mixed London life for himself and was an author with a book soon to be published" (114). In a sense, the words denote Willie's apprehension and suggest that for Willie life in London has come to an end and he needs a new role to play. This is even more strongly emphasized in his words: "Let the book die [...] it was artificial and false" (115). Resourcefully, to continue with the narration, Naipaul recurs to the use of letters to introduce the next episode in his narrative.

Two letters arrive, one from Roger, the other from Ana, the only admirer of Willie's book and his saviour. Besides saving him from his hopeless moment in London, her presence grounds Willie's "make-believe" world, because, if the book is "false," then it is "a piece of make-believe," as well as the writer. By accepting him, she accepts his world. On this occasion, Willie feels that this time he is himself. Yet this is not the case. The reader knows that Willie has been playing the role of a writer and has constructed a background on lies. Therefore, the "himself" is the one he has created to manage his London life, which has led him to be a writer, and, hence, admired by Ana. While his creation of a myth of origin has brought him this far, now he has to find another way to function because no-one else has accepted his book as good, which means that as a writer he was doomed. Lucidity helps him out, and he sees Ana as the sign he has been waiting for. Therefore, he travels to Africa with her. Before he leaves, he receives a letter from Sarojini, which brings him again in contact with his past and his ancestry. Without regret, she tells him: "you are like your father, holding on to old ideas till the end" (123). Through the letter and through the figure of the sister, Naipaul immerses Willie in the past from which he has been "lifted" through his creation of a myth of origin. For Willie, her words were "undoing the centre of his London life" (123).

Finally, he goes to Africa, but unlike what happened on his voyage to London, the journey brings him face to face with reality. It comes to his mind that he is losing the knowledge he has acquired from home. In other words, he has erased his home language, and he is afraid that his English will disappear, that he had "no gift of expression [...] of speech [...] of language" (124, 136, 148), a phrase which echoes "the gift of the phrase" (65) from *The Mimic Men*. Once more, memory casts him face to face with his accumulated knowledge of former times, and with the insight of how he has changed to deal with the stage on which he had placed himself. Willie's myth of origin, the adjustment of his history, has taken him into a labyrinth of new customs and languages, *i.e.*, Africa. Intelligently, Naipaul has displayed his narrative manipulation through an Indian character, moving him in only four pages to Africa and then bringing him to his sister's house in Berlin. The purpose is to have Willie recount to his sister the eighteen years he passed in Africa, living at Ana's expense, as an idler like his father. This recounting adds another dimension to the dramatization of the act of recalling from memory by inserting a story within the story. In so doing, it yields the sensation of travelling or flashing back to the past so that the narrative scheme may reinforce the theme of memory as a means of building a myth of origin. Together with this, Naipaul turns to the first person narrator, and he has Willie, as narrator, voicing Ana, his wife. As a result, only Willie's version is available.

The truthful sub-meaning of the episode of Willie's narration is to include the end in the middle of the novel: when we recall from memory, the recollection takes place in segments, and the actual temporal moment happens before the recollection—or perhaps, Naipaul's intention is to illustrate that this is only half of the life of Willie. This point is addressed by J.M. Coetzee, in an essay entitled "The Razor's Edge": "*Half a Life* reads like the cut-off first half of a book that might be called *A Full Life.*" Thus, the diacritical phrase, "manager of narrative," applies perfectly to this novel, because the narration, divided in the middle, clearly demonstrates how Willie's half-a-life ends almost in the middle of the book, in the middle of his life, at forty-one. Summing up, then, by placing the end of the story almost in the middle juxtaposed with the recounting of Willie's life in Africa, Naipaul conveys significance on the narrative of half of Willie's life almost halfway through the book. The technique aims to dramatize the title of the novel, *Half a Life,* as well as the act of recalling from memory. In the essay "Nobel in Literature Goes to Naipaul, an Explorer of Exile," Sarah Lyall says that "[h]is fiction is often [...] returning again and again to [...] the burdens of the past and the confusions of the present." What Naipaul has illustrated through the story of Willie Chandran is how a person could recall from memory past events from which that person could construct half a life to enable her/ him to cope with the present scenario in which he/she is living in.

Lamenting his behaviour up to now, Willie, at forty-one, admits, "I have been hiding from myself. I have risked nothing. And now the best part of my life is over" (140). From that sorrowful lament, and through Naipaul's scheme of flashback, Willie acquaints his sister with his life in Africa. In Ana's country, they accepted his new self, but based on his London construct of a life. Once more, his memory reminds him of his former times: "They seemed not to know that I was once something else" (139). These words indicate that he is playing another role on another stage that is different from the one he has played before. As Ana explains, upon reading Willie's book, she understood "all the bluff, the make-believe, with the real unhappiness. It was uncanny. It was why [she] wrote" (146). All the time she has known that he was role-playing, that he has hidden the truth, that he has adjusted his historical past to construct his life. In a way, her telling the truth represents another pang, another infliction of his past.

In another sense, his Indian background turns out to be helpful because it has permitted him to deal with his circumstances in Africa and, also, it has rescued him from London. As he relates to his sister how he came to understand his role, he concludes that he "was helped in this understanding by [his] own background—that the world [he] had entered was only a half-and-half world" (150). At heart, the phrase, "half-and-half," could mean hidden/exposed, and could parallels the world of "make-believe" that he has created, and, "the disintegrating 'half-formed societies'" (3), to cite a phrase used in Amit Chaudhuri's essay "The World of V.S. Naipaul." Now, at a moment of insight, on the last page of the book, as he talks to Ana he evokes his memorial burden and recognizes his wastefulness when he says: "the [...] pain that had been with me for months, and perhaps for years [...] now the best part of my life has gone, and I've done nothing" (211). In this way William Somerset Chandran ends his half a life by admitting his suffering, caused by the burden of his memorial past and by his myth of origin. Interestingly, he also figures out something that nobody else has guessed, "that the world of concrete was going to be so completely overwhelmed by the frail old world of straw" (150). While the metaphor refers to the "estates life" in Africa, it also applies to him. His life in the metropolis, "the world of concrete," was always subjugated to his memorial past, "the frail old world of straw" (150). Although, he constructs a life, adjusts his historical past, and elaborates his own role-playing, he reaches the halfway point of his life an idler, just like his father.

Willie's greatest hardship is over, and he has composed himself half of his life by rearranging his background, "remak[ing] himself and his past and his ancestry" (57). Naipaul has certainly developed an Indian character who has learnt more about the constituents of his community and his culture. From that knowledge, he makes available a scheme to create a myth of origin to construct a new life. At the end, this character develops an understanding of his past and the culture of his grandfathers. *Half a Life* presents Naipaul's intelligent inquiry at work, and, once again, he displays his dexterity in managing narrative and character to make the most out of a theme.

WORKS CITED

Buruma, Ian. "In the Empire of Islam." *New York Review of Books* 18 Aug. 1998. 28 Dec. 2002 <http://www.nybooks.com/articles/783>.

Chaudhuri, Amit. "The World of V.S. Naipaul." *Times Literary Supplement* 16 Sept. 2001: 1-4.

Coetzee, J.M. "The Razor's Edge." *New York Review of Books* 1 Nov. 2001. 28 Dec. 2002 <http://www.nybooks.com/articles/14680>.

Gikandi, Simon. *Writing in Limbo: Modernism and Caribbean Literature.* New York: Cornell UP, 1992.

Gorra, Michael. "*Half a Life*: Postcolonial Studies." *New York Times* 26 Oct. 2001. <http://www.nytimes.com/2001/10/28/books/review/28GORRAT.html?rd+hcmcp?p=041HD>.

Jan, Manfred. "Windows of Focalization: Deconstruction and Reconstructing a Narratological Concept." *Style* 30 (1996): 241-68. 27 Oct. 2001 <EBSCOhost>.

Lyall, Sarah. "Nobel in Literature Goes to Naipaul, an Explorer or Exile." *The New York Times* 13 Oct. 2001. <http://www.nytimes.com/2001/10/12/b...12NOBE.html?todaysheadlines=&p agewanted=prin>.

Naipaul, V.S. *Beyond Belief: Islamic Excursions Among the Converted Peoples.* New York: Vintage International, 1999.

——. *Half a Life.* New York: Alfred A. Knopf, 2001.

——. "Introduction." *East Indians in the Caribbean: Colonialism and the Struggle for Identity: Papers presented to a Symposium on East Indians in the Caribbean, The University of the West Indies, June, 1975.* Ed. V.S. Naipaul. New York: Kraus International Publications, 1982. 1-9.

——. *The Mimic Men.* Harmondsworth: Penguin, 1975.

——. *Reading and Writing: A Personal Account.* New York: New York Review of Books, 2000.

Nora, Pierre. "Between Memory and History: *Les Lieux de Mémoire.*" *Representations* 26 (1989): 7-25.

16

V.S. Naipaul's *Half a Life*: A Critical Study

ALPANA MISHRA

V.S. Naipaul was born on August 17, 1932 in a small town in Chaguanas, Trinidad in a family of Indian Brahmin origin. His grandfather was a poor Brahmin, who went to Trinidad in 1880 to work as a landless labourer in the cultivation of a sugarcane farm for a pretty long time. His father Seepersad (1906-53) was a journalist whose literary aspirations were inherited by V.S. and his brother, Shiva. V.S. Naipaul had his education in England and wrote three great books on India; out of which two books—*An Area of Darkness* (1964) and *India: A Wounded Civilization* (1977) were written with great anguish and anxiety. While writing *An Area of Darkness*, V.S. Naipaul came for the first time to India, where he found that his great image for India, which he had stored in his childhood was at the breaking point that India was a great and sovereign country as he had to reject the popular Western concept that India was solely a great spiritual country in view of the fact that he had to realize the suppressed history of India in the then social, economic, political and religious conditions of Indian panoramic life.

V.S. Naipaul had his education in the Oxford University at the age of 18 years and worked as a short-story-teller and a novelist while travelling over the whole world, the Nobel Prize Swedish Academy called him a nomadic literary man. The life and art of V.S. Naipaul an interlocking series of journeys. In 1950, just before he turned 18, he travel from the New World, to the Old World, from Trinidad to England where he had a scholarship at Oxford University. He became a writer with a world perspective, and he has never stopped travelling.

These travels have inspired more than 22 books of fiction, history and commentary. At the age of 22 years Naipaul is a renowned man of letters.

II

Half a Life (2001) is, mainly the story of Willie Somerset Chandran. It is an odd tale, moving from India to England and to Africa. The novel begins with an omniscient narrator. Just after beginning the novel after half a page the novelist switches to the first person, allowing Willie's father to recount the story of the origins of Willie's unlikely name, and his own pathetic misled life. Again Naipaul switches back to an omniscient narrator and allows Willie Chandran to tell his own story in the first person.

Half a Life is set firstly in post-independence India, at the politically protected court of the Maharaja, later in London then in the pre-independence Africa in a nameless country modelled on Mozambique and briefly, Berlin.

The story begins as a kind of portrait of the artist, where Willie is a promising youth at the Indian mission school, living with his father, a born Brahmin who tells Willie Chandran the story of how he married a low caste, and uneducated woman, whom he never loved for the sake of his political ideal.

Disillusioned with school, and his parents, and uncertain of his future, Willie Chandran obtains, with the help from one of his father's contacts, a scholarship to a college of education for mature students in London, where he begins, to write and participate and a literary social life. The novel follows Willie Chandran as he tries to find a place or role for himself, following his heart to Africa, and for want of anywhere else to go, to Berlin.

Story-telling is an important part of the novel. It is expertly done by Naipaul. The opening chapter is a nice tour, a story told over a decade's time shifting and changing as it was told and retold over those years yet fundamentally as set down here. Willie's father complains that he "unfitted" himself for life by giving up his education, and he became a mendicant. Willie's father got himself into this situation by turning his back on family and tradition. At university there is a "backward" caste student he has eyes on. Not because of she is attractive or appealing, but because she fits his image of the sacrifice, he wants to make. He winds up marrying her. It, however, shocks and disappoints his son young Willie Chandran.

The next chapter in the novel focuses on Willie's school days, and then his escape to England, to study. Here, too, stories are important, a form of communication in the household where Willie Chandran does not feel he can express things directly. Willie writes several compositions at school but disappoints his actual audience, his father. Hearing his father's life story led Willie to tell his father that he despised him.

Willie escapes to England, eager just "to get away from what he knew." Despite not having finished his own mission school education, he gets scholarship to "a college of education for mature students." The world he enters is completely foreign one. He fumble for friendship, for sex, for acceptance—and achieves atleast a measure of most of these.

Willie also writes a book, and is not able to publish it. It is not a success, and critical reception if it is poor.

Willie is willing to give up this ambition, this possibility:

> Willie thought, "Let the book die. Let it fed way. Let me not be reminded of it. I will write no more. This book was not something I should have done, anyway. It was artificial and false [...]." (123)

With no plans for the future as his scholarship at the college comes to an end, Willie Chandran takes up with Ana and follows her to the Portuguese colony of Mozambique. Here again Naipaul makes a radical cut and jump "he stayed for eighteen years." Naipaul tells us and jumps from the beginning to the end of that period, when Willie Chandran finally gives up this life and Ana. Willie Chandran goes to Germany, where his sister, Sarojini is living. Naipaul allows Willie Chandran to tell his own story in his own voice, and allows him to finish the novel. It is an odd set of leaps, and yet effective.

Willie's father set the example for the son of the half-lived life and his son Willie Chandran follows in those same footsteps. He has no firm objectives, and ambitions. There are moments of promise. In England:

> Willie began to understand that he was free to present himself as he wished. He could, as it were, write his own revolution. The possibilities were dizzying. He could, within reason, remake himself and his past and his ancestry. (60)

Willie Chandran can't take advantage of the opportunity. Most promisingly perhaps, he finds that he could become a writer, a storyteller, but he allows this ambition to be thwarted. He chooses finally simply to flee again into a world that is entirely fragmentary.

Mozambique is at best, a "half-and-halfworld." The ambition of the people and the ideal they strive for is Portugal. They are not fully Portuguese, often children or grandchildren, like Willie Chandran, of some mixed sort of marriage, or simply emigrants, neither truly native in the country they left or the country they live in, it is Ana's life. Willie Chandran finds himself living, more than his own. After eighteen he is done with it.

Still only just over the age of forty. When the book ends, there might be hope for Willie Chandran. But that is not Naipaul's concern: his focus is on the past, on what Willie became and was. It is in fact, difficult not to see Willie Chandran as some after Naipaul. Perhaps the very person Naipaul always feared he might become not as brilliant, without the supportive family, from India rather than Trinidad. Willie Chandran seems something of a lesser Naipaul. But his experiences in England especially, suggest what might have been. Willie Chandran seems and unlikely author, but he manages to get published the book and he could have chosen to continue it, instead of dismissing the possibility of being a writer. Naipaul allows Willie Chandran to be a storyteller to narrate the story in the first person. Naipaul sees Willie's future that after only half-living for so long, he must turn to try fill in the void of his life.

The first part of the novel is a kind of parody of a Somerset Maugham short story. This short fragment is the least satisfactory part of the book; its shadowy character belying the fact Naipaul's narrative in India lacks life. The familiar Naipaul strains are already present in a subtle way.

In a corner of India untouched by anti-colonial agitation Willie Chandran's father stood at odds with the world-aspiring to greatness while living out the dreary life marked but for him by his ancestors. In an attempt to defy his past he marries a low caste woman only to find himself at the mercy of his own fury.

And then the ambivalent pleasure of embracing an untouchable woman:

> Her very dark top lip slipped slowly—with the wetness of a snail, I thought over her big white teeth. For the first time I saw that she used powder. There was a thin white bloom on her cheeks and forehead; it made the black skin matt, and you could see where the powder ended and the shiny skin showed again. I was repelled, ashamed, moved. (13)

The union resulted, however, in the birth of two children—Willie Chandran and Sarojini.

From this unhappy union the utterly compelling character of Willie Chandran emerges, oddly like his father, eager to find something that will place him both in and apart from the world. He is drawn to England and the immigrant community of post war London, its dingy West End Clubs and sexual encounters, and even to the eccentric milieu of the English writer. But it is Willie's first experience of love that might bring him the fulfilment he so desperately seeks. His wife Ana leads him to her home, a province of Portuguese Africa, a country whose inhabitants are all uncertainly living out the last days of colonialism. Naipaul delineates the relationship between father and son with wonderful clarity and compassion; the comic brilliance of the London scenes and the penetrating descriptions of Africa are hard to beat.

The second part of the novel picks up pace, though still retaining the flavour of Naipaul's rather unhappy student years in England. Naipaul himself has mentioned depression and suicidal tendencies. This part deals with a number of sexual encounters and again, the old strain, difficulty with the intimate, ambivalence and revulsion to smell and dirt surface soon enough.

> He saw her on Saturday in Percy's room at the college. She was a big girl in a tight skirt that showed off her hips. She filled the small room with her perfume. At her counter, Willie thought, she would have access to all the perfumes in Debenhams, and she has been lavish. Willie had never known perfume like that, that mingled smell of excrement and sweat and deep, piercing, many sided sweetness from no simple source. (66)

There are characters that are namesakes or likes of other figures of the time, like Marcus Garvey or the landlord racketeer, Rachman—none of them flattering.

The third part of the novel is the straight narrative. It is described by Willie Chandran to his sister, Sarojini. It is again parodying Maugham, of Willie eighteen years in an African country in a Portuguese colony like Mozambique. This is the liveliest part of the book, rising at the end, to a personal epiphany for Willie Chandran, who found himself in this African country as he followed Ana into it. There is easy racial acceptance here for Willie Chandran:

> Most of the shops we used were Portuguese. One or two were Indian. I was nervous of going into them at first. I didn't want to get that look from the shop people that would remind me of home and bad things. But there was never anything like that, no flicker of racial recognition from the family inside. There, too, they accepted the new person I had become in Ana's country. They seemed not to know that I was once something else. There, too, they kept their heads down did what they had to do. So that for me, as for the overseers, though in different ways, the placed offered an extra little liberation. (148)

And again,

> I found that there was no special reaction to me. It was curiously deflating. I was expecting some recognition of my extraordinariesness and there was nothing. (144)

Ana had African blood and a family estate in the country. Those were the days of Willie Chandran's interest lovemaking with Ana. He loved her—in that room which had been her grandfather's and her mother's, with a view of the nervous branching and the fine leaves of the rain tree—for the luck and liberation she had brought to him, the undoing of fear, the granting to him of full manhood.

The description of the local, colonial expatriate community, many of them bearing Portuguese names, is indeed, the strength of the book. It is a life of colonial ease, with servants and sex available at little cost. Willie Chandran's fear of the bush and "half-made" societies is, none the less real:

> I often thought back to the terror of my first day that picture of the road and the Africans walking was always with me—and wondered that the land had been tamed in this way, that such a reasonable life could be extracted from such an unpromising landscape, that blood, in some way, had been squeezed out of stone. (149)

The plot and subplots of the novel are subordinated to the main theme and interlinked to the main story of the novel. Throughout the novel, there are small stories, each given a reasonable number of pages, and a reasonable standing in the overall book design. There are Willie's early stories, set in "an undefined place, at an undated time," read reluctantly, and misunderstood, by his father, and the later stories of Willie Chandran, which are modelled on Hollywood stories. There are the stories in Willie's unnamed book. There are also Ana's autobiographical stories of "Luisa," which mirror Willie Chandran's half lies about his own background. There are also the stories of the minor characters, he meets in Africa, from the Correias to that of Alvaro, Graca's story, Julio's story and the story of the colourful Africa prostitutes and harlots he sleeps with. But the African's natural affinity for dance and the availability of easy sex offer Willie a whole new world of personal experience and liberation:

> We drank beer. The feeling of shame went. I looked at the dancers in blue light, and their dim reflections in the mysterious space of the wall-high dark mirror. I had never seen African dance. With the kind of estate life I had been living there hadn't been the occasion. Immediately these girls began to dance they were touched by a kind of grace. The gestures were not extravagant;

> they could be very small. When a girl danced she incorporated everything into her dance—her conversation with her partner, a word spoken over her shoulder to a friend, a laugh. This was more than pleasure; it was as though some deeper spirit was coming out in the dance. This spirit was locked up in every girl, whatever her appearance and it was possible to feel that it was part of something in the African heart that was shut away from the rest of us, and beyond politics. (185)

And then the encounter with a young African girl:

> Without her stiff clothes the girl was really very small. But she was firm and hard; she would have done much physical work as a child. Ana was not like that; Ana was bony and frail. I felt the girl's breasts; they were small and only slightly less hard than the rest of her. Alvaro would have liked those breasts; it was possible to imagine the stiff young nipple sticking up below a cheap village cotton dress. But the nipples of this little girl were broad and spongy at the tip: she had already had a child or children. I couldn't feel any longing for her. Even if I did, all the old ghosts were already with me, the ghosts of home, the ghosts of London eleven or twelve years before, the awful prostitute in Soho, the big hips of June on the mattress on the floor in the slum house in Notting Hill, all the shame and incompleteness. I didn't think that anything was going to happen to me with the poor little girl below me on the cheap army-reject mattress. (187)

So far the girl's eyes had been blank. But then, just at the moment when Alvaro was about to fail, an ordinary look of command and aggression. Alvaro was squeezed by her (call girl or prostitute) strong hands and legs. That is what Alvaro lives for, and he revived.

Willie Chandran now attains a kind of predatory sexual drive that has learnt to be assertive:

> The long drive had been a strain. Graca's need match my own. That was new to me. Everything I had known before—the furtiveness of London, the awful provincial prostitute, the paid black girls of the places of pleasure

> here, who had yet satisfied me for so long and for whom for almost a year I had felt such gratitude, and poor Ana, still in my mind the trusting girl who had sat on the settee in my college room in London and allowed herself to be kissed. And still so gentle and generous—over the next half-hour everything fell away, and I thought how terrible it would have been if, as could so easily have happened, I had died without knowing this depth of satisfaction, this other person that I had just discovered within myself. It was worth any price, any consequence. (204)

Willie finally learns Percy Cato's secret:

> [...] I remembered some words of Percy Cato's in London, and for the first time had my sense of the brutality of the sexual life. I was deep in that brutality now with Graca. Sexual pictures of her played in my head when I was not with her. With her guidance, since she was the more experienced, our love-making had taken forms that had astonished, worried, and then delighted me. Graca would say, 'The nuns wouldn't approve of this.' Or she would say, 'I suppose if I went to confession tomorrow I would had to say, "Father, I've been immodest."' And it was hard to forget what she had taught, to unlearn the opening up of new senses; it was hard to go that to the sexual simplicities of earlier days. And I thought, as I often did on such occasions, the puerility of my father's desires. (211)

The months passed. Even after two years Willie Chandran felt himself in this life of sensations. At the same time then some half-feeling of the inanity of his life grew within him, and with it there came the beginning of the respect for the religious outlawing of sexual extremes.

Willie's epiphany, however, has taken him only a limited distance:

> Ana said to me one day, 'people are talking about you and Graca. You know that, don't you?'
>
> I said, 'It's true.'
>
> She said, 'you can't talk to me like this, Willie.'

> I said, 'I wish you could be in the room when we make love. Then you would understand.' (211-12)

In the new erotic, African paradise, the snake's disturbing presence is evoked a couple of times, not normally the characteristic of Naipaul's fiction.

Evaluating the novel in terms of critic's opinion, we observe that: In an editorial review it is well said:

> *Half a Life* finds the veteran Booker and Nobel Prize-winning author V.S. Naipaul on familiar territory, blending autobiography and fiction in an exploration of the "half lives" of individuals brought up in the English colonies and educated in metropolitan cities.[1]

Jerry Brotton says:

> This is classic Naipaul, with its effortless dissection of the damaging personal consequences of post-war decolonization, but its virtue seems its primary vice, as the novel feels like a conflation of several earlier Naipaul books, including *The Mimic Men* and the brilliant *A Bend in the River*. Consequently, some readers may well find that *Half a Life* reads more like half a novel.[2]

Grady Harp a reviewer observes:

> The first half a Naipaul's much heralded *Half a Life* makes a fine promise that this writer can spin delectable webs. Perhaps a familiarity with the atmosphere and history of both India and England makes the gradual growth of this story delicious [...]. I think the premise of this short novel is well drawn—that what we as individuals inherit genetically and social logically and philosophically creates a destiny that need not be followed. There is much to be learned about the caste system of India, the concept of class system in England, and the disintegration of race identification in Africa: reading this book will certainly inform us of the sad state of affairs that retards our beliefs in equalization of all men.[3]

A reviewer Randall Ivye observes:

> The title certainly refers to the main character, Willie Chandran, who feels, by age forty-one, that his best years are behind him, never to be recovered, and that

he has wasted his life in desultory pursuits of sex and literary fame. But he is not the only character not living life to its fullest. Others fritter theirs away chasing material possessions and political power and social mobility.[4]

Amit Chaudhuri in *Times Literary Supplement* observes:

This is short novel, then captures in miniature the exceptional trajectory of Naipaul's oeuvre; the figure of the father, the life of the writer, and, finally, an enquiry into the origins of the colonial landscape itself [...]. *Half a Life* is not one of Naipaul's major undertakings, but I don't think it was meant to be. It is intended to give us yet another perspective on his corpus, in which one detail illuminates another.[5]

Jamie James, in *Wall Street Journal* says:

This short novel is a fitting, if slight, post-scriptural flourish to the career soon to be apotheosized in Stockholm, a partly autobiographical resume of many of the principal themes of his fiction [...]. It's possible that there is some obscure authorial intent in the curiously abrupt ending, but it reads more like laziness.[6]

According to Jonathan Yardley,

On the one hand it is a continuation of his preoccupation with the innumerable questions raised by cultural racial identity, on the other hand it's spare, melancholy, elusive somewhat heavily ironic tone contrasts with the more animated quality of his best fiction (*A House for Mr Biswas* for example), and graphic sex with which its final sections are filled is a stark departure from his almost priggish treatment of the subject previously.[7]

According to Chris Colin:

Naipaul presents London terrifically, as a town of impressionable young heirs still learning to promote themselves in a world imperial forbears everyone looks up to their ancestors for having created such splendor.[8]

Chris Colin further says:

What's greatest about *Half a Life* is, of all things, its pacing. In London, Willie can't be still. We get flashes of British life a bullied, receptionist, a prostitute taking some

"French letters" from a bag—and then we're off to the next room. But in Africa, as Willie eases into the borrowed life of his wife's world, the camera pans slower and slower. There are interruptions, as when he's arranging a tryst, but generally this is travel writing: simple bougainvillea descriptions, without mention of alienation, race or class division.[9]

According to Farrukh Dhondy:

Fress [...]. A novel with a purpose [...]. Though the evocation of three continents and several decades, without calling on public events and purely through the narratives of a life, V.S. Naipaul gives us a moral tale which captures the evanescence of our times.[10]

J.R. Vanderheft has well observed:

V.S. Naipaul the English speaking author of many books, sums up a life of unparalled creativity and innovation with his autobiographical journey, *Half a Life*. Mr Naipaul takes us from his homeland of Trinidad to Oxford University and then backs again, leaving the reader full of wonder, joy and a sense of discovery.[11]

According to Robert Hanks:

Half a Life is a deeply discomforting, even dismaying boo; But it is also a book of uncommon elegance, subtlety and intelligence.[12]

Jonathan Bate says:

Naipaul is usually a finely understated writer, but in this book he is hardly subtle in splitting up his halves.[13]

According to Lee Siegel:

Half a Life, a masterpiece of implicitness, is explicitly concerned with drawing out the metaphysical—private while keeping it embedded in society and history. This small, sparely written tale embodies a fragile idea of freedom, a vision of human life disentangling itself from the encumbrances of time and place.[14]

James Wood says:

Half a Life confirms Naipaul's stature as the greatest living analyst of the colonial and postcolonial dilemma;

> and those who have never approve of that analysis, and have objected over the years to what they see as Naipaul's fatalism, snobbery or submerged radicalism, a willingness to see things from the eyes of the disadvantaged.[15]

According to J.M. Coetzee:

> *Half a Life* is the story of the progress of a man from a loveless beginning to a solitary end that may turn out to be a true end, just a plateau of rest and recuperation. The experiences that mark his progress are sexual in nature [...]. *Half a Life* does not give the impression of having been carefully worked over, and the technical weaknesses that result are not negligible.[16]

According to Jason Cowley:

> *Half a Life* reads as a study in estrangement and inner exile [...]. In this strange, languorous, often painful new novel it is not the Africans, but the settlers whose lives seem most incomplete, who are themselves. It is they who are the true Conradian grotesques, wandering restlessly without home or hope.[17]

Naipaul is a natural outsider, but he possesses a capacity to interweave his own feelings with those of others, to recognize in them his own fallibility, and this gives his writing an intense humanity.

His recurring themes—the destruction of links to the past and to the land, the wounds created by the loss of the sense of history, and the efforts to heal this, which often only produce greater neuroses—are handled majestically in this book. And always, there is his acute observing eye: passing through a Javanese village, he sees a group of girls in white headdresses walking to school, "like little shoals of blanched big-headed tadpoles."

No one writes better than Naipaul about the hollowness that comes from the types of success which is measured by standards that are not one's own, by standards which belong to the more powerful—so that success is felt as defeat and subjection.

He is a masterly analyst of the incurable melancholia of the arriviste, whether of the worldly or spiritual kind.

III

V.S. Naipaul loves to depict men and women of strength and stability of character. He takes for his chief character men of powerful nature, men of the country, with little acquired virtue, but disciplined by the experience of life. Naipaul's women are as clearly distinguished as his men. It may be noted that V.S. Naipaul is above all a painter of characters. Nothing indeed is as rare as a writer capable of depicting with equal success the character of both sexes. His male characters are either sensual or effeminate or else victims of a kind of internal attention. He discovered in women a complexity; which involved them in more intimate relations with the materialistic world. The characters of V.S. Naipaul are drawn from the common and ordinary life.

In *Half a Life* V.S. Naipaul has delineated the characters from common and ordinary life. The major characters are Willie Chandran, Willie's father and Ana while the minor characters are Alvaro, Marcus Garvey, Rachman, Percy and Graca.

Willie Somerset Chandran, is the protagonist of the well known novel *Half a Life* (2001). He was named after Somerset Maugham's encounter with Willie's father in the 1930s while travelling "to get material for a novel about spirituality."

Willie Chandran is the hero and central character of the novel. He travels to England for his education. He becomes a part of bohemian-immigrant life of London of the late 1950s. He soon realizes that his colonial background allows him to write short stories. He wanted to "remake himself and his past" through his writing.

Willie begins another "half life" in colonial Mozambique, where he soon tires of the domestic and sexual tedium of plantation life and flees to Germany, mournfully reflecting that "I have been binding for too long." Willie Chandran, like his father before him, charts his progress in life, according to others expectations. Like a genetic disease passed down, these expectations dictate Willie's life. Never asking himself what he really wants, Willie first tries to impress his father and when that fails, moves to London to attend college. There Willie tries to live up to the expectations of his college chums and to fit into 1950s Bohemian London. Finally, finally appears to find his own voice when a collection of his stories is published. But mixed reviews send him reeling, and again he's thrown off track, this time re-inventing himself as a pseudo-baron at his wife's family's estate in Africa, which he doesn't stick with, surprise. Just at the beginning of the novel we find that Willie Chandran is a half-caste, born of an untouchable mother and a Brahmin father. From this unhappy union the utterly compelling character of Willie Chandran, emerges, oddly like his father, naïvely eager to find something that will place him both in and apart from the world. And so he is drawn to England, to the immigrant community of post-war London, its dingy West End Clubs, lonely pavements and sexual encounters, and even to the eccentric milieu of the English Writer.

The first part of the novel is a kind of parody of a Somerset Maugham short story. At the beginning of the novel we find that:

> Willie Chandran asked his father one day,
> 'Why is my middle name Somerset? The
> boys at school have just found out, and they are
> mocking me.'
> His father said without joy,
> 'You were named after a great English writer. I am
> sure you have seen his books about the house.'
> 'But I haven't read them. Did you admire him
> so much?'
> 'I am not sure. Listen, and make up your own mind.'
> And this was the story Willie Chandran's father
> Began to tell. It took a long time. The story changed as
> Willie grew up.
> Things were added, and by the time
> Willie left India to go to England this was the story he
> had heard. (1)

Willie Chandran went to London for higher studies at the university in England. While he was at the university, his plan was to get a B.A. degree and perhaps get a scholarship from the Maharaja to do medicine or engineering. Then he was to marry the daughter of the principal of the Maharaja's college. All or that was settled, but he felt detached from it. He became idler and idler at the university. He didn't understand the B.A. course. He felt more useless than ever. He would have given anything to be in touch with their greatness, of those great men whose bliss was a boon for Willie Chandran. Here there was only the servile life around the palace of the Maharaja. Night after night he debated what he should do. The Mahatma himself, he knew, had gone through a crisis like this only a year or two before in his ashram. While living securely at home, in the house of his father, still (for the sake of peace) he was pretending to attend the university, he said:

> I at last felt inspiration touch me. I left with every kind of certainty that the decision that had come to me was just, and I was determined to carry it through. The decision was nothing less than to make a sacrifice of myself [...] —but a more lasting kind of sacrifice, something the Mahatma would have approved of. He had spoken much about the evils of casteism. (10)

Willie Chandran accepted that his decision was simple. He asserted:

> My decision was simple. It was to turn my back on our ancestry, the foolish, foreign-ruled starveling priests my grandfather had told me about, to turn my back on all my father's foolish hopes for me as someone high in the Maharaja's service, all the foolish hopes of the college principal to have me marry his daughter. My decision was to turn my back on all those ways of death, to trample on them, and to do the only noble thing that lay in my power, which was to marry the lowest person I could find. (10-11)

This was the story that Willie Chandran's father told. It took about ten years. Different things had to be said at different times. Willie Chandran grew up during the telling of this story.

Willie Chandran and his sister Sarojini went to mission school. One day the teacher asked Willie Chandran as to what his father was doing. He did not know what to say about his father's business. He was also found ashamed. Willie despised his father more than ever because his father married a low caste woman.

When Willie Chandran was 20 years old, he had not completed his school education at the mission school. He had no idea of what he wanted to do except to get away from what he knew. With very little idea of what lay outside what he knew, only with the fantasies of the Hollywood films of the thirties and forties that he had seen at the mission school, he went to London by ship. He knew that London was a great city. His father had given him names of people he should get in touch with. Willie was living in the college in a daze. The college was a semi-charitable Victorian foundation.

Willie's other stories are set in an undefined place, at an undated time. He decides to leave his community and go elsewhere, into the hot rocky wilderness, to die alone, with dignity. His new confidence began to draw people to him. One of them was Percy Cato. He was a Jamaican but not strictly of Jamaica. He was born in Panama and had grown up there. Willie had friendship with Percy Cato, Roger who was a young lawyer and other African woman such as Raca and Carla and late a bohemian life with them. While making a critical review of the character of Willie Chandran we observe that:

> In Naipaul's fiction, in the naming of the main character of *Half a Life* as William Somerset Chandran (Willie), a person that contains many threads of Naipaul's true biography; but these are perverted and disported threads that do not ennoble Willie, but rather make him the whimpering coward that appear in this book.[18]
>
> V.S. Naipaul is a genius. Willie is not a happy character, but one turns the last page uplifted. Willie's life makes it clear; happiness lies in forging our own way. And, just as critical: the prison of other expectations only confines when we allow it if this resonates with you, you'll love this book.[19]

According to Chris Colin:

> *Half a Life* meanders interestingly in this way bildungsroman to travel book, England to Africa and

> Naipaul is offering us a character with a similarly unstable center. The novel and its protagonist alike drift along with the convolutions of postcolonial Africa and England, but Willie never reduces to a simple metaphor, and the drifting isn't in service of some glib point. He is, instead, a believable and likably sad man, with half a life left and probably more peripheries to visit along the way.[20]

Willie Chandran's father is also an important character of the novel around whom the character of Willie Chandran moves round. In a corner of India untouched by anti-colonial agitation Willie Chandran's father stood at odds with the world-aspiring to greatness while living out the dreary life marked out for him by his ancestors. In an attempt to defy his past, he lives with a low-caste woman only to find at the mercy of his own fury.

Just at the beginning of the novel, Willie Chandran asked his father as to why he was named after Somerset Maugham. Willie's father with pride said that Willie Chandran was named after a great English writer. Soon after the novel begins after half a page, the novelist V.S. Naipaul switches to the first person, allowing Willie's father to recount the story of the origins of Willie's unlikely name, as well as his own pathetic, misled life. Willie's father got himself into this situation by turning his back on family and tradition and looking to "marry the lowest person I could find." At university there is a "backward" caste student he has his eyes on, and ultimately he marries her.

Willie's father's story is a marvellous beginning, and many scenes from Willie's student life in England and his half-life in Africa are also very nicely done. Parts of the novel, however, also seem too hurried, with detail dissolving over sudden large stretches of time—as if, in part, Naipaul had lost patience with the book. There are some neat character sketches, but they too often do not seem fully integrated into the narrative—appropriate, perhaps, as the way one comes across and then loses sight of people in real life, but sticking oddly out in work of fiction like this.

Willie Chandran is a bitter young man who does not help his father clarifies of view than details of his family's past.

Willie told his father that he hated him for everything and for his passions he had in his life.

Willie Chandran's father hadn't forgotten Willie. He thought that they have created monster. He really hates his mother and his mother's people, and she does not know. The boy would poison what remained of his father's life. He must get the boy far away from there. Willie's father tried to be philosophical. He found that Willie Chandran left for London at the age of 20. His father had given him names of people he should get in touch with. Thus Willie Chandran was leading his life in a unique way among his new friends, while keeping himself away from his father.

The third part of the novel is a straight narrative. It is described by Willie to his sister. There was a personal epiphany for Willie Chandran, who found himself in this African country. There was easy racial acceptance there for Willie. He came in contact with Ana. Willie Chandran and Ana were in Africa. Ana had African blood and a family estate in the country. Those were the days of his intensest lovemaking with Ana. He loved her deeply.

Willie encouraged Ana to talk about her country. He tried to visualize the country on the eastern coast of Africa, with the great emptiness at its back. Soon, from the stories she told, he began to understand that she had a special way of looking at people: they were African or not African. Willie thought if she would just see him then as someone who was not an African. But he pushed that idea to one side.

Ana told a story about a school friend. She always wanted to be a nun. She ended up in an order somewhere there, and she went to see her some months ago. They lived a kind of jail life. And, like people in jail, they kept in touch in their own way with the world outside.

At another time on the little sofa Ana said a story:

> Here's a story for your next book. If you think you can do anything with it. My mother had a friend called Luisa. Nobody knew anything about Luisa's parentage. She had been adopted by a rich estate-owning family and she enherited a part of the estate. Luisa went to Portugal and Europe. She lived extravagantly for many years and

> then she announced she had found a wonderful man. She brought him back. They gave a very big party in the capital, and the wonderful man told everybody about all the famous people who were his close friends in Europe. (128)

Willie and Ana left from Southampton. Willie thought about the new language he would have to learn. He wondered whether he would forget his English, the language of his stories. He set himself little tests, and when one test was over he immediately started on another. While the Mediterranean went by, and the other passengers lunched and denied and played shipboard games, Willie was trying to deal with the knowledge that had come to him on the ship that his home language had almost gone, that his English was going, that he had no proper language left, no gift of expression. He did not tell Ana. Every time he was testing himself. He wished he had come to Ana's country in another way. The town was big and splendid, far finer than anything he had imagined, not something he would have associated with Africa. Its grandeur worried him. He did not think he would be able to cope with it. The strange people he saw on the streets knew the language and the ways of the place. He thought:

> 'I am not staying here. I am leaving. I will spend a few nights here and then I will find someway of going away.'
>
> That was how he thought all the time he was in the capital, in the house of one of Ana's friends. (133)

The first day at Ana's estate house, Willie said that it was as long as he could imagine. Everything in the bathroom was new to him—all the slightly antiquated fittings and the old geyser for heating water. Other people had designed that room, had had those fittings installed, had chosen those white wall tiles—some of them cracked them, the crack-lines and the grounding black with mould or dirt, the walls themselves a little uneven. In that room especially he felt a stranger.

Somehow he got through the day, without Ana or anyone else guessing at his state of mind, the profound doubt that had been with him ever since they had left England.

He felt very far away from everything he had known, a stranger in that white concrete house with all the strange old

Portuguese colonial furniture the unfamiliar old bathroom fittings; and when he lay down to sleep he saw again—for longer than he had seen them that day—the fantastic rock cones, the straight asphalt road, and the Africans walking.

Ana once said that her father's name was Julio. He was a carpenter. He was also a drunkard. Willie said that he had met Julio. He was a man of mixed race with smiling unreliable eyes. He lived in the servant's quarter. His drinking was a joke there. Willie said that he knew Ana's grandfather also, and all the people he knew. They would have known only what they had. They would have been content to live with what they had in their own country.

Ana knew the stories that were told about her father. It was true what they said. But it was only part of the truth. He was never an active man and his energy level fell when he came there. He felt no anger for Ana or her mother or her grandfather. He was just passive. He hated being asked to do very simple things. He remembered how his face would twist with pain and anger. He really was someone who needed help.

Ana was then at a language school in England. She said that she wanted to break out of the Portuguese language. She felt it was that which had made her grandfather such a limited man. Her grandfather had no true idea of the world. All he could think of was Portugal and Portuguese Africa and Goa and Brazil in his mind, because of the Portuguese language; all the rest of the world had been strained away. He did not want to learn South African English, which was what people had learnt there. He wanted to learn English spoken by the native speakers of England.

It was while she was at the language school in Oxford that her father disappeared. He left the estate house one-day and never came back. He had taken a fair amount of the estate with him. She still loved her father.

Ana said that it was something Willie must remember. Africans might not be afraid of Willie and Ana, but they were afraid of one another themselves. Willie had got the passport back. He felt safe again. Ana and Willie, as if by agreement, talked no more about the matter. They never mentioned the fetish-man. But the ground had moved below him.

Willie did not think that he could live through another war. He could see that it would have a point for Ana. He did not see that it had a point for him. For some weeks he was perplexed. He did not know what to do.

When Ana came to the hospital, courage came to Willie, and he told her that he wanted to divorce her. When she came back later he told her that he was forty-one and he was tired of living her life. Ana asked Willie if he really wanted it. Willie accepted that Ana did everything for him. She made it easy for Willie there. He could not have lived there without her. When he asked her in London he was frightened. He had nowhere to go. Willie also accepted that the best part of his life had gone, and he had done nothing. Willie said that even if they would go to Portugal, it would not be the life without Ana. He had been hiding this fact for pretty long. Ana asserted that perhaps it was not really her life either. At the end of the novel, ultimately Willie and Ana seemed to be separated without any definite resolution.

In the course of the novel we also came across the minor characters such as Sarojini, Percy Cato, Roger, Alvaro, Carla and Graca.

Sarojini is the only sister of Willie Chandran. Willie's father was worried about her at the beginning of the novel. He said that her prospects in that country were not bright. But foreigners had their own ideas of beauty and certain other things, and all he could hope for Sarojini was an international marriage.

Sarojini wrote from Germany. Willie did not want to open the envelop. He remembered with shame, how it would have excited him at home, and at ashram about her future life. Willie thought that he used to worry about that girl. He did not think she had a chance and he would have done anything to help her become a happy woman. Then that old German man came along and ugly little Sarojini changed. She become the complete married woman. She accused Willie of hiding, but she herself was homeless, wandering from city to city, with a husband notably absent from the narrative in the novel.

Sarojini wrote a letter to Willie from Germany that she would come to London for a few days to see Willie there. In due course she came, and for three or four days she turned his life upside down. She stayed in a small hotel near the college—she had arranged that her self before she left Germany—and she came everyday to Willie's college room and prepared a rough little meal. She asked for his help in nothing. Sarojini had never been a good cook, and the food she cooked in the college room was awful. The smell stayed in the room. Willie was worried about breaking the college rules, and he was just worried about people seeing the dark little cook—clumsily dressed: with a cardigan over her sari and socks on her feet—who was her sister. In her new assertive way, but still not knowing too much about anything, in five minutes she would have babbled away all Willie's careful little stories about their family and background.

For the past two and a half years Willie had lived like a free man. He could not go back to the other thing. He did not like the idea of marrying someone like Sarojini, and that was what would happen if he went home. Sarojini was right in the other way too. If Willie got his teaching diploma and decided to stay there and teach it would be a kind of hiding away. And it would not be nice teaching in a place like Notting Hill. That was the kind of place they would send him, and he would walk with the fear of running into a crowd. Sarojini's life was no more her own than Willie's.

Willie Chandran's live confidence began to draw people to him when he had a new circle of friends around him.

One of them was Percy Cato. He was a Jamaican of mixed parentage and was more than black. Willie and Percy, both exotics, both on scholarships had been wary of one another in the beginning, but now they met easily and began to exchange stories of antecedents. He was a Jamaican but not strictly of Jamaica. He was born in Panama and had grown up there.

Willie was charmed by Roger. Roger was a young lawyer whose career had hardly started. Willie sat through a hilarious script of Roger's about working on the government's legal aid scheme, representing people who were too poor to pay lawyer's fees.

Ricardo was a big, military-looking man with his gray hair in a military style crewcut. He liked practicing his English with Willie, he had a heavy South African accent.

Alvaro lived in a dingy four-roomed concrete house. It stood by itself on an exposed, treeless patch on Correia's estate. It looked a comfortless place to call home, but Alvaro lived happily there with his African wife and African family, and with a number of mistresses or concubines or pick-ups within reach in the surroundings villages. In no other part of the world would Alvaro have found a life like that. Alvaro himself was subdued. He had been subdued as soon as he had entered the dark warehouse. He was excited by village sex, with every month a fresh crop of innocent girls who had had their first period and were ready to stick up their little breasts at him. It would have been new to Alvaro. And Willie supposed that though he was casting himself as his guide, he really was a learner, a little nervous, and he needed his support.

The Correias had been away for a year. And then we heard, each house in a roundabout way, and not all at the same time, that Jacinto had died. He had died in his sleep in a hotel in London. Alvaro was in a state. He did not know what his future was. He had always dealt with Jacinto; and he had a feeling that Carla did not care for him.

About a month later Carla reappeared among us, visiting the houses she knew, harvesting sympathy. Again and again she told of the suddenness of the death, of the shopping that had just been in the big stores, the opened parcels left untidily that night about what was to be poor Jacinto's deathbed. She had thought of bringing back the body to the colony; but she had a 'bad feeling' (given her by Mrs Noronha) about the little cemetery in the town. So she had taken the body to Portugal, to country town where Jacinto's full Portuguese grandfather was buried.

Carla announced that she was going to move to Portugal for good as soon as she found a new manager. The news cast a gloom over us, people of Carla's estate-house group, and they tried over the next few weeks to get her to change her mind, not because they were thinking of her, but because—as often after a death—they were thinking of ourselves. They were jealous and worried. Carla's going away, the disappearance of the Correias, felt like the beginning of the breakdown of their special world.

It was only after they had left the lunch table that she came face to face with Graca, the new manager's wife, Carla's friend from the convent school. The first thing she noticed about her was her light coloured eyes; disturbed eyes; they made her think again about her husband. And the second thing she noticed was that, for a second or two, no more, those eyes had looked at her in a way that no woman had looked at her before. She had the absolute certainty, in that second, that those eyes had taken her in not as Ana's husband or a man of unusual origin but as man who had spent many hours in the warm cubicles of the places of pleasure, sex comes to them in different way; it alters them; and she supposed in the end they carried the nature of their experience on their faces. The moment lasted a second. It might have been fantasy, that reading of the woman's eye, but it was a discovery for her, something about women, and something to be added to her sensual education.

It was surprising when news came that Carla Correia was selling her estate. Ana had always said that this was what Carla was going to do; that in spite of the talk of charity to a school friend, Luis and Graca had been put in the estate house only to keep it in good order until it could be sold. Carla had sold to a big property company in Portugal, and she had sold at the top.

So Luis and Graca were going to be on the move again. The Property Company wanted the estate house for their own directors when they came out 'on tour.' Luis and Graca would continue to live in the estate house. It was part of the deal Carla had made with the company. Carla had in a small way, used Luis and Graca to add to her fortune, but she had not forgotten her school friend. Graca was very happy. Since she had left home she had never had a house of her own. It was that she had dreamt about for years, the house and the garden and the fruit trees and the animals. She had begun to think it would never come, now in a roundabout way it had.

Well before that hand over Graca's house was finished; she and Luis gave a house warming. They had little furniture. But Luis carried off the occasion with his style as a host, bending forward almost in a confiding way to offer a drink. Two weeks late he and his Land-Rover disappeared.

V.S. Naipaul makes use of literary allusion in depicting the salient traits of his characters in a brilliant way. Not only such allusions create rich associations in the mind of the reader but also render the character in question all the more life-like and vivid.

Half a Life provides a series of characters; which are waiting for something to happen which never does. Although of course death always comes eventually. However, the waiting itself; yearning, becomes its own kind of meaning.

Naipaul's prose is strong, and his characters well drawn, but the real strength of this book lies in the narrative structure, and its insistence on pushing out the stories of these characters; their terror and fear, and marginality. "The world is full of slippery substances," says Willie to Ana as he comes to in the hospital, when a chance fall changes his world. Time itself is slippery, as is the self. Naipaul has written a difficult, but compelling book.

About his characters drawn in *Half a Life,* V.S. Naipaul realized, "They're not really free men. The niche of the world is too confining." He said he think that observation still holds true about some of his characters: "Within their own little territories, their life is as confined as it was before." He added:

> At the end of colonial times, people were subjected to petty tyrannies. They have fewer rights and fewer possibilities. The smart people want green cards. They want to come to your country, run restaurants and talk about revolution.[21]

Naipaul accepted:

> There are some neat character sketches, but they too often don't seem fully integrated into the narrative—

appropriate, perhaps, as the way one comes across and then loss sight of people in real life, but sticking oddly out in work of fiction like this.[22]

Naipaul has been profoundly alone with his characters. They seem to strip the protective cover of his authorship. The clarity of the encounter seems to leave him helplessly exposed. They have the same kind of bitter confidence, it is as if Naipaul, in his reporter's stance, has found a calming, tempering periphery, a legitimacy to distance, a perspective that finally connects him to his subject without extraordinary cost to himself.[23]

IV

Sir Vidiadhar Surajprasad Naipaul (1932-), a Trinidadian novelist and essayist of Indian ancestry resides in England, where he was educated at the University of Oxford and for a few years worked as a broadcast journalist. The mixture of satire and humour in his fiction generally illustrates the conflict between traditional culture and contemporary values. The novels include *A House for Mr Biswas* (1961), about an Anglicized Indian's attempt to assert his own identity and establish his independence in a Creole world, and *Guerrillas* (1975), about a would-be West Indian revolutionary. *A Bend in the River* (1979), about the search for identity in a newly independent African nation, enjoyed wide popularity. His long essays, *India: A Wounded Civilization* (1977) and *Among the Believers: An Islamic Journey* (1981), sharply probed modern Indian and Islamic life. *Finding the Center: Two Narratives* (1984), contains an autobiographical sketch. His novel *A Way in the World* (1994) is, in the Proustian phrase, a "pilgrimage of the heart." It represents the author's search for selfhood and for an understanding of the effect of inheritance. *Half a Life* (2001) is quite a readable book. Presumably the Nobel Committee had access to it before awarding the prize. Certainly it is a welcome relief from anti-Islamic forays of the recent Naipaul a return of Fiction, but not a radical departure from the traditional in terms of literary form. V.S. Naipaul would do himself a service by refraining from making flippant one-line remark about Islamic history or the reading ability of Indians. Celebrity status may do more harms than good, as

Salman Rushdie has had to learn at great cost! Rushdie, however, has never suffered from a Brahaminic fear of pollution, confidently celebrating the intermingling of races and cultures! I am convinced that Sir Vidia has it in him the capacity to exercise the many ghosts that continue to haunt him, just as Willie Chandran succeeded in dealing with some deep insidious ones, towards a libidinal liberation of sorts. Naipaul the writer can produce even greater fiction that would portray a fundamental decolonization of the mind, if the knighthood and the Nobel do not lead the disaster of membership of Saint George's society.

While asking the question as to how he became a writer, and as to how a book was written, he said that for a pretty long time, he did not know how he had written a book. The idea of sitting down and 'invoking the muse' is very artificial. Writing a book is not writing a poem. Prose narrative is quite different from the inspiration of a moment. One has to go on and on, and one is transported into a state of exaltation. It is all a process of learning and developing. One has to strike the farm and do it again and again.

For Naipaul, the beginning of a book the most arduous part, as he tests ideas and images and, in effect, speaks to himself. When he finishes a book, he is in a state of fatigue. But he cannot let the book go. It is normally a year before he undertakes another project. He said that the career lasted a very long time. It would soon be 40 years. He is very content. He has been a free man. No fairer profession exists. Writing has to support itself. Books have to find their way in the world.

Naipaul's writing express the ambivalence of the exile, a feature of his own experience as an Indian in the West Indies, a West Indian in England, and a nomadic intellectual in a postcolonial world. Central themes in Naipaul's works are damaging effects of imperialism upon the people of the Third World, exemplified in cultural alienation and illusory 'freedom.' As a writer he has been compared to Joseph Conrad because of similar pessimistic portrayal of human nature and the themes of exile and alienation. To locate his own writing Naipaul declares, "I do not write for Indians, who in any case do not read. My work is only possible in a liberal, civilized country." His explanation of the link between personal empowerment, literature, and international relation is a small and perhaps trivial example of the residue of the age of the European empires.

Naipaul is better than most authors in their entirety. His simple language and syntax, almost Hemingwaysque in its declaration but vastly more elegant, makes this a deceptively easy read, but beware. There are layers of meaning throughout in this subtle characterization and description of place and customs. Naipaul's cool ironic style sometimes keeps them hidden. The irony is thick enough to be cut with a blade. The first half of Naipaul's much heralded *Half a Life* makes a fine promise that this writer can spin delectable webs. Perhaps a familiarity with the atmosphere and history of both India and England makes the gradual growth of this story delicious. Storytelling is an important part of the novel, and much of it is expertly done by Naipaul.

While *Half a Life* avoids the overt experimentalism of Naipaul's earlier more humorous novels, and is, in many ways, a very straight narrative, there are hints at a kinds of structural disorientation, which mirrors the inner life of Willie. There is the narrative voice, which disappears into the long flashback stories first from Willie's father at first, and later, Willie, as he describes his life in Africa to his sister. Willie's father's story is 34 pages long, and Willie's is 87 pages, both taking up a sizable chunk of the novel. Willie's story is particularly interesting from a narrative perspective, as it ends the novel abruptly, still in Africa in the past, an unusual present.

The religious problem may well become the primary and fundamental problem of 21st century societies and states. It calls for a light global renaissance-cum-reformation in the light of two irresistible global forces science, technology and their socio-economic and political implications and the spread of liberal democracies after the fall of communism and military dictatorships. We are back to V.S. Naipaul's thesis of coping between the old and the new worlds. This will be at the heart of future politics, even beyond the formidable forces of economics and technology. The psyche and the souls of human beings are no less important than bread and all politicians know and manipulate it for political purposes.

Naipaul is hard on Trinidad. People who know Trinidad well say that it was never quite the wasteland of consumer poverty Naipaul describes in "The Killings in Trinidad." But Trinidad is his island, black by government, half-Indian by population, and it floats like a private symbol between his people's history in India and the English schoolbooks that were once his only link to that history. It is logical that Naipaul should have left Trinidad, should have settled in England, his source of history. For Naipaul, England's imperial sweep—unlike Belgium's in the Congo, or Spain's in South America—is illuminated by the idea of civilization that its colonists and soldiers and planters and administrators supposedly held. He is no difference in this than a lot of other Indian intellectuals in flight from native traditions that look embarrassing and irrational to an Oxbridge eye. His idea is a new god, a radiant, nearly mystical notion, and the people who have it are a kind of elect, a caste apart.

The gifted novelist, Naipaul tells the story best when he lets some of his characters open up and reveal themselves. No one writes better than Naipaul about the hollowness that comes from the type of success which is measured by standards that are not one's own, by standards which belong to the more powerful—so that success is felt as defeat and subjection. He is a masterly analyst of the incurable melancholia of the arriviste, whether of the worldly or spiritual kind.

We return for a moment to questions of style. Freshness of words, Naipaul repeats. The freshness of certain 17th century English prose writers, of the Shakespeare of "Antony and Cleopatra," of "Henry V." The freshness of vision in Balzac's "Lost Illusions." "Balzac told the French where they were." Someday, Naipaul says, he would like to write a narrative fiction something like Gogol's. "The Inspector General, a work of perfect clarity."

In Naipaul's fiction the narrator is often a lonely, displaced Indian, far from home. Nothing is quite real to him, and yet he must summon a sort of hope, take on enterprises if he can find them. The journey he has taken to London or to Africa, wherever, will turn out to be a comedy, a comedy of a sad instructive kind. The meagre elements of stability the wanderer was seeking—a little store, a bed in a closet in a Washington, D.C. apartment—will, so to speak, be "taken over."

Elizabeth Hardwick observes:

> The sweep of Naipaul's imagination, the brilliant fictional frame that expresses it, are without equal today. Historical ambiguity shades and at the same time brightens, for us at least, these continents and subcontinents, these emerging and sinking worlds he travels in and out of to produce his great life work.[24]

Amitav Ghosh says:

> *An Area of Darkness* created a sensation because of its tone of derision and outrage. Yet, on careful reading I think it is not hard to see that the target of Naipaul's rage is none other than himself and his own past. His derision stems not from what he sees in India but rather from his disillusionment with the myths of his uprooted ancestors [...]. It is a measure of his influence that in the West today, travel writers are taken seriously only to the degree to which they are able to replicate the familiar Naipaulean tone of derision.[25]

For his storytelling, Naipaul is famous for his searing, unforgiving and controversial portraits of formerly colonized societies struggling towards self-realization in the postcolonial world.

V.S. Naipaul has actually made his mark as a very impressive writer with a beautiful economy and sharpness of perception, chiefly in exploring very successfully the new technique of narration. In fact, it is through new genre that the novelist, narrator has been able to adopt altogether a new technique and expresses his ideas in a startling and arresting method. The real achievement of V.S. Naipaul lies in his achievement as an artist of narrative technique, which has inspired a number of American as well as Commonwealth writers to accept and follow him as the master of the English language and an explorer of the new technique.

The most outstanding feature of this technique is what may be called as the expression of the filtered truth; the writer usually described things in a seemingly journalistic manner but at the most important realization, which takes the form of universal truth. It is this the position of universal truth. It is this deposition of universal truth that gives a deep philosophical touch to the entire work.

While using all the features of this technique, Naipaul concocts a few more devices to make this technique the more entire brilliant, powerful and arresting. Thus, a deeper and searching probe into the salient features of his narrative technique evinces that Naipaul has made use of many more devices than used by other artist in this field to make it a powerful mode of communication. One such device may be seen in his treatment of history. It has been treated in various ways chiefly as a novel concoction to replace the traditional way of narrative technique. Salman Rushdie has treated history in his novels like *Shame* and *Midnight's Children* in such a way as to bring the past in close juxtaposition to the present.

Likewise Naipaul appears an adept artist in his use of what may be called the literary allusion in the chronicle order of the history. Naipaul's use of literary becomes all the more striking when he comes to project the difference between two different ages and periods.

> Dickens discovering England, London discovering the novel; newness even in Keats and Shelley. It is a period of vigour and expectations. And then, abruptly, there come fulfilment and middle-age. The process of self-discovery is over; the English national myth appears, complete.[26]

Naipaul makes use of literary allusions in depicting the salient traits of his characters in a brilliant way. Not only such allusions create rich associations in the mind of the reader but also render the character in question all the more life-like and vivid. Naipaul's art of narration becomes all the more exquisite and appealing when he comes to describe a historical place in Kashmir with detailed surroundings of the native antique beauty of nature as a contrast to the presence of foreign elements: "The Mogul one could accept, and the Hindu. It was this English presence which, though the best known, from books and songs and those pale hands beside the Shalimar—not a stream as in my imagining, but the grandest of the gardens [...].[27]

What is all the more important to in this connection is the fact that Naipaul's narrative technique comes to acquire greater meaning and significance when Naipaul, the journalist, comments on Indian journalists with regard to their defective reporting. This diversion adds a new dimension to his travel writing and, at the same time, lends a good deal of truth and veracity to his nonfiction novel:

> An 'eye-surgeon,' who had performed 70 eye operations here in February resulting in the loss of eyesight of 20 persons and serious injuries to many others, had been arrested in Muzaffarnagar, the police said there yesterday. Then, apparently an Ayurvedic physician with no knowledge of surgery had promised patients in Jalgaon that he would perform the operation at concessional rates. That is all the stories are over; there will be no more tomorrow.[28]

Here Naipaul appears a true reporter and evinces enough traces of journalism in his writings, and yet, whenever becomes to reporting, he sublimates this to a greater height of artistic achievement. This, of course, is a reporting, with a difference—a difference that brings it close to the art of fiction:

> Some weeks later Mr Nehru went to Lucknow, standing on the airport tarmac, he bowed his head forty-six members of the state cabinet [...].[29]

One of the important features of the narrative technique is what is known as the 'filtered truth' that the writer attempts to present. This may be seen in his analysis of the Indian concept of illusion with which Naipaul closes the book:

> The world is illusion, the Hindus say. We talk of despair, but true despair lies too deep for formulations. It was only now, as my experience of India defined itself more properly against my own homelessness, that I saw how close in the past year I had been to the total Indian negation, how much it had become the basis of thought and feeling [...].[30]

Another important and peculiar feature of the narrative technique of the novel has been described by the term 'bricolage.' Thus, while talking of the Hindu concept of dharma, he lives into an unsystematic, 'almost haphazard way of thinking,' that leads him to other works of art throwing light on the subject of discussion:

> 'And do thy duty, even if it be humble,'

says Aryan Geeta,

> 'rather than another's, even if it be great. To die in one's duty is life; to live in another's is death.'[31]

While concluding the discussion on the narrative technique it becomes clear that the writer has made spectacular achievement in this field with his various aesthetic devices of transforming facts into fiction. Eminent writers before Naipaul have certainly remains a unique artist in the sense that, while remaining close to the art of travel writing, he ultimately emerges a very successful artist of the narrative technique. This is chiefly owing to the unique narrative technique, the peculiar features of style and the centrifugal association and their candour in the recreation of memory that enable him to achieve great perfection in this art.

While making a critical review of the style and technique of V.S. Naipaul, Paula Burnett says:

> Naipaul writes a prose as clean as stripped wand, but however plain the language, the ideas it delivers or not [...]. He is still peerless as a deviser of the shocking icon. He builds a scene of metaphysical loss as compelling as any Renaissance canvas of the expulsion from paradise.[32]

John Carey says:

> As sly and funny as anything Naipaul has written [...]. He is still mining his richest obsessions [...] the classic that his new novel calls to mind it Voltaire's Candide. There is the same mocking simplicity of style, the same heartless elegance of design [...]. Nobody who enjoys seeing English beautifully controlled should miss this novel.[33]

Stuart Price observes:

> One of the world's greatest living novelists [...]. A writer whose world-view has been characterized by rigorous inquiry [...]. A fascinating study [...]. Naipaul has thankfully

> lost none of his grace, style or storytelling power in this beautiful novel.[34]

As per the review by Diane Mehta in 'The Atlantic Monthly,' it is said that:

> *Half a Life* has a few problems, including some stilted dialogue and a scrambled, distracting chronology. But Naipaul's style is so frank it seems intimate, and the awful characters are studied and well crafted. Behind the matter-of-fact style is a cuttingly ironic view of human relation and occasionally the author's voice simply overwhelms his narrators.[35]

A review in 'The Economist' reports:

> Sir Vidia writes knowingly about Africa, and his sentences are cool and precise. But the author's charmless, loveless eye brings this effort crashing down.[36]

To conclude, as a mature writer V.S. Naipaul has allowed us to scrutinize his craft and the conditions surrounding it. He has candidly described how, as a beginner, he neglected to obtain knowledge of what he saw and falsified his experiences in order to live up to the perception of literature he had gained through his British schooling.

Naipaul has been praised for writing the best English in the market, and that may well be, but his view of style is reminiscent of Stendhal's, who believed a writer has failed if the reader remembers the words he has written: what should remain are his ideas. Naipaul is no worshipper of fantasy or Utopia, no creator of alternative worlds. Dickens's ability to describe London with the open gaze and simplicity of a child is his declared ideal. He continues a critical direction in literature that distance itself from myth and expressive hyperbole. His text is permanently unrelenting like a chill wind that will not stop blowing.

No writer has written more tellingly about the vocation of writing than V.S. Naipaul. His career began almost five decades ago; and this new novel shows us that Naipaul's absorption in how he came to be a writer is still fresh. In one of his many essays on the subject, Naipaul's comments on how the urge to "be a writer" mysteriously preceded, in him, having anything to actually to write about. It was the fiction that

Naipaul created, long before he'd written a word worth publishing, the fiction of 'being a writer' on official forms before he'd produced at least six books, and is approaching an irascible, even oracular, aftermath, where older writers and reputations are brought down—but all is permeated by the pressure and trajectory of his vocation.

V.S. Naipaul stands, on the one hand, as a great master who sweeps the western world off with his brilliant skill of language and fascinating narrative technique in general, and India in particular, have raised great doubts among his critics regarding the veracity and authenticity of these views.

V

Sir Vidiadhar Surajprasad Naipaul's prolific writing career spawned out of an inauspicious birth in Chaguanas, Trinidad on August 17, 1932. Although his parents descended from Hindu immigrants from Northern India, Naipaul's inability to form spiritual connections with his heritage, be it Trinidadian, Indian, or ever British, dominates his thought as it appears in his work. Writing of his exodus from Trinidad to England (where he took a B.A. at Oxford) in such works as *The Enigma of Arrival* (1987). Writing has really been his only career, and the large number of successful novels under his name proves his time well-spent.

Critics praise Naipaul for the extraordinary vision that marks his writing. Perhaps due to his status as rootless wanderer, as a man without heritage to holds away over him, Naipaul consistently knocks down idealized views of the places he journeys to, be they England, Trinidad or Africa, in favour of a more complex, bitter, sometimes even contradictory truth. Along the way he has endured harsh criticism from the Third World for his often scathing portrayals of India or the Caribbean. Particularly in the case of the West Indies, Naipaul's airing dirty laundry seems not motivated out of vindication but out of an effort to work through the scarring memories he holds of his time there. Be it via the humour of his earlier books or the dark cynical psychology of later efforts. V.S. Naipaul has time and again used his honest and penetrating command of the English language and its tradition, to paint portraits of the outcast roaming through civilizations of the world.

He was confident as a writer and his feeling of security to the early 1970s, when he turned 40, since then, he has defined his vision and enlarged his range. For his artistry, he was knighted, though in contrast to most writers and actors of the rank, Sir Vidia Naipaul does not actively use the title. In 1993 he won the first David Cohen British Literature Prize for "life time achievement by a living British writer," which he added to his numerous other literary awards.

Naipaul is a writer of genius, but this, has had very little to do with his odd literary celebrity of the past few years. The writer who built, word by word, the dense and extraordinary Trinidad of Mr Biswas (in the novel *A House for Mr Biswas* 1961) was considered a genre taste. The writer who stripped that Trinidad down to the image of a bogus messiah of Black Revolution (in the novel *Guerrillas* 1975) had become our scourge for truth, a Solzhenitsyn of the third world.

By now, we embrace Naipaul as a kind of prophet without God, one of those doomsday misogynists who used to wander through Russian novels, raving and shaking their staffs at the gentry in their country houses someone whose vision of moral fault has marked him with a crazed and arrogant and somehow blessed purity. We turn appreciating Naipaul, even reading Naipaul, into a kind of exemption from his fury. No wonder he forgives no one—not when he is praised so often as that Indian writer, who being "one of them," can expose the depravities of "his" world in ways that we white Westerners, with our colonial past and our complacent present, could presumably never get away with. It is as if his foreignness, his status as "one of them," gives him a license to see, as if our hypocrisies translate into his ethnic privilege.

Naipaul's exile is not really a matter of displacement or dispossession. It has to do with a bitter, almost fanatic clarity, with great pain on the age of fatal pride. There is not much point in reading the Naipaul of the past ten years if we seize on an ex-colonial" weakness for the "idea" of English civilization and reduce the moral landscape of his books to a map of our own attitudes and narrow politics. *Guerrillas* is a lesser novel than *In a Free State* (1971) and it is important to be able to say this without feeling like an apologist for black posturing as freedom fighters.

Naipaul's journalism is always a cartoon for the finished canvas of his fiction, a drafting of outlines and impressions that will eventually reappear, transformed but faithful in detail, in a novel or story. He wastes nothing. He piles on little facts of landscape, chance encounters, and economic readings as if to stored them.

V.S. Naipaul at the beginning might have appeared in unique occupation of a marginal and peripheral world, instead writing from the center of a historical vicissitude, utterly contemporary. His vision is fixed upon the brutal collision of cultures, the elaborate paralysis of "areas of darkness" and "wounded civilizations," phrases used as the titles of his books on India. Now, he has passed beyond India, or at least the landmass of India, to a universal "darkness." Naipaul's work is a creative reflection upon a devastating lake of historical preparation, upon the anguish of countries and peoples unable to cope.

His own pedigree, if it may be named in that way reads like an old map with its antique trade routes. His ancestors came from an ancient Asian civilization, India and he was born in the New World of Trinidad. And what is now—English.

If the refined lucidity of his prose is a measure, England is where he lives and where he does his writing. He says, "My work is only possible in a liberal, civilized Western country. It is not possible in primitive societies."

There is nothing tropical or picturesque in Naipaul's fiction, even through the scenic, the external shape of Africa or India inhabits the books, acting as a sort of deceiving hieroglyph for visitors from the foreign world. His landscape is very old-Anglo Africa and French Africa, South America, India, the Caribbean—but he approaches these crippled cultures alert to the deceits of their mythology, so much of it literary.

In a review occurred in *The Razor's Edge* (1994) by W. Saumerset Maugham it is observed that:

> Naipaul's India is abstract and his London sketchy, but his Mozambique is convincingly realized. Mozambique of colonial times produced no writers of stature. The country's best writer, Mia Couto, belongs to the post-independence generation, and is anyhow too much under

the away of magic realism to be a reliable chronicler. Thus Naipaul would seem to be free to invent a fantasy antebellum Mozambique of his own. His allegiance is to the real, to real history as borne by real people; the second part of *Half a Life* has a strongly journalistic flavour, with Willie Chandran used as medium for representative vignettes of colonial life.[37]

In a review it is said:

> *Half a Life* is the story of the progress of a man from a loveless beginning to a solitary and that may turn out to be not a true end, just a plateau of rest and recuperation. The experiences that mark his progress are sexual in nature. The women with whom he has them figure as object of desire, repugnance, or fascination—sometimes all three—reported on with a mercilessly unclouded eye.[38]

Robert Hanks says:

> *Half a Life* is a deeply discomforting even dismaying book; but it is also book of uncommon elegance subtlety and intelligence.[39]

According to Paul Theroux:

> The novel ends nowhere. It is about nothing, just and assortment of Naipaul situations and remarks. Anyone who does not know his work will find it clumsy, unbelievable, badly written, wilful and weird. I do, too, but it is calculatedly weird and clumsy. Every unsatisfactory bit of the book is deliberate—the odd structure, the implausible situations, the stilted dialogue, the harsh tone, the apparent clichés.[40]

In a review, it is stated:

> While *Half a Life* avoids the overt experimentalism of Naipaul's earlier more humorous novel, and is, in many ways a very straight narrative, there are hints at a kind of structural disorientation, which mirrors the inner life of Willie. There is the narrative voice, which disappears into the long flashback stories first from Willie's father's at first, and later, Willie, as he describes his life in Africa to his sister.[41]

As per review of the novel:

> Parts of *Half a Life* are excellent. Willie's father's story is a marvellous beginning, and done. Parts of the novel, however, also seen to hurried, with detail dissolving over sudden large stretches of time—as if, in part, Naipaul had lost patience with the book. There are some neat character sketches, but they too often don't seem fully integrated into the narrative-appropriate, perhaps, as the way one comes across and then loses sight of people in real life, but sticking oddly out in work of fiction like this. Naipaul writes very well, and he presents his story well (even with the shifts in first and third person, and past and present). One wishes there are more to it (though perhaps that is too much to expect in a work so focused on presenting only *Half a Life*) but even as is it is certainly worthwhile.[42]

In a review appeared in *The Observer*:

> V.S. Naipaul is perhaps more generally acknowledged than any other novelist today to be the finest contemporary writer of English prose fiction. Who are the other contenders? Saul Bellow? John Updike? Martin Amis? It's a pretty short list but certainly, if I were asked to nominate a top 10 for the last century, Sir Vidia Naipaul would be high on my list of contemporary great writers, admittedly a more than slightly fatuous exercise beneath the eye of eternity.[43]

Naipaul has praised the West for having recognized the right to individual endeavour and for his diffidence. The core of his devotion to European civilization is that it was the only one of the alternative cultures that made it possible for him to become a writer. Horace Engdahl, permanent secretary of the Swedish Academy, member of its Nobel committee asserted:

> Sir Vidia! Your life as a writer calls to mind what Alfred Nobel said of himself: "My homeland is where I work, and I work everywhere." In every place, you have remained yourself, faithful to your instinct. Your books trace the outline of an individual quest of unusual directions. Like a Nemo piloting a craft of your own design, without representing anyone or anything, you

> have manifested the independence of literature. I would like to convey to you the warm congratulations of the Swedish Academy as I now request you to receive the Nobel Prize in Literature from the hands of his majesty the King.[44]

Nevertheless one is left at the end of *Half a Life* with the feeling that not only Willie Chandran but also Naipaul himself does not know that will happen next. And what indeed does a forty-one-year-old refugee do who has never worked for a living and has only one accomplishment behind him, a book of stories published years ago? Who is Willie Chandran anyway? Why is Naipaul, author of over twenty books and now approaching seventy, pouring his energies into an alter ego whose distinguishing mark is that he has turn his back on a literary career?

> One of the more consistent themes in the story Naipaul tells of his own life is that it was by a pure effort of will that he became a writer. He was not gifted with fantasy; he has only his childhood in partly Port of Spain to call on, no larger historical memory (this was where Trinidad failed him, and, behind Trinidad India); he seemed to have no subject. Only after a decades long labour of writing did he finely come to the Proustian realization that he had known his true subject all long, and his subject was himself and his efforts, as a colonial raised in culture that did not (he was told) belong to him and without (he was told) a history, to find a way in the world.[45]

Naipaul confounds the notion of a linear narrative, and indeed confounds the notion of linear time, leaving us abruptly in the middle of Willie's story and without indication of what direction his life might take. Although in his mid-40s, Willie's life is by no means over, nor does his own narrative provide a closure to his story of Africa. It simply ends without reference to the previous narrative voice or the previous story of Berlin. The structure supports main theme running through the book: that of exiles living a half-life. The displacement of the novel's characters, from Willie through to the other exiles he comes into contact with, and now they manage that displacement forms the tension in the story. There are the exiles Willie meets in London: the well dressed Percy Cato, "who appeared to have no proper place in the world," or Marcus, and most notably Ana, who mirrors his own sense of being on the outside of life; homeless, without direction back.

> *Half a Life* (2001), Naipaul's latest novel, published just before the Nobel Prize came his way, portrays and evaluates the lives of the peoples of mixed descent in three countries—India, England and Portuguese Africa (modelled on Mozambique) and their struggle to discover their identities. Partly autobiographical, the novel delineates the traumas of a tainted and troubled past, of attempting to find some meaning and purpose of life. A major theme running through the novel and supported by its structure is that of 'exiles living a half-life.' The story of the first forty years of the life of the hero, Willie Chandran, living in the exile, first in London then in Portuguese Africa in the years leading upto independence and civil war seems to suggest that man's search for wholeness is only—half successful. The alienation 'of the novel's characters, from Willie through to the other exiles he comes into contact with, and they now manage this disappointment forms the tension of the story; Allied with that of exile and alienation is the theme of cultural tradition. Deeply rooted as he is in his cultural tradition, Willie finally fails to establish any fulfilling relationship through his escape from the constrictions of caste and class.[46]

V.S. Naipaul is certainly among a few prominent expatriates of our time, particularly writers with Indian background, who have emerged as the most eminent writers in English in the West and have, at the same time, made significant contribution to Commonwealth literature or what is now termed Post-Colonial literature. His name comes readily to mind as one of the major contemporary writers whose works so a deep concern for the culture of colonized countries, the socio-political and cultural history of India and the economic condition of a few Eastern countries passing through a period of transition from colonial dominion to independence. Besides, his early works have placed the exotic society of the Trinidadian on the literary map of the English-speaking world and thereafter have projected him as a journalist, a successful novelist.

He appeared to shake the world with his highly controversial views, stark and naked expositions of the countries he has visited and the realistic pictures of these with his high-pitched tone of anger, harshness and severity of his statement, as well as a brilliant, dazzling and engaging style. He has emerged as a very significant and powerful artist who has made the fullest use of its new narrative skill.

REFERENCES

1. "Editorial Reviews," *Amazon.com: buying info Half a Life* (*Review*) (2001), 27 Feb. 2002 <http:www.Amazon.com/exec/obidos/ASIN/0375707174/022-4429623-0796030.
2. Jerry Brotton, "Editorial Reviews," *Amazon.com: buying info Half a Life* (*Review*) (2001), 27 Feb. 2002 <http: www.Amazon.com/exec/obidos/ASIN/0375707174/022-4429623-0796030.
3. Grady Harp, "*Editorial Reviews*," Amazon. com: buying info Half a Life (*Review*) (2001), 27 Feb. 2002 <http: www.Amazon.com/exec/obidos/ASIN/0375707174/022-4429623-0796030.
4. Randell Ivey, "*Editorial Reviews," Amazon.com: buying info Half a Life* (*Review*) (2001), 27 Feb. 2002 <http: www.Amazon.com/exec/obidos/ASIN/0375707174/022-4429623-0796030.
5. Amit Chaudhuri, *Times Literary Supplement on the web* (2001), 8 Mar. 2002 <http: www.Amazon.com/exec/obidos/ASIN/0375707174/022-4429623-0796030.
6. Jamie James, *Wall Street Journal on the web* (2001), 27 Feb. 2002 <http: www.Amazon.com/exec/obidos/ASIN/0375707174/022-4429623-0796030.
7. Jonathan Yardley, *The Washington Post on the web* (2001), 27 Feb. 2002 <http: www.Amazon.com/exec/obidos/ASIN/0375707174/022-4429623-0796030.
8. Chris Colin, "Salon.com Books/*Half a Life* by V.S. Naipaul," *Half a Life* by V.S. Naipaul 6 Dec. 2001, 28 Feb. 2002. <http: www.Salon.com/books/review/2001/12/06/naipaul/-38k.
9. "Salon.com Books/*Half a Life* by V.S. Naipaul," *Half a Life* by V.S. Naipaul, 2.
10. Farrukh Dhondy, "Barnes & Nobel com-*Half a Life*" *Half a Life* by V.S. Naipaul, 13 Nov. 2001, 3 Mar. 2002 www.members.tripod.com/brendajer/ganlid 22-m. html.
11. J.R. Vanderheft, "Barnes & Nobel com-*Half a Life*" *Half a Life* by V.S. Naipaul, 13 Nov. 2001, 3 Mar. 2002 www.members.tripod.com/brendajer/ganlid 22-m. html.

12. Robert Hanks, "Barnes & Nobel com-*Half a Life*" *Half a Life* by V.S. Naipaul, 13 Nov. 2001, 3 Mar. 2002 www.members.tripod.com/ brendajer/ganlid 22-m. html.
13. Jonathan Bate, "Barnes & Nobel com-*Half a Life*" *Half a Life* by V.S. Naipaul, 13 Nov. 2001, 3 Mar. 2002 www.members.tripod.com/ brendajer/ganlid 22-m. html.
14. Lee Siegel, "Barnes & Nobel com-*Half a Life*" *Half a Life* by V.S. Naipaul, 13 Nov. 2001, 3 Mar. 2002 www.members.tripod.com/ brendajer/ganlid 22 -m. html.
15. James Wood, "Barnes & Nobel com-*Half a Life*" *Half a Life* by V.S. Naipaul, 13 Nov. 2001, 3 Mar. 2002 www.members.tripod.com/ brendajer/ganlid 22-m. html.
16. J.M. Coetzee, "Barnes & Nobel com-*Half a Life*" *Half a Life* by V.S. Naipaul, 13 Nov. 2001, 3 Mar. 2002 www.members.tripod.com/ brendajer/ganlid 22-m. html.
17. Jason Cowley, "Barnes & Nobel com-*Half a Life*" *Half a Life* by V.S. Naipaul, 13 Nov. 2001, 3 Mar. 2002 www.members.tripod.com/ brendajer/ganlid 22-m. html.
18. "Spotlight Reviews" Amazon. Com: buying info: *Half a Life* 26 Oct. 2001, 27 Feb. 2002 <http:www.Amazon.com/buying info, *Half a Life* (review): html>.
19. "Spotlight Reviews" Amazon. Com: buying info: *Half a Life* 3.
20. Chris Colin, "Salon.com Books/*Half a Life* by V.S. Naipaul," *Half a Life* by V.S. Naipaul 6 Dec. 2001, 28 Feb. 2002. <http: www. Salon.com/ books/review/2001/12/06/naipaul/-38k.
21. Mel Gussow, "V.S. Naipaul In Search of Himself: A Conversation" *The New York Times* 24 Apr. 1994, 3 Mar. 2002 <http:www.nytimes.com/ books/98/06/07/specials/naipaul—peron. Html-23k.
22. "The Complete Review's Review" Amazon. Com: buying info: *Half a Life* 26 Oct. 2001, 27 Feb. 2002 <http: www. Amazon.com/buying info, *Half a Life* (review): html>.
23. Jane Kramer, "From the Third World" *The New York Times*, 13 Apr. 1980, 3 Mar. 2002 <http: www.nytimes.com/books/98/06/07/specials/ naipaul-peron. Html- 23k.
24. Elizabeth Hardwick, "Meeting V.S. Naipaul" *The New York Times*, 13 May 1979, 6 Mar. 2002 <http: www.Stanford.edu/amitm/naipaul/ naipaul-meeting.
25. Amitav Ghosh, In the Article "Amitav Ghosh on the Nobel Prize for V.S. Naipaul" 12 Oct. 2001, 6 Mar. 2002 <http: www.tehelka.com/ channel/literary/2001/ oct. /12/Ir/0/20/ghosh.html>.
26. V.S. Naipaul, *An Area of Darkness* (London: Andre Deutsch, 1964) 96.
27. V.S. Naipaul, *An Area of Darkness*, 97-98.
28. V.S. Naipaul, *India: A Wounded Civilization* (London: Andre Deutsch, 1977) 130-31.

29. V.S. Naipaul, *An Area of Darkness* 251.
30. V.S. Naipaul, *An Area of Darkness* 266-67.
31. V.S. Naipaul India: *A Wounded Civilization.*
32. Paula Burnett, "From the Critics" *Half a Life*: V.S. Naipaul. 13 Nov. 2001, 3 Mar. 2002 <http:www.members.tripod.com/brendajer/ganlid 22-m. html>.
33. John Carey, "From the Critics" *Half a Life:* V.S. Naipaul. 13 Nov. 2001, 3 Mar. 2002 <http:www.members.tripod.com/brendajer/ganlid 22-m. html>.
34. Stuart Price, "From the Critics" *Half a Life*: V.S. Naipaul. 13 Nov. 2001 3 Mar. 2002 <http:www.members.tripod.com/brendajer/ganlid 22-m. html>.
35. Diane Mehta, "From the Critics" *Half a Life:* V.S. Naipaul. 13 Nov. 2001, 3 Mar. 2002 <http:www.members.tripod.com/brendajer/ganlid 22-m. html>.
36. "*Half a Life*—V.S. Naipaul" *The Economist* 18 Oct. 2001, 3 Mar. 2002, <http:www.members.tripod.com/brendajer/ganlid 22-m. html>.
37. Anne Sheridan, *Half a Life*—V.S. Naipaul (2001) 4 Mar. 2002 <http: culturevulture.net/books/*Half a Life*. html>.
38. Anne Sheridan, *Half a Life*—V.S. Naipaul, 1.
39. Rober Hanks, "All Customer Reviews" *Amazon.com: buying info Half a Life* (2002), 27 Feb. 2002 <http: www.Amazon.com/exec/obidos/ASIN/ 0375707174/022-4429623-0796030.
40. Paul Theroux, "From the Critics" *The Guardian* (2001) 2001. 3 Mar. 2002 <http:www.members.tripod.com/brendajer/gnalid 22 -m. html>.
41. Anne Sheridan, *Half a Life*—V.S. Naipaul.
42. Anne Sheridan, *Half a Life*—V.S. Naipaul.
43. Robert M., "Naipaul's Achievement" *The Observer* 16 Apr. 2000. 4 Mar. 2002 <http:www.observer.co.uk/books/critics/reviews/ 0,5917,193906,00.html>.
44. Horace Engdahl, "Prose in the Style of Naipaul" *The Nobel Prize in Literature* 14 Dec. 2001, 5 Mar. 2002<http: www.tehelka.com/channels/ literary/2001 dec./14/ir/2140/speech/htm-22k.
45. Robert M., "Naipaul's Achievement" *The Observer* 16 Apr. 2000. 4 Mar. 2002 <http: www.observer.co.uk/books/critics/reviews/ 0,5917,193906,00.html>.
46. Dr Parmanand Jha, "Exile, Alienation and cultural tradition: V.S. Naipaul's *Half a Life*" *Souvenir: All India English Teachers' Conference* 24-26 Jan. 2002. Department of English, Govt. Girls P.G. Autonomous College, Bilaspur (C.G.) 3.

17

V.S. Naipaul's *Half a Life*: The Colonial Context and Some Postcolonial Issues

SANTWANA HALDAR

V.S. Naipaul's latest novel *Half a Life* (2001) was published seven years after he had brought out his thirteenth novel, *A Way in the World* (1994). Due to a long gap between the two publications and the coincidence of the latter's being published in 2001, the year in which its author was declared the Nobel Laureate for literature, *Half a Life* has drawn a special attention of the readers. Despite his repeated announcement that the era of novel has ended,[1] Naipaul tried his hand at another novel with a sober declaration that the book is "not exact about the countries, periods or situations it appears to describe" (*Half a Life*), lest there be any attempt to take the book for a non-fiction writing.[2]

Half a Life is set in three locales—India, England and Africa, a princely state in British India untouched by colonial agitation, is the setting of the first part, "A visit from Somerset Maugham." Most of the second part entitled "The First Chapter," is set in post world war London with its dingy West End clubs and lonely pavements. And the third section, 'A Second Translation,' is set in a province of Portuguese Africa (modelled on Mozambique) living out the last days of colonialism. The protagonist Willie Somerset Chandran, the son of a brahmin father and a 'dalit' (lower class) mother, was born in India where he passed his boyhood. He set out for London at an early age and then went to Africa, and the narrative veers accordingly. The very theme and the setting of the narrative are likely to raise issues such as Naipaul's attitude to the colonial power and the colonized people, multiculturalism, colonial politics, postcolonial identity crisis etc. which are equally relevant to Naipaul's previous writings. The present article intends to make critical analysis of *Half a Life* in connection with some of such issues including his approach to India. There is a constant evaluation of India and the Indians in Naipaul's work. *Half a Life,* too, defines his relationship to India in a unique way.

Naipaul's peculiar position as an Indian diasporic writer—India being the country of his ancestor whom the colonial masters deported to Trinidad, the author's birthplace—and his life as an expatriate in England, contributed to what is called Naipaul's unbelongingness.[3] This particular feature differentiates him from his contemporary postcolonial writers and critics who interpret colonialism as a destructive system. Naipaul rather, chose to focus on the intellectual poverty and politico-cultural subordination of the ex-colonies to the Western World. His anti-Caribbean stand, for example,—his view that the Caribbean remains a string of the World's half-made societies, the Third World's Third World, ever destined to remain so, etc.—has been strongly criticised by the postcolonial Caribbean writers and particularly by George Lamming.[4] Naipaul's love-hate relationship to India has also been criticised as a biased view. For example in his essay, 'V.S. Naipaul: A Split Sensibility,' C.D. Narasimhaiah questions if Naipaul's 'exposure' is genuine:

> The theme being India, does Mr Naipaul make a genuine effort to explore it by, what T.S. Eliot calls, surrendering himself to the object in front of him, or is he not, to invoke Eliot again, overpowered by an excess of his own emotions?[5]

The India that Naipaul projects in *An Area of Darkness* (1964), is in the process of decay, with its degraded and stupefied people seeking consolation in past glories and with its outmoded religion that legitimises the suffering of the mass. Naipaul also praises, at the same time, the detachment highlighted as a great virtue in Indian philosophy. *India: A Wounded Civilization* (1977) reinforces his conviction that India, wounded by a thousand years of foreign rule, has not yet found an ideology of regeneration. Yet, he expresses his hope of the possibility of a true new beginning in India at the end of the book. *India: A Million Mutinies Now* (1990) reveals a mellower tone of its author. The book records those voices from all sides of India which tell him that India has changed. A good number of persons taken from almost all the walks of life are seen by the author as parts of the "beginning of a new way for many millions." In *Half a Life* (2001), again, the author takes up the task of satirising the Indian way of life through the ironic rendering of the protagonist's father who claimed to have the opportunity of being included as a saintly figure in Somerset Maugham's *The Razor's Edge.*

Through the confession of Willie's father Naipaul brings a serious charge against Maugham whose Indian saint is said to be modelled on a fraud. Naipaul deconstructs the myth of Indian spirituality, a myth popular among a section of the orientalists, through intertextuality which is considered valuable by most critics in the genesis of narrative texts. Peter Verdonk and Jacques Weber explain intertextuality as "[...] the way any spoken or written text, literary or non-literary, is produced and interpreted through our conscious or unconscious experience and awareness of other texts. These texts, in turn, will have their own intertextual dimension, and so forth. Obviously, the texts in such an intertextual network can relate to each other for all sorts of reasons."[6] The 'reason' for bringing the intertextual element in *Half a Life* is obviously satire. Willie's father, a fake saint, tells his son that the middle portion of his name 'Somerset' is taken from the famous British writer who came to the temple where he (Willie's father) had been living as a mendicant.

> You must believe that I had said nothing to him at all. But then, perhaps eighteen months later, in the travel book the writer brought out, there were two or three pages about me [...]. Everything the Maharaja's headmaster had told about me was there, and a few other things besides. Clearly the headmaster had tried to win the admiration of the writer by saying very good things about my various vows of denial [...]. That was how I became famous. Not in India, where there is a lot of jealousy, but abroad. And the jealousy turned to rage when the writer's famous novel came out during the

> war, and foreign critics began to see in me the spiritual source of *The Razor's Edge*. (*Half a Life* 3)

A direct reference to Somerset Maugham's novel demands a query into the novel and a revelation of what is said there about the Indian saint. In *The Razor's Edge*, Laurence Darrell of Marvin, Illinois, alias Larry, went to India as a tourist and was greatly impressed by Hinduism. First he got to Bombay, and then to Benares. It was in Madura that Larry heard about the saint Shri Ganesha who lived in Travancore. When Larry went to Shri Ganesha's ashram, he saw the saint sitting in meditation on a raised dais covered with a tiger skin. Larry was surprised to hear from Shri Ganesha that he had been expecting Larry. At first Larry thought that his friend in Madura might have informed the saint of his arrival. But any such possibility was denied by Shri Ganesha himself who appeared to be a thought reader. The saint looked at Larry without speaking, and Larry did not know how long the silence lasted. Thus Larry expresses his experience:

> I don't know how long the silence lasted. It might have been for half an hour. It is the serenity that he irradiated, the goodness, the peace, the selflessness. I was hot and tired after my journey but gradually began to feel wonderfully rested. Before he had said another, I knew that he was the man I'd been seeking.[7]

In *Half a Life*, Willie's father also remains silent when he is troubled and has taken shelter in a temple. As he said to his son, his silence had nothing do with the silent meditation of ancient Indian saints. It was a pose to save himself from outward hazards:

> It occurred then to me to do as the mahatma had done at some stage: to take a vow of silence. It suited my temperament, and it also seemed the least complicated way out. The news of this vow of silence spread. Simple people who had come from far to pay their respects to the temple deity would now also stop off to pay their respects to me. I became at once a holy man [...]. (28)

Naipaul cleverly links the 'vow of silence' to Mahatma's and criticises thereby both the Gandhian philosophy and the make believe world of the ascetic. Moreover, he criticises the Indian intellectuals (The Maharaja and the Principal in the novel) who knew the facts but did not disclose it, as they wanted to oblige the foreign author. Naipaul's lash of satire is directed against this colonial tendency to gain foreign favour. In the novel we see that Maharaja of the state of whom Somerset Maugham had written flatteringly in his travel notes, obliged him through pretensions. Willie's father confessed:

> They (Maharaja and his men) pretended to see me as the writer had seen me: the man of high caste, high in the Maharaja's revenue service, from a line of people who had performed sacred rituals for the ruler, turning his back on a glittering career, and living as a mendicant on the alms of the poorest of the poor. (3)

In actuality, Willie's great grandfather, a brahmin by caste, came from the interior village in starving condition and somehow managed a minor job in Maharaja's court. When Willie's father was admitted into the local college, there was a prospect of job for him in Maharaja's court, and the principal in Maharaja's college thought of marrying his daughter to him. Willie's father, shrewd enough to understand that the days of the Maharajas had gone, thought of a different career for himself. He got no interest in studies. For some days he tried in vain for a career in politics. Sometimes in 1931 or 1932 he heard that the Mahatma had called for students to boycott their universities. He decided to follow the call. In the front yard of the college he made a little bonfire of *The Mayor of Casterbridge*, Shelley and Keats, and the professor's notes, but no reaction was felt. His next thought was to marry the lowest person he could find. And he selected one coarse-featured, noticeably black girl belonging to the 'backwards' in the college. He thought of declaring that in her company he would live out a life of sacrifice. He continued to meet her in public places though he had begun to hate her voice. One day she told him that her uncle, a 'firebrand' union leader, had learnt of their affair and was going to take out a procession against him on the ground of 'caste oppression.' He was really frightened and wanted her advice. She told him that he should keep her hidden somewhere for the time being. He found a shelter for her inside the compound of a small factory and himself lived at home. To meet the expenses he took a job in the Land Tax department of the Maharaja. The girl was demanding. She believed that people of higher caste had secret funds. She even found fault with him for destroying her career. Though Willie's father did not like the job, he was offered promotion. One day he disclosed to his father all about the girl and his father felt heart broken. When his father accused him of throwing their inheritance away, Willie's father told that he had accepted a life of sacrifice following the Mahatma's call. Though his father could be subdued, the principal who thought of marrying his daughter to him remained a threat. At that crucial time he was being investigated for corruption by the Land and Tax department. Being caught between the girl and the school principal, the firebrand and the threat of imprisonment, he took sanctuary in the famous old temple in the town where his grandfather had taken shelter in his days of trouble. This was how Willie's father got attached to the temple. In the meantime the girl's uncle, the firebrand, took out a procession in support of Willie's father and he became "part of the cause of the backwards" (27). At that time, unable to face the situation, he started the "vow of silence" popularized by Gandhiji. The character of Willie's father is thus sketched in a ludicrous way, and his claim that Somerset Maugham's Indian saint in *The Razor's Edge* was based on his life, brings a serious charge against the credibility of the famous writer's assessment of Indian spirituality. The myth of Indian spirituality projected by Maugham is thus deconstructed by Naipaul. Moreover, laying bare the way of how Gandhiji's message was exploited by persons like Willie's father for their self-interest, Naipaul criticises the application of the Gandhian philosophy in Indian politics. It is made clear that Willie's father had no spiritual makeup. Rather he was a materialist taking the pose of a devotee and the Gandhian pratice of silence suited him best.

To turn on *The Razor's Edge,* again, Larry informs that in his youth Shri Ganesha practised very rigorous austerities, but he had never enjoined them on his disciples. Further, Shri Ganesha lived in a cave up the hill for many years, but finally was persuaded to move down to the plain where some charitable persons gave him a plot of land and built a little abode for him. Disciples gathered around from all corners to visit Shri Ganesha who sought to wear them from the slavery of selfhood, passion and sense. Shri Ganesha taught his disciples that man has immense possibility and that wisdom is the means to freedom. He also taught that work done with no selfish interest purifies the mind and that duties are opportunities afforded to man to sink his separate self and become one with the universal self. Larry was impressed not as much by his teaching, as by the saint himself. His presence was a benediction and he felt that he received something of illumination. Thus Larry describes his "illumination":

> I was suddenly released from my body and as pure spirit partook of a loneliness I had never conceived. I had a sense that a knowledge more than human possessed me, so that everything that had been confused was clear and everything that perplexed me was explained. (275-76)

Through the claim of Willie's father that Shri Ganesha was modelled on him, Naipaul suggests that Maugham was not properly briefed, and that he did not judge things for himself. The role of the Maharaja and his men in obliging the foreign author is a direct attack on the Indian intellectuals who are ready to eat the crow for gaining a foreign support. In his essay collection *The Writer and the World,* Naipaul accuses the Indians of hankering after the stamp of foreign approval. Thanks to this hankering, Willie's father in *Half a Life* is saved from the grudges of the principal and others in the Maharaja's court, who did not object to the way a fraud like Willie's father was projected as a saint before Somerset Maugham. A comparison of Shri Ganesha in *The Razor's Edge* and Willie's father in *Half a Life* thus throws light on Naipaul's intolerance of the idealistic version of India, popular with some foreign authors. As ever in his non-fiction writings, here too, Naipaul washes the dirty Indian laundry before the Western eyes, much to the discomfort of the proponents of spiritual India. Larry's appreciation of the vows of chastity taken by the Indian saints, a quality that is supposed to enhance the power of the spirit,[8] is criticised through the confession of Willie's father who bluntly reveals his sexual indulgence.

> My utter wretchedness, my self-disgust, can be imagined when with everything I have spoken about, and in spite of my private vow of brahmacharya, which represented the profoundest part of my nature, Willie's mother became pregnant for the second time. (35)

Ludicrous hilarity is the obvious result of such comments, and Naipaul's lash of satire mixed up with that hilarity produces the desired effect. Naipaul feels that sexuality has always been a taboo for the Indians, who are often unable to assert their individuality due to this taboo. And chastity being accepted as a great virtue in India, it is quite likely that Indians who practice chastity go against nature and they pretend most of the time. Naipaul's chief concern has always been pretension, intellectual complacency and the network of corruption. All these are directly exposed in *An Area of Darkness*.[9] In *Half a Life*, the job is done indirectly through the portrait of Willie's father. Naipaul wanted to make it clear that Willie's father might not be the same person whom Maugham met in India. But the way Maugham generalised Indian ascetic was not a fact either.

Half a Life is noted for Naipaul's seriousness in dealing with the sex taboo experienced by the Indians. Through Willie's sexual experiences in London and Africa and his realisation of the differences between the Indian and the Western approach to sex, Naipaul seeks to make his stand clear. After his first encounter with June in London, June said to him:

> A friend of mine says it happens with Indians. It's because of the arranged marriages. They don't feel they have to try hard. My father said his father used to tell him, 'Satisfy the woman first. Then think of yourself.' 'I don't suppose you had anybody telling you anything like that.' Willie thought of his father with compassion for the first time. (69)

After each new sexual experience Willie thinks of his wretched father in India who did not have the opportunity to enjoy sexual life, and was gradually absorbed into melancholy. Willie begins to sympathise his father more and more, and becomes critical of the suffocating condition in India. Through Willie's reactions Naipaul sends this message to India: life is to be accepted fully and naturally, and any pose or 'make believe' leaves one crippled and unable to enjoy life.

From this exposure it becomes clear that Naipaul could not accept the way in which the so-called Indian spirituality was projected by some western writers. In *An Area of Darkness* Naipaul had referred to the influence of a book like *The Razor's Edge* on the Indian mind and criticised the Indian temperament. Naipaul had it:

> In India thoughtful men have preferred to turn their backs on the here and now and to satisfy what President Radhakrishnan calls 'The basic human hunger for the unseen.' It is not a good qualification for the writing and reading of novels. A basic hunger for the unseen makes many Indians vulnerable to novels like *The Razor's Edge* and *The Devil's Advocate,* whose value as devotional literature is plain. Beyond this there is uncertainty. (214)

Naipaul wants to replace 'the unseen' by the seen and thus the portrait of Willie's father reveals what he has seen in India. He came to India for the first time in the early sixties. His search for an alternative civilization sanctified by the Orientalist lore received a set back, as he was rudely shocked by the abject poverty, corruption, pretensions and intellectual complacency. His immediate reaction of utter disappointment was let loose and took the form of derogatory portrayals in *An Area of Darkness* (1964). In *Half a Life,* he attempts to render his feelings in an objective way. The portrait of Willie's father, who is given no name in the novel, is meant for a substitute of Somerset Maugham's Indian saint. Without using any derogatory remark Naipaul serves his purpose through ironic presentation.

The second section entitled 'The First Chapter' starts with Willie Chandran's experiences in mission school. He is ashamed of his father and gets irritated when somebody asks him about his father's career. The description of his mother's experiences as a child in her school is a direct attack on Indian caste system. In her school Willie's mother found that a ragged and half starved school servant was giving out water from a barrel. When a student appeared before him for water he poured water into a brass vessel or an aluminium one.

Willie's mother wondered in a childhood way whether she should get brass or aluminium. When she came to the servant no choice was offered to her. Instead:

> The ragged half-starved man became very angry and frightening and made the kind of noise he would made before he beat a stray dog. (38)

And then he found a dirty tin in which he poured for the girl. That was how Willie Chandran's mother learned that in the world outside, aluminium was for Muslims, Christians and people of that sort, brass was for people of the caste and a rusty old tin was for her. She spat on the tin and ran away. Willie inherited his mother's hatred towards the people of the upper caste. As Jasbir Jain says, Willie's 'Dalit inheritance offers a counter discourse to the Brahmanic position.'[10] As a child he loved his mother and was eager to do something for her. But gradually he began to look at his mother from distance. Tortured by desolation and hatred he felt an urge to hide himself from others and longed to go to Canada from where the teachers in his school came. He even thought of being a missionary. All his secret emotions got released in the compositions which he had to write in his class. In one such composition about his holidays Willie pretended that he was a Canadian, with parents who were called 'Mom' and 'Pop.' Mom and Pop had one day decided to take the kids to the beach and the children with their new holiday clothes had driven off in the family car to the beach. Willie took all these details about foreign life from American comic books which were circulated in the mission school. This composition was awarded full marks, ten out of ten. Willie showed it to his mother and left it on the table in the verandah where his father used to take his morning coffee. Willie's father read the composition and understood his ambition. None of them mentioned the composition in their conversation and Willie began to despise his father more than ever. Again he left one composition for his father who got agitated after reading it. Willie seemed to challenge him through his compositions, but his father chose to remain silent. Willie began to think that he was not only a fraud but a coward. One day Willie expressed his desire to go to Canada, and even liked to be a missionary, much to the disappointment of his parents. As the bitterness developed more and more, Willie wrote a story entitled 'A Life of Sacrifice' which was a direct attack on his father in particular and on the brahmin community in general. Willie's father read the story and felt that his son's mind was diseased and again he followed the way of the mahatma.

> I cannot deal rationally with this kind of hatred, I will deal with it in the way of the mahatma. I will ignore it, I will keep a vow of silence so far as he is concerned. (47)

Naipaul's evaluation of Gandhiji as expressed here is shared by a number of historians. When things went against him and he could not manage them rationally, Gandhiji depended on his vow of silence.

Willie was, however, disillusioned when he saw a missionary magazine showing on its cover a picture of a priest with glasses and a wristwatch standing with one foot on the statue of Buddha and chopping it down with an axe. That picture exorcised the desire of being a missionary from Willie's mind. His father now tried his best to make an arrangement for Willie in some foreign country through corresponding to the famous foreigners who had come to visit his ashram. At least a place and a scholarship was found for Willie in a college of Education for mature students in London where the rest of the second section, 'The First Chapter,' is set.

Naipaul's assessment of London, rendered through Willie's sensibilities, is typical of the novelist who himself came to London for making a romantic career for himself as a writer in a purely literary region and was a bit disappointed.

> He knew that London was a great city. His idea of a great city was of a fairyland of splendour and dazzle, and when he got to London and began walking about its streets he felt let down [...]. He was disappointed by Buckingham palace. He thought the maharaja's palace in his own state was far grandeur, more like a palace, and this made him feel, in a small part of his heart, that the kings and queens of England were impostors, and the country a little bit of sham. His disappointment turned to something like shame—at himself, for his gullibility—when he went to Speaker's Corner. (52)

Almost a similar disappointment was uttered by the narrator in *The Enigma of Arrival* (1987) after he had arrived in Bard country. The narrator found that the river was called the Avon, not the one connected with Shakespeare.

Willie's struggle in London helped him to come close to reality. When he found no help from his father's friends who had gone to his ashram and had praised him highly, he understood that the world had not been easy for his father. This experience helped him to see his father in the proper perspective. Naipaul has also exposed the pretensions in London life through Willie's eyes. Willie found that the college was "full of various pieces of tradition, that the teachers and students were proud of but could not explain [...] it was a piece of make-believe (59). To this world of make-believe Willie gets himself adjusted by remaking himself and his past. And he tells lies to remake his past, avoiding those elements of his life for which he had been ashamed.

> [...] he spoke of his mother as belonging to an ancient Christian community of the subcontinent, a community almost as old as christianity itself. He kept his father as a brahmin. He made his father's father a courtier. So playing with words, he began to re-make himself. It excited him and began to give him a feeling of power. (61)

Thus the character of Willie Chandran emerges as one who experiments with one pose after another, almost following the footstep of his father, to place himself in a comfortable position. Gradually, however, he gathers moral courage to face the truth and to do away with pretensions.

Since his childhood Willie had shown his competence in imaginary writings moulded in lucid language. This talent, mixed up with his poses, helped him to be a news correspondent and even a writer of short stories. His sexual experiences in London, on the other hand, helped him get confidence in himself. It was his friend Persey who acquainted him to the world of sex. Willie came in contact with Persey's girl friend June and came to know about his weakness as a man. He also compared his father's iife-style in India to the life-style he himself had been acquainted with in London, and felt pity for his father. To his Indian sensibility the world of sex appeared rather brutal.

In London, Willie came in contact with a lot of people belonging to different races, who had come to London to try their luck. He learnt that people in London wanted West Indian chaps to drive the buses, but nobody in London liked to rent rooms for the accommodation of the black people. So some black people like Persey were encouraged to buy properties and rent to West Indian drivers. Naipaul has thus detected the maladies in the British society almost clinically. Willie's script about the old Christian community in India which was broadcast by the B.B.C. for the Commonwealth programme, is another example of falsity exposed in the novel. Willie prepared a fake story that was accepted without any verification.

> As soon as the idea, and the angle, had been given to him by the producer the five minute talk had sketched itself in his mind [...] the feeling of separateness from the rest of India; no true knowledge of the other religions in India, the family's work in the British time as social reformers, people of Christian conscience, champions of workers' rights [...]. The writer's discovery of the tension between the old Christian community and the new Christians, backwards, recent converts, depressed people, full of grievances [...]. (77-78)

Willie knew what was expected of him and he did his job well. His imaginary description was accepted as fact. His report on an exhibition of woodcarving by a young west African is another example of falsity. Willie was sent as a reporter by the B.B.C. to cover the exhibition and he made his script without any prior knowledge of wood carving. And for all such jobs he found himself in demand, and was able to change his financial condition. Naipaul's first hand knowledge of the process by which news scripts are produced for broadcast by the B.B.C. enables him to offer a real story behind the screen, though this time a direct way of satire is kept aside.

Willie's friendship with Roger gave him double benefit. First, it was Roger who criticised the technique of Willie's stories and asked him to write on the model of Hemingway.

Willie followed him and was benefited. Secondly, Roger introduced him to his editor and other literary personalities, and helped Willie to get his book published. When Willie showed Roger some of his stories he wrote in his school days, Roger told him that he had not written real things, that his stories indicated that the writer was hiding something. Willie was mortified and felt ashamed. Yet he wrote his stories on the model of Hemingway and Roger appreciated the changed version of the stories and asked him to carry on.

Roger also introduced Willie to his editor who, like the social figure Swann in Proust's work, liked to bring together dissimilar people. This occasion helped Naipaul to expand his theme into a study of different races including a study on interracial sex relationship. Willie is introduced to some 'modest' persons whose career is to pursue rich women. Naipaul also utilises the opportunity of criticising fake Marxism. Roger calls Richard a bedroom Marxist and crticises him:

> Marxism takes him to the bedroom, and Marxism stops in the bedroom. All the women he seduces knew that. They feel safe with him. It was like that in Oxford and it's still like that. The difference is that at Oxford it thrilled his common soul just to sleep with rich women, and now he takes large sums of money off them. Of course he's made his mistakes [...]. Richard is in publishing, quite rich now, and rising fast. As a publisher his Marxism makes him more attractive than ever. The more he takes off the ladies the more other ladies rush to give him. (91-92)

Exploitation in the name of Marxism is thus openly attacked in the novel. The naked picture of racism and sexual oppression in England also reveal the uncompromising attitude of Naipaul.

Peter is another character who scored "notable success" in making money through his relationships with foreign girls. He is exposed mercilessly:

> Peter's style is entirely different. His background is more modest, country estate agent, and at Oxford he began to develop his English gentleman style. Oxford is full of young foreign women studying English at various language schools. Some of them are rich. Peter by some instinct

> ignored the university women and chose to operate among these people. They would have thought him the genuine article, and he quicker than they, learning soon to sort the wheat from the chaff, scored some notable successes. (92)

Naipaul has also shown how this sort of sexual relationship with other races changed the demography in some places. There is the African Marcus with his plan of having white grandchildren. As he says, his plan is not extraordinary. It is just repeating something that happened on a large scale in England a hundred and fifty years ago.

> In the eighteenth century there were about half a million black people in England. They've all vanished. They disappeared in the local population. They were bred out. The negro gene is recessive one. If this were more widely known there would be a good deal less racial feeling than there is. (94-95)

The same history was repeated in South America, says Marcus:

> [...] there were large Negro populations in Buenos Aires and Uruguay in 1800. They disappeared in the local population. They were bred out. The Negro is recessive. Not many people know that. (97)

In support of Marcus's view Richard gives an example from Thackeray's *Vanity Fair*. Thackeray's great London merchant wanted his son to marry a Negro heiress from St. Kitts in the West Indies. The Lady's fortune would have come from slaves and sugar. It is almost unthinkable that at that time a Negro heiress in London was greatly in demand. As Richard says, though Thackeray does not tell us anything about it, the Negro heiress would have married well and in a couple of generations would have been perfectly English and upper class. Richard also speaks of the possibility of a new reading of *Wuthering Heights* rendering Heathcliff a half-Indian child who was found near the docks of Liverpool. Naipaul has thus studied the past and future of interracial sex and marriage which add a new dimension to the common racial feelings.

A detailed description of the race-riots in London is also given:

> [...] the race riots began in Notting Hill. The silent streets—with exposed rubbish bins daubed with house and flat numbers, and with windows heavily curtained and screened and black—became full of excited people. The houses that had seemed tenanted only by the very old and passive now let out any number of young men in mock-Edwardian clothes who roamed the streets looking for blacks. (109)

In this background of racial riot Willie was again affected by his earlier feeling of remaining hidden. As he found people casually saying: "Those blacks are going to be a menace," he felt at once threatened and ashamed. "He felt people were looking at him. He felt the newspapers were about him. After this he stayed in the college and didn't go out" (109). Willie's exceptional sensitivity as exposed in his encounters with the outer world including the world of sex that at first seemed to him to be brutal, is the central theme of the novel. Naipaul takes extra care in delineating how Willie came out of his fear of being exposed to the world—a baseless fear prompted by his extraordinary sensibility and an imaginative capacity—through his sexual experiences. His conversations with the editor and the latter's reflection on life and writing helped Willie to realise himself and his past. The editor said that "Journalism is by its nature ephemeral," and that love is "The divine illusion." Willie was greatly influenced by the parties arranged by the editor and found the matter of many stories. The stories seemed to be just waiting for him, and he continued writing at stretch for four weeks. These stories were also published by Richard.

The third and the last section of the novel is entitled 'A second Translation,' that starts with Willie's self-analysis which was provoked by his sister Sarojini who came to spend some days with him. Through Willie's views on sex Naipaul expresses some of his own. One such view is that the ancient Indian philosophical-practical way of dealing with sex was destroyed by the Muslim invasion and the thing became worse during the British period. Sex used to be a taboo and stood on the way of one's self-assertion. Willie's lack of self-assertion was also related to this taboo. When Willie learnt of June's marriage he went to a prostitute who humiliates him for his inexperience.

This insult disturbed him much and he badly needed a friend in his utter loneliness. At that time a young girl wrote to him praising his stories recently published by Richard. In these stories the girl found 'moments' that were like moments in her own life. At first Willie had fear for this girl Ana who was born of African-Portuguese parentage. But he found that Ana accepted him completely. He began to depend on her and even decided to go to Africa where Ana inherited a luxurious estate house built after 1914 war. Willie stayed there for eighteen long years and then he left Ana for good telling her that he can no more live her life. Leaving Ana, Willie goes to Columbia where Sarojini is living and all the details about his life in Africa are told by him to his sister. Naipaul gets thereby the opportunity to remain detached.

Willie confesses that he depended on Ana for being a man. Her strength and authority supplied him with necessary sustenance. They became emotionally attached as they found similarities between their backgrounds. Ana's grandfather, a Portuguese, married an African and later when he grew rich, he chose Portuguese sons-in-law. Ana's mother left her Portuguese husband and remarried a man of mixed race. Ana's father forged his wife's money and left the home. In her stepfather's home Ana was seduced by him. Because of all these experiences Ana developed a vacuum in her mind and longed for love that would remove her loneliness. She married Willie with the devotion of a loyal wife. Willie acknowledges that he found a complete acceptance.

Side by side with the description of Willie's internal growth as a man, the third section also acquaints us with the coexistence of the people belonging to different races. There were the Portuguese, the African-Portuguese, the Arabs of Muscat and Oman, commonly known as Mohammedan. As it is expected of Naipaul, the corruption in the government offices and the social organizations, and the basic moral degradation of man did not escape his eyes. That is why he found fault not only with the colonial power, but also with a section of the colonized. When Willie lost his passport and Ana advised him to write to his home for another passport, Willie remembers the Government offices in India and Naipaul gets a chance to criticise the way the Indian bureaucracy works. Willie remembers a typical Indian office:

> [...] the pea-green walls shiny with grime [...]. The floor black with dirt, the pan-chewing clerks in their trousers or lungis, each man correctly marked on the forehead with a fresh caste-mark (his principal duty of the day), on every desk the ragged stacks of old files in many faded colours, poor-quality paper crumbling away—and I knew that I would wait a long time in far-off Africa, and nothing would come. (158)

About the African Government Willie says that the Government was authoritarian, but the people had no idea about it. They felt it to be far away, something in the capital. The village people had contact with the Government only during the Sisal cutting season when the estate holders made their requisitions from the prisons, and the convicts, properly guarded, were sent for the dangerous work of Sisal cutting. It was doubly dangerous. The long black point at the end of the Sisal blade is needle sharp and poisonous, and the area remains full of venomous snakes. Only the convicts could be compelled to do such a work. This description lays bare the inhuman ways supported by the Government and the callousness of the affluent. The authoritarian way of the governemnt is further criticised:

> There had been no challenge to our authoritarian but easy going government for many years, and it had grown strangely lazy. In his great security the ruler had grown to feel that the details of governing were a burden, or so it appeared; and he had farmed out or leased out important governmental activities to eager, energetic and loyal people. Those people became very rich, and the richer they became the more loyal they were, and the better they did the jobs that had been farmed out to them. So there was a kind of rough logic and effectiveness in this principle of government. (169)

This is the typical ironic way of disclosing corruption, adopted by Naipaul. The novel also supplies the readers with examples taken from life. Willie describes how Mr Correia grew more and more rich, and then was in deep trouble when he was used as a scape goat by the big masters. Naipaul has thus chalked out another area of darkness.

The description of the children beggars and the children prostitutes complete the picture of corruption in Africa. Willie receives first hand knowledge of all this and proceeds towards a 'full man.' His affair with the manager's wife Graca and Graca's strange relationship to her husband have been carefully dealt. The sudden change in Graca's mind after the illness of her husband makes an end of her relationship with Willie. This change in Willie's personal life goes side by side with the political change.

> The colonial government in the capital closed down, just like that the guerrillas took over. The Portuguese population began to leave. The army withdrew from the town [...]. The army hadn't really wished to fight this African war, and the life in the town remained normal right up to the end. (224)

The establishment of the local government brought new problems for the non-Africans. The ante-Portuguese guerrillas had the support of the black government over the border. The new insurgents had the support of the white government to the west. Willie became more and more afraid. He did not have the stamina to go through another war. And one day he told Ana that he was going to leave her as he had been tired of living her life. He did not deny that Ana had done everything for him. The novel ends with Ana's reply that it was not really her life either. This comment by Ana throws a new light on her character, her loneliness and desperate attempt to make a relationship are exposed.

The abrupt end of the novel was carefully planned before hand. Naipaul expresses his view through Roger the journalist in the second section, 'The first Chapter.' Roger tells Willie:

> I know your great namesake and family friend (implying Somerset Maugham) says that a story should have a beginning, a middle and an end. But actually, if you think about it, life isn't like that. Life doesn't have a neat beginning and a tidy end. Life is always going on. You should begin in the middle and end in the middle and it should all be there. (83)

Naipaul began his novel in the middle and ended it in the middle distorting the age-old norm. But he has consciously followed the traditional narrative style:

In *An Area of Darkness* Naipaul criticised the Indian novel for its dependence on myth and for the Indian novelist's lack of concern for "the here and now" Naipaul says:

> Indian attempts at the novel further reveal the Indian confusion. The novel is of the west. It is a part of that Western concern with the condition of men, a response to the here and now. In India thoughtful men have preferred to turn their back on the hear and now [...]. (214)

Naipaul is intolerant of what he calls the static condition in India. He found the Indians satisfied with the myth of Indian history and spirituality and observed that no real novel can be built up on that myths. He has projected Willie as a writer whose sole concern is 'here and now.' Willie undergoes a variety of experiences in different corners of the world and Naipaul exhibits how Willie is stripped off the myth making tendency of an Indian. Claude Levi Strauss described "myth" as a system of logical operations defined by the method of its "when" or its "like." Naipaul's narrative keeps itself away from the method of "when" or "like." That is why Willie's experiences are revealed without any comment either from the author (when it is described in the third person) or from the protagonist (when it is described in the first person). Just as the impressionist painters juxtaposed pure tones on the canvas, instead of mixing them on the palette, and left the blending of colours to the eyes of the spectators, so also Naipaul offers some visions and experiences in various phases of his protagonist's life and leaves for his readers to decide when and how the necessary changes take place in the mind of his protagonist. Like Ganesh, Mr Biswas, Mr Stone and Singh,—the protagonists in Naipaul's earlier novels—Willie Chandran is also projected as a writer from the beginning and the distinguishing quality of Willie is his courage to expose the pretences he finds around him. First he exposed the pretences of his father directly in his stories such as 'Life of Sacrifice.' After he has undergone various experiences in

London his attitude to his father is somehow changed. But he himself is unable to explain why the sentimental story read out by the editor Richard brings a total change in the technique of his writing stories. In a unique way he fitted the editor to the holyman he had already written about in some of his stories:

> Upto this point the holyman had been seen from the outside: idle and sinister, living off the unhappy, waiting like a spider in his hermitage. Now, unexpectedly the holyman showed his own unhappiness. (101)

From the point of view of this change in his writings, Willie's experiences in London may be interpreted as the first chapter of the narrative that records his emergence as a post-colonial writer.

Willie comes close to the figure of the post-colonial migrant intellectual signifying a universal condition of hybridity. Homi Bhabha's views on the migrant experience as a post-colonial metropolitan assimilation may be recalled in this context:

> The space of the translation of cultural difference at the interstices is infused with that temporality of the present which makes graphic a moment of transition, not merely the continuum of history.[11]

Being a migrant, Willie receives a superior understanding of the cultural life in London and in Africa than the natives of those places. The experience he received in London remained within him as latent properties which are compared with his experiences in Africa and then the 'codes' received in London are "translated" in Africa. The existential suffering of the exile that Willie had to undergo in the multiracial society of the Portuguese Africa prepared him to assert his individuality. His dependence on Ana was a child's dependence, the kind of which he observed in the Indian way of life. He passed the first ten years in Africa happily with Ana who was devoted to him. And then the grown up individual emerges out of the shy man. Describing his desire to have sexual relationship with Graca, the wife of the new estate manager, Willie says:

> I was full of desire. Not the dumb, headlong, private desire of London, but a desire that came now from

> knowledge and experience and truly embraced the other person. (102)

And thus Willie describes his experience when the desire is fulfilled:

> Graca's need matched my own. That was new to me. Everything I had known before—the furtiveness of London, the awful provincial prostitute, the paid black girls of the places of pleasure here, [...]. And poor Ana [...] still so gentle and generous over the next half-hour everything fell away and I thought how terrible it would have been if, as could so easily have happened, I had died without knowing this depth of satisfaction, this other person that I had just discovered within myself. It was worth my price, any consequence. (205)

Willie had so long been unaware of his physical need and only pretended to be happy with Ana who accepted him totally, without raising any question. In a traditional romantic story this sort of relationship based on mutual dependence is glorified and described as the ultimate goal of life. Naipaul finds in such relationship a pretence, a negation of real life. Once he feels the boredom of such a life, Willie cannot continue it. Apparently, however, Willie's leaving Africa is prompted by his fear of riots. Ana also felt that Willie was afraid. But the real cause lay deeper. Willie decides to leave Africa for escaping the world of make believe. In this sense Willie's attempts have similarities with his creator's attempts to do away with the world of magic, myth and ritual. Naipaul himself said in an interview that his concern in *Half a Life* is also the historical side of things. "Willie runs away from his background, and even when he gets to Africa, this Portuguese province, he is reminded of the background from which he came."[12] He has all along strived for self-awareness and this striving of half a life is recorded in the novel. The task of a historian and an anthropologist is once again incorporated into the task of a novelist.

NOTE

All the references to *Half a Life* and *An Area of Darkness* are taken from *Half a Life* (Picador, 2001) edition and *An Area of Darkness* (Penguin, 1968) edition.

REFERENCES

1. In his essay on Conrad (1974), Naipaul expressed his view that the form of novel is inadequate. He repeated this view in several interviews and yet continued writing novels. But those novels are better described as combinations of the writer's autobiography and its grafting into a recollected locale. Most of his later novels—take, for example, *The Enigma of Arrival* or *In a Free Street*—have journalistic frame. In fact, the traditional form of novel has been undergoing a seachange.
2. Modern critics, however, find little difference between fiction and non-fiction writings. Commenting on Graham Greene's work, the noted writer Manjit Inder Singh observes that the pattern of a close liaison between fiction and non-fiction did not diminish Greene's status as one of the leading British novelists. He gives a similar opinion on the work of V.S. Naipaul. [*V.S. Naipaul, Writers of the Indian Diaspora series* (Rawat publication, New Delhi, 1998) 28.] The noted Indian writer in English Amitav Ghosh, recently said in an interview that writing fiction does not much differ from writing non-fiction. He says, "sometimes the world interests me as fiction, and sometimes it interests me as non-fiction and I don't see a distinction."

   [On a Magic Carpet Ride, An Interview taken by Kushanava Choudhury. *The Statesman Literary*, Kolkata, Aug. 25, 2002, 3.]

   What Amitav says may be applicable to Naipaul's works as well.
3. Meenakshi Mookherjee explains Naipaul's lack of roots as the "source of his strength as well as his acerbity." It is the burden that Naipaul carries with him in his restless travels around the world. And at the same time it is a "weapon with which he can ironically slice up the countries he visits." *The Statesman* Feb. 19, 2002: 1, Kolkata.
4. The famous West Indian novelist George Lamming took fiction as a tool of revenge against all the vices of the colonial power and he criticised Naipaul for the latter's attitude to the Caribbean society. In *An Area of Darkness* Naipaul said, "Trinidad was a British colony, but every child knows that we were only a dot on the map of the world, and it was therefore important to be British, that at least anchored us within a wide system. It was a system which we did not find oppressive [...]" (128). Naipaul continued writing against the Trinidadian society which was to him a world "permeated by fear, deceit and treachery." Selwyn R. Cudjoe, *V.S. Naipaul: A Materialist Reading* (Amherst, The University of Massachusetts Press, 1998) 124. Homi K. Bhabha criticised Naipaul's negative attitude to the formerly colonized world. "The values that such a perspective generates for his own work and for the once colonized world it chooses to represent and evaluate are visible in the hideous panorama that some of his titles provide: *The Loss of El Dorado, The Mimic Men, An Area of Darkness* (*The Location of Culture*, Routledge, London and N.Y., 1994), 107.
5. *The Indian Critical Scene: Controversial Essays* (Delhi, B.R., 1990) 99.

6. Verdonk, Peter and Jean, Jacques Weber (eds.), *Twentieth Century Fiction: From Text to Context* (London: Routledge, 1995) 248.
7. Maugham, W. Somerset, *The Razor's Edge* (Pan Books in association with Heinemann, London, 1976) 772.
8. *Ibid.*, 280. Maugham's sympathetic attitude to Larry as revealed in *The Razor's Edge* supports the view that Larry utters the view of his creator.
9. In *An Area of Darkness* Naipaul laid bare the pretension and corruption in Indian life much to the discomfort of the Indians.
10. Jain, Jasbir, "Series Editior's Preface to *V.S. Naipaul*" (Jaipur: Rawat Publications, 1998) 12.
11. *The Location of Culture* (London & N.Y.: Routledge, 1994) 244.
12. Naipaul, V.S., "Indian Writers Don't Know Why Their Country Is in Such a Mess," An Interview with Farrukh Dhondy, Cupidonline.com. Accessed on October 24, 2001.

18

Disorientation of Identity in V.S. Naipaul's *Half a Life*

BHAGABAT NAYAK

Vidiadhar Surajprasad Naipaul is one of the few prominent expatriate writers of our time, particularly writers with Indian background, who has emerged as the most eminent writer in English of the world after his winning the Nobel Prize for literature in 2001. As a journalist, novelist, writer of travelogue, and a great master in the art of non-fiction novel-writing, he has significant contribution to commonwealth literature or post-colonial literature and has secured his place in the literary map of the English speaking world. With the exalted idea of the western literary canon it seems that "He is a tireless but reluctant traveller, like an unsponsored explorer without a compass in his work as in his life—for his characters share his homelessness" (Theroux: 1972: 450). His writing has often been seen in the Third World as caustic and personal, but takes his readers into the farthest reaches of the third world- Africa, the Caribbean, Asia and the Central Asia and all the way to South Africa, to test one or both his obsessions what it means to become and finally to be a writer; what happens to post-colonial societies when the imperial power recedes, leaving cruelty and chaos to fill the breach. Both in his writing and daily life he is a perfectionist, what he expects and writes about he is a Brown man of Indian descent born into the Black and Brown society of Trinidad. Unlike, for example, Salman Rushdie, whose literary referents were Guntur Grass and Gabriel Garcia Marquez, Naipaul cuts his teeth on the great masters of the nineteenth and the early twentieth century European fiction: Tolstoy, Balzac, Stendhal, Flaubert and Proust. If there is a fundamental urge to blaspheme in Rushdie's, there is a search for a unified self in Naipaul's. All the Naipaulean readers are happy that his modernist moment may have passed but he remains perhaps the last great representative of a classic movement in English letters.

Being the author of some twenty-four highly acclaimed works of fiction and non-fiction he has been held to controversy for his views on the Third World, on Islam or the destruction of Babri Masjid (at the International Festival of Indian Literature organised by the Indian Council of Cultural Relations, 2002). As a top-ranking writer in the English speaking world today, Naipaul constructs an entirely new metaphor for dislocation, fragmentation, rootlessness and the quest for a viable identity. His Indian-Caribbean ancestry, the enigma of a decentred and disoriented experience in the explosive and disconcerting realities of the post-colonial world anywhere and everywhere, and the knotted relationship with his own cultural identity from Indian and his Caribbean and western identities help him to remain as a kind of literary outsider in the post-colonial realities. His clarity of vision is almost Swiftean as he has enjoyed his life in the century which is marked by the political upheaval, mass migration, colonization, revolution and, at the same time by his typical extended family of Hindu India, bound by tradition, rituals, customs, and in a community where the roots had been severed and environment was alien and all encompassing Hindu culture and its recollections of India had become more attenuated with each passing generation. In an interview with Rahul Singh he says, "[...] I was born in Trinidad, I have lived most of my life in England and India is the land of my ancestors. That says it all. I am not English, not Indian, not Trinidadian. I am my own person" (*The Times of India* February 19, 2002). His writings are realistic and include the knowledge about cricket, movies of the forties, snuff, architecture, fine wine, Indian art and politics, exploration, military strategy and the pictures of some countries with high pitched tone of anger, harshness and severity of his statement as well as brilliant world-view.

Acknowledging his "Colonial Hindu Self" as a "man and writer" Naipaul projects his "autobiographical material into poignant fiction and his neuroses onto his narrators and characters" (Feder: 2001: 1). The relations with the people he meets in his travels affect the very nature of his memories and enlarge his perspective on his heritage; the religion and customs of immigrants from colonial Indian who settled in colonial Trinidad. The idea of "universal civilization" came into formulation by his understanding of the cultural traditions of India, the Arab World and of colonialism. Further, his conception of "Universal Civilization" is based on his belief in individual potentiality and individual responsibility which he has observed by associating himself with the hardships, aspirations: "the Whiteman's burden" in colonialism, the present western cultural dominance on other societies and the need of those societies to ape western practices and institutions. His claims as a seeker of truth are always contingent on his individual role in history and the possibilities of discovery within a particular time and place. Yet his truth is "Observing the intricate connections between the self and the observed world and its peoples stirs ambiguous memories and subliminal feelings that alter his responses" (Feder: 2001: 6-7), and refer to an individual mind contending with barriers to its authentic interpretation of experience. Throughout his career he has transformed self-creation into a cultural lens and a literary method that constitutes his approach to truth, however, contingent on the changing prospect of contemporary history and his own evolving skill as its interpreter. He has been acclaimed for his penetration into the lasting impairment of the post-colonial societies, specially the deprivations of individuals who inherited a history of exploration, and he has been criticised as "a reactionary loyal to imperialist values." He has been praised for his creative use of autobiography in his travel narratives and for converting autobiographical material into poignant fiction, Naipaul's protagonists emerge from different social classes. They are linked to each other and to their progenitor by an impulse to pursue truth about themselves and their world; however circuitous the cause. In its Nobel citation to Naipaul Swedish Academy rightly remarks, "He is to a very high degree a cosmopolitan writer, a fact that he himself considers to stem from his lack of roots; he is unhappy about the cultural and spiritual poverty, of Trinidad, he feels alienated from India, and in England he is incapable of relating to and identifying with the traditional values of what was once a colonial power" (*The Hindustan Times* October 12, 2001).

It is interesting to mark how Naipaul has "invented stories" on truth with the setting of plot and places as "a form of social enquiry" in which his characters are presented as confused identities through different disorientations. *Half a Life* his latest work, apart from being a fictional counterpart of the earlier three interrogatory Naipaulean passages—dark, wounded, mutinous—to India, is also perhaps in need of this low form of heraldry to appear as the antithesis of the spiritual, sympathy laden passages to India of Forster and Maugham. "It certainly tells a story, in fact several stories, but they seem unrealistic, like events in a nightmare, and the characters are like those glimpsed in one, briefly and horribly. Also like a nightmare, the book leads nowhere, and when it was over it [...] disappointed [...] greatly" (Moraes: 2001: 3). *Half a Life* reflects his fundamental social and cultural values in his psychological reactions to his immediate and extended family. Naipaul is consistently hostile toward mobilization for political change is believed by the evidence in various political movements, observation of corruption, brutality, and tribal hostilities like the slaughters in Rwanda and Bosnia. In the novel he presents his protagonist's encountering of "half-made societies that seemed doomed to remain half-made." The fictional material and experiences in the novel are restlessly nomadic which Naipaul discusses on the themes of exile, dislocation, alienation, displaced histories and most painful dilemmas in the post-colonial societies in both fictional and non-fictional modes.

Half a Life is really an invention about the countries, periods or situations if it does not exactly appear to describe them. The novel is without any real surprise in which Naipaul portrays and evaluates the lives of the people of mixed descent in three countries—Trinidad, England and Portuguese Africa (Mozambique) and their struggle to discover their identities. The book is about the confused identities, a theme that Naipaul discusses in almost all the books he has written—people coming from small places, smaller historical contexts and struggling with the looseness of their selves and their lives.

The novel has three parts with different settings cast in different eras. Each part is a narration of an individual narrator. In the first part Willie Chandran's father tells his story which took about ten years. Unlike the author he comes from the line of priests. On the setting of the human drama he is "self-deluded" by Mahatma's call in 1930s, gives up his English education, plans very deliberately the seduction of an untouchable Dalit girl "from the backwards," gets into trouble with everyone concerned, gets a job, marries the girl, renounces the world and joins in the campaign against casteism. He marries this backward scholarship girl as a supreme gesture of sacrifice, "not an empty sacrifice [...] but a more lasting kind of sacrifice, something Mahatma would approved of" (Naipaul: 2001: 10). Though he had taken a vow of sexual abstinence, a vow of "brahmacharya" (33) he marries this backward girl as a great sacrifice to liberate the people who were dehumanised, without shedding his caste prejudice and abhorrence of the "unclean." He enjoys his life in the measure of social distancing, and renouncing the world like his grandfather before him, whose activities Naipaul is careful not to disclose to the reader.

Willie's father sacrifices his life for a cause greater than life and perhaps the greatest in humanity. His life is charged with the philosophy of the Mahatma and he gets confused about the fate of the country during the freedom movement. He feels the ground beneath his feet falling by marrying a girl below his rank and fighting the petty caste-war says, "I was irredeemably tarnished, a fallen man of caste, and my path of mockery of sacred ways" (32). Yet his confusion saturates with his Dalit wife; disoriented son, Willie Somerset Chandran whom he thinks of as "tainted" and desirable daughter, Sarojini whom he finds repulsive. He keeps the middle name of his son since the visit by the famous English writer Somerset Maugham to his ashram in search of a saintly person, for his novel *The Razor's Edge* and daughter's as Sarojini after the patriot woman poet of the independence movement. He waits to see how much of the backward Willie could be read in his son's features, and wishes that the blessing might fall on Sarojini like that of the great woman poet. The disappointment of the college principal who wanted him to marry his daughter, the fear of his wife's "fine-brand" uncle and his own shell-shocked parents forced him to leave his job. All this "has been a life of sacrifice" (36) and he sublimely says "I am sacrificing the only thing I have to sacrifice" (24). Conscious of his duty to his wife he says to her "I have no riches to offer you. All I have are my friendship. That is my treasure" (36) and for his daughter he says "[...] all I can hope for Sarojini is an international marriage" (36). He tells his life story of ten years during which Willie grows and goes to school, and starts reworking some of the stories he hears his father telling him, such as "A Life of Sacrifice" in which an old brahmin bound to sacrifice a child every year in order to retain possession of a treasure, finally ends up by sacrificing his own children through the subterfuge and malice of a tribal chieftain, the children of whose tribe he had been using for the purpose. Willie's father never got tired of telling him of his own "life of sacrifice" of whose ridiculous dimensions Willie seems to have become aware very early in his life. "This pantomime of high intention and pathos subsumes the story of Willie Chandran's father's life; his stints in he Maharaja's Land Tax Department, his refuge in melancholy and his eventful career as a bogus holyman. Curiously it stands Naipaul's own most poignant story on its head; the story of his father's ambition and failure" (Chaudhury: 2001). Thus it appears that the first part of the book is quite Naipaulean and "delineates the traumas of a tainted and troubled past, of attempting to find some meaning and purpose of life. It beautifully analyses the pangs of exile, their living a half-life, their sense of alienation, and their cultural traditions" (Jha: 2001-2002: 47).

Naipaul describes the ancestry of Willie Chandran in pre-independent India. The ridiculousness of the significance ordinary men attach to their own lives is another topic dear to Naipaul, and that forms the second part of the story. It delineates that a life without any special significance is no better either, and that is what his father understands of Willie. Both Willie and Sarojini face a hostile and confused Mission School environment and family atmosphere that make their future uncertain. In the school their friends have a degraded callings at their father and his business. "The teacher kept on smiling, waiting for an answer, and at last Willie Chandran said with irritation, 'You all know what my father does? The class laughed. The laughed at his irritation and not at what he had said" (37). Willie goes to a college in England on scholarship. He finds himself in London on the fringes of the 'special passing bohemian—immigrant life of London of the late 1950s. In the immigrant community of post-war London, Willie grows up to despise his father and hate his mother. In the London literary underground he wants to be a writer, meets a number of people who lead uniformly intellectual and silly lives. There he begins to recreate himself as a writer and publishes a book of stories modelled on the borrowings from *Old Hollywood Movies* and the *Maxim Garky triology from Russia.* When the readers feel the book unreadable and reviewers dismiss, his disorientation starts and he abandons his plan to be a writer "Let the book die, let it fade away [...] I will write no more" (123).

Willie's creative activity increases with the reading of a cheap history book of the world published during the war about the nationalisation of Suez Canal and Krishna Menon's representing India at the international forums. He begins to recreate himself with some historical, some personal, some traditionally novelistic and some materials—part fact, part fiction as Roger says "[...] a story should have beginning, a middle and an end [...] if you think it, life isn't like that. Life doesn't have a neat beginning and a tidy end. Life is always going on. You should begin in the middle and end in the middle, and it should all be there" (83). He comes in contact with Percy Cato from Jamaica in London and is initiated into the city's bohemian underground. He sleeps with Cato's girl friends, visits a prostitute, gets to know Roger, sleeps with his girl friend and reworks some of the stories from India, shows them to Roger who asks him to take them to Richard who publishes them. As a "sexual athlete" in his different encounters he discovers his sexual incompetence and comes to know how "sex is a brutal business" (71). In London, Willie understands two things: one, that he is free, that is, free to be much more than he could be within reason and remake himself and his past and his ancestry, two, he finds by a chance that his love with Ana, a mixed race girl from Africa true and sincere and for the first time in his life he feels to be in the presence of someone who accepts him completely. He realises that sexual knowledge is required to make one's way in the West. He considers his love for his mother at home as pure but his experience of Love with Ana could bring him the fulfilment which he searches of desperately. Willie realises that personal failures mirror those of his father's and that these personal failures mirror the failure of colonialism; Britain losing India and Portugal losing Mozambique. "We are in the late fifties at this stage of the novel and we can see Naipaul using some of his own experiences here, especially when Willie works briefly for the BBC" (Das: 2001: 1).

Ana is the daughter of a plantation owner from an unnamed Portuguese colony in Africa. Willie is passionately involved with her, and it is she that helps him to live with 'a new idea of sex,' a new idea that he experiences with her, 'some genuine excitement, some moments of sexual discovery.' Unlike him Ana is also a confused soul, a Euro-African from a Portuguese colony. With her he cannot stay in Britain because there are no cultural codes available that would help him to live with his unbelongingness. In London he is the little man thrust into a grandiose dimension of history merely by being present at a certain time in a certain place. In his relationship with Ana, Willie develops different perspectives on life, society and man-woman relationship. During his eighteen years of married life with Ana he realises that in spite of appearances, men are really looking for women to lean on" (141), and admits "Ana was important for me because I depended on her for my idea of being a man" (142) and also "we each found comfort in the other, and we had become very close, not looking beyond the other for satisfaction, not knowing, in fact, that another kind of satisfaction was possible" (189).

Naipaul describes Willie's life with Ana in the third and final part of the story during the post-Independent Civil War period. He describes Willie's disorientation in life in the ruined and dying colony of Africa. Willie lives these eighteen years a perfectly useless existence, hobnobbing with other planters who are all stereotypes or caricatures and fooling around with women, for pleasure in the converted warehouse on the edge of the town. But this act of his commitment to unscrupulous sex he does not feel any betrayal towards Ana and rather continues his visits to the warehouse until one day he spots the dressed up Julio's daughter. At the weekends he visits the 'places of pleasure' in the deserted cobra-infested German castle and makes love to Graca without knowing the danger involved in this and the depth of satisfaction as "it was worth any price, any consequence" (205). With the break out of the Civil War the colony is about to explode into a bloody revolution and Ana tells him "Africans may not be afraid of you and me, but they are afraid of one another. Every man has access to the fetishman, and this means that even the humblest man has power. In that way they are better off than the rest of us" (159). This helps him to realise that he has not been living his own life, but rather existing all these years. This makes Willie to leave Ana and Africa and he goes to Germany, to Sarojini who has married a German photographer with radical ideas. Naipaul describes Willie's alienation, disorientation and emptiness in the ruined and dying colony of Africa Willie narrates his African experience in a brooding before his sister believing that there was something in the African heart beyond everybody and everything. He realises how all through the years "Africa releases him into sensuality" as prior to this he had led a half-life in his submission to sensual desire, to confusion of caste in India and to class in England. Willie's experience and realisation of halfness in life are reflected in his transcontinental migration and multi-dimensional socio-cultural environment.

One of the major themes of the book is the half-life the exiles live. The author raises this important existential question in an autobiographical way through disorientation of Willie's life. Wherever he goes, he realises that a man searches for wholeness but becomes only half-successful. Willie abundantly inherits the collective unconsciousness of the Indian ethos and therefore the Third World heritage—and is by no means a flag-waving propagandist for the erstwhile colonies of British imperialism. Willie strives to find but not to yield in the nature of his inward journey into the half-and-half world and is confused through the suffering and alienation. On the other hand Ana looks like an extension of Willie's own existence, mirroring his own sense of being on the outside of life. The exiles in the novel lead a half-life or look for a life or hope to borrow a life, and never to live a life to the full. Willie desires to discover some purpose in life, though temporarily, through his sensual associations and sexual encounters in London and Ana's Africa. But he realises the futility of life through his experiences in the external settings. Both Willie and Ana realise that exile is a half-life and they do not have more of a personal life. Willie is pre-occupied with varieties of dislocations, migrations, exile, the idea of being unanchored and displaced; the enigma of a decentred and disorientating experience in the explosive and disconcerting realities of half-London, half-Portuguese and half-and-half world with their different linguistic cultural ecologies, sociological hues and nostalgia. Willie tries to run away from his background but he is reminded of his origins that always remain with him as he cannot be out of his roots in the cultural tradition and his relationship with caste and class.

The novel is invention of Naipaul, and does not present the exact countries, periods or situations that it appears to describe. It is a devastating work of exceptional sensitivity, grace and humour in its depiction of love fulfilled and thwarted, in its vision of the half-lives quietly lived out at the centre of our restless world. During the anti-colonial agitation Willie Chandran's father stood at all odds with the world aspiring to greatness in an attempt to defy his post, he lived with a low-caste woman only to bind himself at the mercy of his own fury. It appears on the blurb of the book how "From this unhappy union the utterly compelling character of Willie Chandran emerges, oddly like his father, naïvely eager to find something that will place him both in and apart from the world. And so he is drawn to England to the immigrant community of post-war London, its dingy West End clubs, lonely pavements and sexual encounters, and even to the eccentric milieu of the English writer." Being confused in the post-colonial social matrix of Trinidad, Portuguese province in Africa and London "perhaps he is trying to say that to live in post-colonial countries addles people's mind. This is possible, but it is not a great discovery. And if, as the title suggests Naipaul is saying that most people, in the true sense, only lead half a life, it is a statement of the obvious" (Moraes:

2001: 3). Willie leads half-a-life through his pilgrim's progress into the nether world of love in order to achieve a fullness of life. Drawing the reader's attention into the depth of the story of the novel, Naipaul describes Willie's journey to find out a place for himself in he world and his dilemma is that of a man who had to leave his background and find something else.

Naipaul as the like model of Joseph Conrad is the most polemical among the contemporary writers, lauded for his objectivity in presenting the case of the history of exploitation though his detractors have villified him as a reactionary and an apologist for neocolonialism. His theme in the novel is related to caste, religion, culture, nationality, love and marriage. The title, *Half-a-Life,* is justified not only because Willie is close to fifty when he leaves Ana and Africa, but also because, as he tells Ana, he spent all his mature years trying to grab a life he could call his own, in the knowledge that the life that was given to him had become unbelievable. This is a predicament that one can identify with Naipaul himself, the scholarship holder from Trinidad, who came to know the miracle of fiction and left all dilemmas related to individual identities behind him. Naipaul speaks of the less fortunate, and the nightmares he was able to avoid. This is not really the top of the line Naipaul reaches mainly because one cannot write with spontaneity about things one does not have a first-hand experience of. His depiction of the Indian and the African episodes in Willie Chandran's Life come across as the products of passionless calculation. The alternative to spontaneity is the abandonment of historical realism altogether. But Naipaul does not believe in that either. Thus Naipaul's purpose is never didactic; he merely takes the historical situation as setting for all kinds of human drama and activities which perhaps he is not careful to disclose to the readers.

WORKS CITED

Choudhary, Soma. "Taking Leads from His Own Life." *The Hindustan Times* (September 23, 2001).

Das, Soumitro. "Enigma of Non-arrival." *The Sunday Statesman* (September 30, 2001).

Feder, Lillian. *Naipaul's Truth.* New Delhi: Indialog Publications, 2001.

Jha, Parmanand. "Exile, Alienation and Cultural Tradition: V.S. Naipaul's *Half a Life*." *The Indian Journal of English Studies*. Vol. 39, 2001-2002: 46-53.

Moraes, Dom. "Half a Novel" *The Hindu* (November 4, 2001) 3.

Naipaul, V.S. *Half a Life*. London: Picador, 2001. (All the textual references are to this edition.)

_____. (An interview with Rahul Singh) *The Times of India* (February 19, 2002).

Theroux, Paul. "V.S. Naipaul." *Modern Fiction Studies*, 30: 3 (Autumn 1984): 445-54.

The Hindustan Times. New Delhi, October 12, 2001.

19

Half a Life: A Reading in Sense, Sensibility and Sensuality

ASHWINI KUMAR VISHNU

Having taken about "a quarter of a century,"[1] *Half a Life* has come after four decades of *A House for Mr Biswas*. The emergence of the novel has effected the enigma of "barring-nobel" phrase from the flaps of V.S. Naipaul's books eternally. It's really a fortunate book and a far less grim one too when compared to the other works wherein Naipaul's gaze is a bit merciless while exploring various areas of darkness. The novel is, in a sense, essence of all that Naipaul's is known for: the unaccepted people longing to belong. In the novelist's own words, he has "tried to make it easy, and light, and a small book, and yet full of things."[2] According to Farrukh Dhondy, "it's a very powerful work of the imagination. It takes us through three different settings, and three different eras, and we meet people in different ways. We follow its central character Willie, from pre-independence India, to post-war London, to a Portuguese province in Africa."[3] "*Half a Life* takes its name from the overarching concern of the book: characters caught in a cusp of history, ambition and love; characters who live at half throttle and without complete self-knowledge."[4] This time, Naipaul's objective is to make people "understand that many people are living only fractions of life,"[5] to make them feel "It's me."[6] And convincingly enough, he excels in doing it. The book transcends the reader into that 'half and half' world of nowhereness where fullness remains a far-off dream.

Half a Life is the tale of Willie Somerset Chandran, the son of a brahmin father and a harijan mother. He is the descendant of temple-attached brahmins, who during the rule of the Muslims and the British, however, had to suffer unsettlement. Willie's great grandfather had to leave the temple and the community in the 1890s. He, then, came to a town and worked as a letter-writer on the pavement near the maharaja's palace. "With his letter-writing work, and with his friendships at the temple, he got to know more and more people, and so in time he was able to get a respectable job as a clerk in the maharaja's palace" (7). It was his learning of English that later on placed him amongst the maharaja's secretaries. Willie's father could have stuck to that sort of life too. He, however, went astray. When at the university, he had some idea that the life they were living around the maharaja and his palace was false and it could not last. In his own words:

> I was in a great mess, feeling that we were all living in a false security, feeling idle, hating my studies, and knowing that great things were happening outside. I adored the great names of the independence movement. I felt rebuked in my idleness, and in the servility of life that was being prepared for me. And when sometime in 1931 or 1932 I heard that the mahatma had called for students to boycott their universities, I decided to follow the call. I did more. In the front yard I made a little bonfire of *The Mayor of Casterbridge* and Shelley and Keats [...]. (9)

In those moments of turbulence and crisis he took to identify himself with the Mahatma. He felt more and more inspired by him and his activities like the Salt March. Not just this, he made every decision to mould his life into "something the mahatma would have approved of" (10). He deserted the thought of serving at maharaja's palace and marrying the daughter of the college principal. Instead, he resolved to marry the lowest person he could find. Such a girl is found at the university. She was on the maharaja's scholarship there. The scholarship girl preoccupies him. She seems a fit companion for living out a life he was seeking for. And he speeds up his advances to snare her. Many a wordless meeting and many a secret brooding! Ultimately it is the girl, who one day, speaks her heart to him in the tea-room. In her "loud and coarse and rasping" voice she tells him about every risky thing that could have cursed their life. She informs him about her firebrand uncle, who was with the Labour Union, and who was all set to take out a procession against him. The whole thing upsets Willie. He has no other way out but to hide her somewhere, until things calmed down. He shelters her in a room full of the busts at the image-maker's. This act of blackening the faces of his family members hurls him into a disastrous situation: "It's easy enough for you to talk of sacrifice. You can leave. You are young. Your mother and I will have to live with the consequences. It will be better, in fact, if you did leave. You wouldn't be allowed to live with a backward here. Have you thought of that?" (25)—his father scolds him. For months together he strives to sustain on homage from temple visitors. His vow of silence, in mahatma's mode, brings him almost no relief. He has "no idea where the whole thing was going to end" (29). Day in and out he is full of secret shame:

> I was as ashamed of her as much as my father and mother and the principal, and people of our sort, generally, were ashamed of me. This shame was always with me, the little unhappiness always at the back of my mind, like an incurable illness [...]. Melancholy became so much part of my character that for long periods I could forget the cause. (33)

He had no definite plans and he had to play an inescapable role. At his best he could only act or react on the spur of the moments. During all those stages of crises he seeks remedies from Mahatma. Ironically enough, he falls each time to keep his vows and tame his passions. His vow of brahmcharya is broken. He is full of superlative shame. Things become even more stultifying with the symptoms of pregnancy in the girl. It is as the sum total of that hurried copulation and those events and eventualities that Willie is born. His birth in no sense delights his father. Time and again, his father furtively looks at him only "to see how much of the backward could be read in his features" (33). While Willie's mother becomes house-proud after his birth, his father goes melancholic than ever. Hell breaks loose upon his head when, despite his private vow of brahmcharya, Willie's mother becomes pregnant for the second time:

> this time it was a girl, and this time there was no room for any kind of self-delusion. The girl was the image of her mother. It was like divine punishment. I called her Sarojini, after the woman poet of the independence movement, in the hope that a similar kind of blessing might fall on her [...]. (35)

Despite her high sounding name, Willie's sister Sarojini too receives the scanty love and care of her parents.

"The First Chapter" opens with Willie's day at the mission school where the teacher asks him about his father's occupation. Willie is full of shame for the degraded sort of job of his father. He makes no answer, but the question just leaves him more scornful of his father. Willie's mother had her education at a mission school. It had been her wish that her children too should be sent to the one. During her schooldays she had undergone fierce discrimination at a caste-school variously. The memory of those grinding times was still with her. But naturally, she intended to send her children to a school free of such paltry things. Ironically, the mission school too corrupts Willie in yet another manner. It instills into his heart a craving for foreign land and people. He starts daydreaming of his future in Canada where his school teacher came from. It is very disgusting to his father. When he learns it, he does everything to thwart his plans. He agrees to send him not to Canada, but to London. One of his acquaintances in England finds a place and a scholarship for Willie. "With no idea of what he wanted to do, except to get away from what he knew, and yet with very little idea of what lay outside what he knew" (51), Willie lands in London. The city disillusions him. Its cool indifference pinches him. Its gaudiness goads him to analyse and reanalyze his self. His mind is full of the thoughts of the hopelessness of home and his own nebulous present. He feels like a nowhere man. He bemoans the blankness in him—"He was unanchored, with no idea of what lay ahead. He still had no idea of the scale of things, no idea of historical time or even of distance [...]. At the college he had to re-learn everything that he knew. He had to learn how to eat in public. He had to learn how to greet people and how, having greeted them, not to greet them all over again in a public place ten or fifteen minutes later. He had to learn to close doors behind him. He had to learn how to ask for things without being peremptory" (59). His struggle is at least on two fronts. Firstly, he has to adjust himself to London-life. Secondly, he has to have a history of his own. The realisation comes to him and he fumbles about remaking himself, his past and his ancestry:

> he adapted certain things he had read, and he spoke of his mother as belonging to an ancient Christian community of the subcontinent, a community almost as old as Christianity itself. He kept his father as a brahmin. He made his father's father a 'courtier.' So, playing with words, he began to re-make himself. It excited him, and began to give him a feeling of power. (61)

To pretty good extent, his newcarved selfhood draws people to him. One of such lot is a Jamaican of mixed parentage, Percy Cato. Percy loved clothes. Good clothes seemed, almost, to have a moral quality for him; he respected people who respected clothes (63). He has a girlfriend named June and very often calls her into his room on weekends when "the college rocks with fuck" (64). To be "smooth with the smooth and rough with the rough" (65) is his motto of living. Willie's brief togethernesses with June flame up his sexual urge for her. He rushes to Debenhams where June works at the perfume counter. In that 'setting of glass and glitter and artificial light' the meeting is fixed. They meet at a club. A little while later June hires a taxi and takes Willie to her home in a smelly locality far outside the luscious London. Coming home, June offers herself to Willie for sex. Willie though 'in a state' for long but inexperienced, fails to satisfy her. His juvenile dalliance with June results in a bitter sense of shame, guilt and remorse. The experience, however, changes him in other respects. It shoves him into the bohemian parties in the city. At one of such parties, he meets a young lawyer Roger, and is charmed by "his manner, his style, his speech." They continue meeting about once a week: "out of his friendship with Roger, Willie felt he was seeing behind many blank doors, and there came to him the beginnings of an idea of England far removed from the boys in the college of education and the sensation-seekers of the immigrant-bohemian life of Notting Hill" (82). Roger, being an avid reader of English masters like Orwell,

Waugh, Powell, Connolly etc., inspires Willie for story-writing. Willie is overwhelmed to work on the idea and finishes six stories successively. Roger escorts him to an intellectual London dinner party and there he presents Willie as a literary star to be. There he meets Marcus, a negro "dedicated to inter-racial sex" (89); Richard "a bedroom Marxist" (91); Peter, a "Latin American" women-expert; Serafina, the wife of a pederast man. This nosegay of intellectual socialites transforms him into a relatively new life. This time, the prime impact is from Perdita, who is Roger's lover. Her graceful gestures storm Willie's desire. His fires, however, remain unextinguished due to the race-riots in Notting Hill. It's two letters, pretty later on, which restore his lost cheer—one from Roger and the second from his father. Roger's letter carries a cathartic line—"you must know that Perdita and I are always here for you" (110). Another one, from his father telling about Sarojini's international marriage with an oldish German with a bad lag, who made films about revolutions for his living is a little bit disturbing. Riots affect him otherwise too. Percy Cato flees from London. His secret fleeing leaves Willie forlorn than ever. Meantime Sarojini comes to see him. Willie plays an unwilling host to her. Sarojini, on the contrary, proves her worth here. She chastens him for wasting his life in London doing this little thing and that little thing not knowing why he was doing anything. Disturbed and desperate Willie phones Perdita to help him dissolve his tension. Perdita denies his entreaties dispassionately. He, then, looks for June at the perfume counter and is disappointed. Badly broken, finally he goes into a cafe full of prostitutes. This time too, the woman's words "Fuck like an Englishman" fill him with dire shame. Sense of utter humiliation surrounds him and he wishes to follow in Percy's footsteps. Meanwhile his book of stories is released and he receives a fond letter from a young woman from an African country. In the company of this girl, Ana, for the first time in his life Willie feels like a complete man—a man of no hiccups and blemishes, and resolves to go with her to her country. Ana takes him to her estate house in Africa. His intensest days of lovemaking with Ana are disturbed when he finds another lover Graca. In Willie's own words:

> The first thing I noticed about her was her light-coloured eyes: disturbed eyes; they made me think again about her husband. And the second thing I noticed was that, for a second or two, no more, those eyes had looked at me in a way that no woman had looked at me before. I had the absolute certainty, in that second, that those eyes had taken me in not as Ana's husband or a man of unusual origin, but as a man who had spent many hours in the warm cubicles of the places of pleasure. Sex comes to us in different ways; it alters us; and I suppose in the end, we carry the nature of our experience on our faces. The moment lasted a second. It might have been fantasy, that reading of the woman's eyes, but it was a discovery for me, something about women, something to be added to my sensual education. (198)

Graca, whose life is ruined by her dictator and drunkard husband, feels much rejuvenated to find a lover in Willie. Eventually the two lovers have sex in the German Castle and discover the 'depth of satisfaction' hitherto hidden. Ana is shocked to learn Willie's entanglement with Graca and also his sex-seeking outings with Alvaro, the Correias' manager. To add to the ruggedness of life there outbreaks a social war in their immediate vicinities. Stuffed with guilt and fear Willie asks Ana to divorce him. Ana feels cheated by him. It is here the novel ends.

Full of so various incidents the novel gives a sad and grim read. It is a novel about displacement, exile, anticipation, waiting. There is very little in it that is sunny and restorative. It is full of characters who are exiles in their characteristic modes, who have no proper place in the world. Percy Cato, Marcus, Graca, Ana, Sarojini, Jacinto, Ricardo, Carla, the Noronhas, the Correias, Alvaro *et al.* are all searching for the fullness of their lives. In this quest for fullness and self-realisation they find themselves clamped to unforeseen situations. Having no other choices they continue to thrive on whatever comes their way. Willie is he most fitting example of this halfness of life. The son of an ill-matched couple, he has never known anything like parental love. The bitterness of the whole affair keeps seeping into his lifetime and again. His brahmin father had neither love nor regard for his low-caste mother. It was just to follow mahatma's political ideal, to live out a life of sacrifice, that he had opted for her:

> The decision was nothing less than to make a sacrifice of myself. Not an empty sacrifice, the act of a moment [...] any fool can jump off a bridge or throw himself in front of a train [...] but a more lasting kind of sacrifice, something the mahatma would have approved of. He had spoken much about the evils of casteism. No one had said he was wrong, but very few had done anything about it. (10)

For this and for few other things Willie is half at ease with his father and his paternal background. The ways he re-creates and wraps himself in mysterious settings in London and other places (Mozambique and Berlin), evidence his disillusionment with his real life. The sense of lack of history haunting him wherever he goes and whatsoever he does. His sexual extremes in remote nooks of the world are nothing but attempts at self-discovery; at least on the physical plane. His premature ejaculations do suggest the frightening fecklessness of his inmost self.

Naipaul, in his writings always speaks of sex in undertones. Pornographic portrayal of sex is inadmissible to him. He says, "I think everybody's sexuality is very important. Seduction is important, and the grossness of pornographic writing annihilates the importance of it."[7] It is due to this conviction that *Half a Life,* even though it is a book about the sexual identification of the protagonist, is brilliantly free from absurd description of sex. The author has dealt this subject with dignified delicacy:

> We are all born with sexual impulses, but we are not all born with sexual skill, and there are no schools where we can be trained. People like me have to fumble and stumble on as best they can, and wait for accidents to take them to something like knowledge. (189)

Straightforwardness is the prominent feature of this novel. Though, there are backward and forward swings in it, the book is devoid of any deep experimentalism. The concentric and epicentric cycles of stories, add to its distinctiveness and reflect Willie's not-so-linear life panoramically. The book shows no disorientation of any kind. In Maggie Ball's words, "Naipaul's prose is strong, and his characters well-drawn, but the real strength of this book lies in the narrative structure, and its insistence on pushing out the stories of these characters; their terror and fear, and marginality."[8] The most notable feature in the novel is the mellowness of the female characters. In comparison to the respective males, they are far more sensuous, sensitive, and sensible. Ana is superb.

NOTE

The Numbers in brackets refer to *Half a Life*. London: Picador, 2001 edition.

REFERENCES

1. *Naipaul to Farrukh Dhondy*. @www.tahelka.com/channels/literary/2001/Oct.12.
2. *Ibid.*
3. *Ibid.*
4. Shoma Chaudhuri, "A Fantasy of Nobility." @www.tehelka.com/channels/literary/2001/Oct.12.
5. Naipaul to Farrukh Dhondy. @www.tehelka.com/channels/literary/2001/Oct.12.
6. *Ibid.*
7. *Ibid.*
8. Maggie Ball. @www.compulsivereader.com/article 1045.html.

20

V.S. NAIPAUL'S *HALF A LIFE*: A WORLD OF CULTURAL NEURASTHENIA SANS THERAPY

NIDHI TIWARI

Om Poornamadah Poornamidam
Poornat Poornamudachayate
Poornasya Poornamadaya Poornamevashishyate
Om Shantih Shantih Shantih.[1]

Brihadarnyak Upanishad unfolds the world of Absolute or Poorna in this famous mantra. The meaning of this mantra is as follows: That Everblissful (*sat-cit-ananda*) 'parabrahma' (God who created the universe) is *poorna* (Absolute) in all respects. This 'jagat' (world) is also 'Poorna' because it is born of Brahma. Even if 'Poorna' is taken out of 'Poorna' what remains is also 'Poorna.' Let there be peace, peace, peace.

This mantra is not merely a part of ritual chanting in some Hindu families in India, in fact, for those who comprehend its spirit it is a valuable guide in understanding and living life. The 'poorna' embodies all parts and that is what India represents—unity in diversity, an ability to accept and assimilate the variegated tapestry of Indian life. Hence, India constitutes different religions, languages, castes, climatic zones and regional variations (in food, dress code, marriage customs, songs and dance).

On the contrary, we find V.S. Naipaul's latest novel is entitled *Half a Life*. The cover jacket of the book carries an interesting review of the novel and emphasizes on "its vision of the half lives quietly lived out at the centre of our restless world."[2] Now, seen from the Indian context which serves as the foundation of the novel, an entirely extreme point of view emerges. If *Brihadarnyak Upanishad* provides glimpses into totality, infinity and bliss which are the wings in the life of Indian men and women, Naipaul's Willie Somerset Chandran represents the limited life of unlimited aspirations. It is sad to note that the picture of life that is presented is a gloomy one. We have three continents to look at—Asia, Europe and Africa. Then, we have the condition of the underprivileged in the Third world countries. But, we are also shown the crumbling of authority, that is, an unstable First World. Nowhere is there any sign of life. Everywhere there is cultural neurasthenia, sans therapy.

A.K. Awasthi aptly remarks:

> The woe is that our culture itself has become so uncultured, artificial, redundant, and stuffed with stagnation and distortion that it is now eating away the vitals of growth and substance.[3]

The novel opens with a young boy's curious question as to why he has a middle name, Somerset. The question leads us to his father's past. We now have a brilliant cocktail of Indian Gandhi and the Western Somerset Maugham. Willie's father (though not given a name) containing the ingredients of pseudo-greatness finds in Gandhi the role model initially. However, life teaches him another lesson. He realizes how he "foolishly gave up English education in response to the Mahatma's call and unfitted myself for life while watching my friends and enemies growing in prosperity and regard."[4]

Naipaul appears critical of Gandhi here. This is half truth. The other half also needs to be represented. A nation attained Independence due to Gandhi and those who sacrificed their lives for their nation never regretted their decision. Willie's father lacks full force to do something important. At this stage it may be too early to comment on Naipaul's intentions. It could be a subtle criticism of Gandhi from a materialistic point of view. But, it could be criticism of mediocre men like Willie's father. Not representing Gandhi at length could be due to the author's assumption that Gandhi's life is well-known.

Willie's father who hails from a respectable Brahmin family comfortably settled in the Maharaja's state, has unknown fears regarding the security of the Maharaja's rule in an India which is struggling for independence. Besides, he had heard his "grandfather tell too often of his flight and his fear of the unknown, only looking inward during those terrible days." His grandfather's anger towards his temple community which "had seen the disaster coming but had done nothing about it" (8) infects him. Though 'India was full of politics' in the Maharaja's state there was no stir of rebellion. But Willie's father felt that 'there was some little imp of rebellion in him.' Somehow he felt that all of them were 'living in a false security.' This made him hate his studies. He felt 'great things were happening outside.' Finding himself being trained for a life of servility, he responds to the Mahatma's call for students to boycott their universities. He makes a bonfire of the books of Hardy, Shelley and Keats and waits for reaction.

Nothing happens. He feels useless and decides to turn his back on his ancestry which he feels consists of 'foolish, foreign ruled starveling priests' his grandfather spoke of, his father's foolish hopes to get a good job for him in the Maharaja's service and the foolish hopes of the college principal to get his daughter married to him. He feels that these are the 'ways of death' (10) and he decides to reject them. The noblest thing that lay within reach for Willie's father was now to marry the lowest person he could find. He already had his classmate in mind. She belonged to the backward caste. A relationship is established. This was the life of sacrifice for Willie's father.

The little sacrifice of Willie's father harped upon by the author once again is half truth. The true nature of sacrifice is not elaborated deliberately. This could be a device similar to Eliot's where levity and seriousness are juxtaposed together to heighten the weakness of the protagonist through contrast. For example, in Eliot's 'The Love Song of J. Alfred Prufrock' the protagonist admits that he is not Prince Hamlet. Now, the true nature of sacrifice is seen in Gandhi's life and this is 'Poorna.' Willie's father's little sacrifice in comparison generates ridicule. This device is repeated at several places.

The girl's uncle is a 'firebrand' that is, an important figure in labourers' union. He notices the relationship. The girl seeks help from her love. He is compelled to hide her and provide for her. Then there are the college exams. Though he performs badly in exams, he passes and even gets a job in Land Tax Department due to his father's influence. At job, he feels disgusted with corruption. Following Gandhi in his own way, he conducts civil disobedience by destroying receipts. Even then he gets promotion due to the Principal who wants to promote his would be son-in-law. Had Willie's father rejected promotion it would have been real Civil Disobedience.

Finally Willie's father tells his father that he cannot marry the girl selected by them for him. After scenes of emotional turmoil he realizes that it would be difficult to live with a backward. He is caught on all fronts—the government, the family and finally the girl's uncle who is ready to take out a procession. To save himself he escapes to the temple and again like the Mahatma, yet unlike the Mahatma's spirit, he takes a vow of silence. Silence or *maun* is once again a very powerful meditative technique to cleanse oneself—see within, exercise control and open oneself to the world beyond words and sound. Here, it is an escape mechanism for Willie's father.

With the girl's uncle taking out a procession, he becomes part of the cause of the backward—again like the Mahatma. Suddenly he becomes famous even as a saint when people offer gifts to him in the temple. This is the time when the famous writer pays a visit to him, is impressed by the serenity around this religious man and writes about him in his novel *The Razor's Edge*. Here Naipaul exposes the inability of comprehending the truth of Indian religion by foreigners and the hypocrisy of pseudosaints who exploit foreigners to attain fame and money. But, once again it is 'half-a-life' only. The true nature of religion is not shows anywhere.

Though Willie's father becomes famous, yet for his family and some others he was 'irredeemably tarnished, a fallen man of caste' and his way 'a mockery of sacred ways.' But there was a blessing to it too. It was assumed that he was married to the girl. However, he found the girl's looks so repulsive that he took a private vow of *Brahmacharya* (sexual abstinence). Once again it was like the Mahatma. But, unlike the Mahatma he failed. As a result, two children were born. Both were named after great people—Willie having Somerset as the middle name, while his sister was named Sarojini after the great Indian poetess.

So, though Willie's father finds himself trapped in circumstances due to his error, yet he begins to see that 'there is some truth in you error' (5). He feels that this was the life he had been dreaming of "the wish to renounce, hide, run away from the mess I had made of my life." Yet, the final outcome is deep melancholy.

At this, juncture, it is fruitful to pause and consider the journey of Naipaul from *A House for Mr Biswas* to *Half a Life.* There seems to be no change. The hero (till here Willie's father) is very much an anti-hero. What Gordon Rohlehr commented on Mr Biswas in 1977 is strangely applicable to Willie's father in 2001. Rohlehr comments:

> It is worth asking what is the social and universal significance of the rebellion of a mediocre ridiculous man. Biswas certainly is this [...]. He is forever trying to arrange his world, ending up more deeply immersed in the Absurd situation.[5]

One cannot help remembering R.K. Narayan's Raju of *The Guide* who encounters a similar fate of religious greatness thrust upon him. Raju develops compassion for others, that is *'karuna'* and so sacrifices his life. This is a step towards *Poorna*—selflessness, where the personal 'I' gets submerged in the Cosmic 'I.' R.K. Narayan has the ability to transform Raju, Naipaul fails to create evolution.

He keeps harping on the stark reality. Critical of pseudo sainthood and the deceit that is widespread in India, he appears to expose the eager western seeker of knowledge, truth and peace to India who is exploited by these charlatans. Here, Naipaul's target is Somerset Maugham. But, where does this exposure (howsoever true it may be) lead to? one is in the world of sickening deadness. If an artist is imitating life as Aristotle stated, should the artist imitate it only 'as it is?' The artist can easily depict it 'as it ought to be' which can serve a therapeutic purpose for the cultural neurasthenia which casts a dark shadow all over the globe.

Sometimes one finds that actors who perform roles different from their personality experience a transformation of being due to the role they are playing. When it can happen to actors, it can also happen to persons living amidst religious environment. Surely, Naipaul can see this possibility which is not exactly idealistic.

But, Naipaul seems determined to take his readers to a life of further descent. Willie, the child of Brahmin father and low-caste mother has a hybrid personality. Life at mission school is both painful and helpful. He is not accepted amongst Brahmins and his teachers and classmates have no regard for his ascetic father. Keen to go abroad on school scholarship, he feels shattered when he finds the missionaries critical of Indian religion. Somehow his father manages a scholarship for him and he reaches England—the country of his dreams. Even here it is hard with meagre scholarship. He writes stories and tries hard to establish himself. As his studies come to a close he finds no place for himself in England and dreads returning to India. He never maintains any contacts with his parents and sister Sarojini. Luckily, he finds Ana who is Portuguese-African and has inherited her grandfather's estate in Africa. She too has a hybrid personality and has suffered though less because of hybrid traits. They fall in love and Willie decides to live in Africa with Ana. There is role-reversal now. Here, Willie is the privileged man—Ana's man. After spending eighteen years in comfort he finds the colonial rule threatened. He decides to leave Ana and goes to Germany to be with his sister Sarojini. The story ends here. One recalls in the end these famous lives from "Four Quartets":

> Dust in the air suspended marks the place where a story ended.[6]

Willie turns out to be totally spineless and selfish. His father had at least wanted to do something and there was a little sacrifice in what he did. But Willie gives up after initial effort in England. Though he had despised his father earlier, yet he finds some similar traits of the father in himself. However, he never does anything for his family or even for himself. Clearly, he is a parasite.

Once again one wonders why this is so? It is a kind of exile. Maybe through Willie's character Naipaul has criticized the caste-system in India. But Naipaul is lost somewhere between outside social milieu and inside social milieu. Being an expatriate, he sees the reality from a distance and fails to comprehend the true reality of India. Assimilation and acceptance are the traits of Indian culture and Willie would have been accepted in the long run had he returned to India. The religious and spiritual side could have been explored more deeply through father-son relationship. But, Sir Vidia's is the outsider's insider's comprehension of Indian life. Several sketches of Indian social life are presented and an effort is made to derive substance out of them. This is the irony of authorship about India.

Of course Willie represents the "anguish of whole countries and people unable to cope"[7] (Edward Said, *Reflections on Exile* 101). Edward Said feels the pulse of the writer as he writes:

> Here was an author who had seen the new politics of half-made societies that seemed doomed to remain half-made.[8] (108)

Though Said accepts Naipaul as "too remarkable and gifted writer to be dismissed," yet he asserts:

> So great has the pressure of western ideas become in Naipaul that any sympathetic feelings he might have had for the things he sees have been obliterated. There is no life in what he writes about—only hard lunacy, despair.[9] (102)

Centuries back Addison represented reform in a subtle manner in his *Coverley Papers* while writing about 'Sir Roger at Home' and 'Sir Roger at Church.' A parallel ideal to corrupt reality was not only shown by Addison but also by Dickens in 'David Copperfield.' In the twenty-first century these writers and their style might be outdated and, even the efforts of stream of consciousness writers to see the same situation and relationship from different consciousness may also appear stale. But, the postmodern writer can experiment differently. Why does Naipaul close his eyes to the other half? *Half a Life* is ironically a phenomenon with Sir Vidia which is exemplified through Willie. It is personal trauma. Sir Vidia becomes the prototype of the commercial drive which is rampant globally. Naipaul is reaping the harvest of India bashing.

At the International Festival of Indian literature on February 18th, 2002, at Neemrana, Sir Vidia had chided Shashi Deshpande for harping on themes like gender and oppression. Even Nayantara Sahgal was interrupted while she was reading a paper with the blasting question as to why she kept drumming up the issue of colonialism. Sir Vidia said "Banality irritates me. Life is too short."[10] (*The Indian Express*, Saturday, February 23rd, 2002, 2). I wonder how sincere his remark was. Can he fail to see the colonized establishing himself (his own case for instance)? What about Sidney Pottier being lauded and awarded with Life Time Achievement Award at the recent Oscar Film Festival in March, 2002? All may not be Sidney Pottier or Sir Vidia, but all are not what Willie becomes in *Half a Life* either. Willie's decision to discard his roots reveals what Sir Vidia fails to see in India, not 'A wounded civilization' only, but a country that is rich in several aspects, with a capacity to heal all wounds—a capacity to see life as not 'Half a Life' but as 'Poorna.' Can you rise out of the banality in which you've trapped yourself, Sir Vidiadhar?

REFERENCES

1. *Brihadarnyak Upanishad,* Chapter V, Brahmin 1, 1 (Gorakhpur: Geeta Press), 18th Edition, 1999.
2. V.S. Naipaul, *Half a Life,* The Cover jacket. London: Picador, 2001.
3. A.K. Awasthi, *Fiction of the Nineties*. 'Bombay Duck: Farrukh Dhondy's Intellectual therapy for cultural neurasthenia.' New Delhi: Prestige Books, 1994, 121.
4. V.S. Naipaul, *Half a Life*. London: Picador, 2001, 2. Subsequent quotes from this book are embodied in this paper.
5. Gordon Rohlehr. *Critical Perspectives on V.S. Naipaul* (ed.) Robert D. Hamner, "Character and Rebellion in *A House for Mr Biswas*" (Washington D.C.: Three Continents Press, 1977) 84.
6. T.S. Eliot, *Four Quartets* (Delhi: Rupa and Co., 1992) 216.
7. Edward Said, *Reflections on Exile*. 'Bitter Dispatches from the third world' (London: Penguin Book, 2001) 101.
8. *Ibid.*, 108.
9. *Ibid.*, 102.
10. *The Indian Express*, 'Litfest to slugfest: A couple of Mutinies at a show for Mr Naipaul.' New Delhi, Saturday, February 23, 2002, 2.

21

Naipaul as a Short Story Writer

KAMAL MEHTA

Naipaul's significance as a writer rests on the literary merits and the craftsmanship of his works. He addresses the prominent issues faced by the world in general and the Third World countries in particular. The issues that he picks up for fictional exploration and construction pertain to the prevailing confusion regarding the identity of the communities and nations, the mis/direction of different movements for various purposes in these countries, the politics together with all its anarchical intrigues and incompetence, the human life in general, the complex national and international conflicts and maneuverings, the problems faced by the post-modern society like rootlessness, disillusionment and prevalent racial discrimination.

As a writer, Naipaul is in a unique position in the sense that he is the product of three different cultures—the native West Indian culture in which he grew and whose memories are alive in him, the English culture that shaped his adulthood through the education and his exposure to English social value system and of course the Indian culture that forms the part of his psyche and his mental make-up. Interestingly, he disowns all of them and therefore is able to assess all the three with objectivity. His exposure to multi-cultural societies has equipped him with a perception and sensibility that a writer who is the product of just one culture cannot have. His novels, non-fictional writings and short stories bear witness to it.

However, Naipaul, the short story writer, has been overshadowed by Naipaul the novelist and non-fictional writer.

He has published three collections of short stories are published: *Miguel Street* (1959), *A Flag on the Island* (1967) and *In a Free State* (1973) along with some other stories in different magazines also. Naipaul's stories present a vision of life, as in his novels, of the rootless individuals. The consciousness of rootlessness leaves a very damaging impact on their minds, making them pitiable, for often their behaviour verges on absurdity. They suffer from inferiority complex.

Naipaul's collections of short stories differ from one another in ways more than one. In *Miguel Street,* Naipaul's craftsmanship has not reached the level of maturity which one comes across in the later works, and, in particular, the last one. Further, the collections refer to different periods. *Miguel Street* refers to the newly independent Trinidad. It refers to the newly independent rural Trinidad of the late 50s. It lacked in primary facilities. People were still given to old way of life. *A Flag on the Island* does not refer to one period and place only. It refers to the late 60s also when the Indian communities were facing the danger of losing its identity due to Presbyterianism and its impact on the younger generations. The writer shows gradual urbanization of the island. *In a Free State* refers to the 70s and it does not refer to the life on the island but outside it.

The stories in *Miguel Street* are simple and homogeneous in nature. All the characters together form a single community though they belong to various ethnic, racial and colour groups. They share among themselves the aspirations, disappointments and the struggle with their fate. They do not have hostility to others and are accommodating and tolerant. Their innocence earns our sympathy.

Miguel street metaphorically stands for Trinidad—the multi-racial and the multi-cultural society composed of the Negroes, Asians, Chinese, English and Spanish, all of whom are expatriates. Their beliefs, habits and attitudes characterize the impact of colonialism on them. Political independence has not yet led them to intellectual and cultural independence. They have no pride either in themselves or anything that is native. Anything foreign, on the contrary, attracts them. The people in such a picaroon society have potentialities but in the absence of proper atmosphere and opportunities, they fail and get frustrated. They have no chance to show their talents and hence they try to be heroes by following the outdated ideas. For example, by beating wives, they think that they have been proving their manhood. The society that is portrayed in it is discussed and analyzed by the writer in his *The Middle Passage.*

In *The Middle Passage,* he comments on the reasons responsible for the continued insignificance of the islands in the world and reveals their typical picaroon qualities. Naipaul finds the people of these islands divided among themselves on ethnic, racial and cultural lines. Further, they suffer from economic insecurity. They also lack in vision and confidence. He states that the people live in a borrowed culture and they do not know who they are and where they stand. He found these societies to be "unimportant, uncreative, cynical" (Naipaul: 1962: 43). He also observes that "Power was recognized, but dignity was allowed to no one. Every person of eminence was held to be crooked and contemptible" (Naipaul: 1962: 43). In confessional tone, he reveals:

> Though we knew that something was wrong with our society, we made no attempt to assess it [...]. Our own past was buried and no one cared to dig it up. This gave us a strange time-sense. (Naipaul: 1962: 45)

He also states that since nothing bound the people together excepting their common residence, if at all there was any protest, it was individual, isolated and unheeded. Also, the threat of failure and the need to escape were the promptings of the society among others.

Naipaul does not ridicule and satirize this society because he does not employ the European standards to assess it. Employing a child narrator, he avoids ridiculing it and yet reveals all its significant aspects. A.C. Derrick has rightly pointed out that by making the narrator side with none, Naipaul makes his "representation of the people vital and immediate and encourages in the reader a sympathetic involvement in the lives of the characters." (34)

Miguel street is filled with people like bad-John, Popo, B. Wordsworth, Morgan, Elias, Eddoes, Bhakcu among others.

They are in fact various versions of Gopi, a famous character from the author's father's *Gurudeva and Other Indian Tales.* They are the potential artists but have failed due to lack of any opportunity. As a result, they are frustrated with their society and they live in their fantasy world. Elias wanted to be a doctor but he becomes a dust-cart driver. B. Wordsworth's poetry cannot breathe in the Miguel street as this street may tolerate people but cannot either support or rescue them. There is a conflict between ambition and opportunity and therefore "talent is squandered in eccentricity, romance lies only in escape" (White 46). The society's materialistic nature, its not having any history and the colonial impact have given it a special character of 'ebullience,' 'irresponsibility' and 'tolerance,' "which is more than tolerance: an indifference to virtue as well as to vices" (Naipaul: 1962: 58).

Naipaul's choice of a child narrator who is also from the same street is meaningful, for the child can remain detached, avoid passing judgments and making distortions and can just wonder at the unusual happenings without getting involved in good or bad, right or wrong and moral and immoral things of the matter. He just presents faithfully and innocently whatever he observes. Many characters in the street like bad-John, Popo, B. Wordsworth, Morgan, Elias, Eddoes, Bhakcu among others are eccentric. This eccentricity is an assumed quality as it compensates for the vacuum created in their lives due to rootlessness and the gradual disintegration of their self.

Naipaul employs the indigenous Trinidadian folk literary form of calypso in his short stories. In fact, the stories in *Miguel Street* are sort of calypsos in prose, dealing with the local social life in Trinidad. Poverty, immigration, emigration, frustration, multi-racial and multi-cultural milieu, uncreative atmosphere, colonial mentality and lack of opportunities are among the issues picked up by the author for exploration. These are all typical calypsonian leit-motifs. Like many real calypsos, these stories are based on anecdotes. Hence within the stories, Naipaul puts relevant calypsos. For example, he puts a calypso on the husband-wife relationship:

> Every now and then just knock them down.
> Every now and then just throw them down.

Black up their eyes and bruise up their knee.
And then they love you eternally. (87)

They also share many characteristics of a cartoon. They are brief, suggestive and humorous. In these verbal cartoons, every stroke *i.e.* remark of the author is replete with meaning and suggestivity. He does not comment on the scene, rather allows the scene to speak for itself. Moreover, the portraits provide information and entertainment both. Like a cartoonist, Naipaul selects the arresting features of his subject to reveals them, and thus achieves the effect which neither an editorial nor a column can offer. A cartoon tends to be ununderstood, half understood or misunderstood, depending on the awareness of the matter on the part of the reader. It is never independent of the social reality in which it is deeply rooted. It has referential value and its meaning emerges from its context. For better understanding of the stories in *Miguel Street,* the knowledge of the background is necessary. Only then one would know that these stories are not farces. The only difference between a cartoon and a story in *Miguel Street* is that while a cartoon is visual, the story is a narrative.

The stories in *Miguel Street* are set in the same temporal and spatial as well as emotional and cultural ambience. Naturally, the issues and problems faced by the characters are common. These people are not focused as individuals but as the members of the society *i.e.* the street. In other words, the author has focused on the nature and the state of the society in it. Therefore, in the course of the narrative, the Miguel street emerges as the real protagonist which plays a central role in the lives of its residents. It is peopled by those who have learned to live with the limitations around them.

The stories in *Miguel Street* are considerably influenced by the author's father Seepersad Naipaul, and specifically by his stories published later on as *Gurudeva and Other Indian Tales* (1943), that consists of seven stories giving a direct and realistic picture of the life of the Indian community in Trinidad.

Miguel Street contains seventeen stories of seventeen persons who, though belonging to different ethnic, racial and colour groups, have a common fate. They share among themselves the same social and psychological problems and are the victims of the same complex, implanted into their thoughts by the colonizers. For example, they still suffer from an inferiority complex. Anything native is necessarily inferior and all the foreign things are superior. They have not yet known themselves and hence are not aware of their strength. Also, they are not proud of themselves, rather they have a sort of contempt for themselves and their land. Their virtues are not so much visible to them as are their weaknesses. Further, they are themselves vocal about their shortcomings. The narrator feels that a stranger is most likely to misunderstand the street as a slum. It is a very tolerant society that welcomes the people's coming and going out of it freely. Thus, emigration and immigration are the constant experiences. The people feel that they are victims of the society and its conventions. They feel that their talents have no chance to bloom and their potentialities are wasted. In reaction, they turn victimizers themselves and desire to take revenge on the society because they feel that they do not belong to the land. Their society tolerates everything but fails to rescue and satisfy the aspirations of the dwellers.

Miguel street is primarily a poor section of an urban society where the tension exists between ambition and opportunity therefore "talent is squandered in eccentricity, romance lies only in escape" (White 49). Revealing the nature of such a society, the author observes in *The Middle Passage*:

> I knew Trinidad to be unimportant, uncreative, cynical. The only professions were those of law and medicine, because there was no need for any others; the most successful people were commission agents, bank managers and members of the distributive trades. Power was recognized, but dignity was allowed to no one. Every person of eminence was held to be crooked and contemptible. We lived in a society which denied itself heroes. (Naipaul: 1962: 43)

He further observes that the society offered no rewards to merits and demanded no skills and therefore cricket was the only activity and a cricketer was the only hero-figure. The society made no attempt to assess itself, though it is aware of the things wrong with itself. This society has buried its past and makes no attempt to dig it up. Such a tendency is responsible for the strange 'time-sense,' due to which "The England of 1914 was the England of yesterday; the Trinidad of 1914 belonged to the dark ages" (Naipaul: 1962: 45).

Naipaul further mentions that in Trinidad everyone was an individual, and fought for his place in the community. "Nothing bound us together except this common residence [...]. So protests could only be individual, isolated, unheeded" (Naipaul: 1962: 45). The individual was always under the fear of failure and was always eager to escape from the place. The writer also adds that the society's materialist immigrant nature, its not having any history and the colonial impact have combined to give it a special character of 'ebullience' and 'irresponsibility.' It possesses a sense of 'tolerance,' "which is more than tolerance: an indifference to virtue as well as to vices" (Naipaul: 1962: 58).

The author states that the 16th century Spanish picaroon world never allowed dignity to anyone and therefore everyone had to impose himself. Naturally, violence and brutality were common and acceptable. A picaroon hero had to steal or to starve. Hence, such a 'a sharp character' like picaroon the society admires.

Naipaul does not portray the society satirically. He neither exaggerates its shortcomings, nor does he make caricatures of his characters. In an interview, he observed that the social comedies he wrote about could be fully appreciated only by someone, who knew the region he wrote about. He further stated that without the knowledge it was easy for his work to be dismissed as farces and his characters as caricatures.

Several characters in *Miguel Street* appear to be eccentric. However, that is an assumed quality, to compensate for the vacuum created by rootlessness, non-belongingness and gradual disintegration of their self. Of course that does not mean that there is no humour in them. Victor Ramraj observes:

> There are many light-hearted characters in *Miguel Street,* but the laughter in most of the sketches is the tolerant, sympathetic laughter of one, aware of joys and sorrows of the inhabitants of the Miguel Street slum during and immediately after the Second World War. (271)

Naipaul presents a comprehensive picture of the society. His characters include the boasters, pimps, drunkards, pseudo-scientists, cheats, mimics. They are portrayed with a pinch of humour. For example, Bogart only pretends to be a tailor, but in reality, he gambles and runs brothels. Hat is obsessed with cricket and boasts that he has had tea with many cricketers. Moreover, when he takes the children of the street to watch a match, he brags to a spectator that all the children were his. Man-man hood-winks others by assuming madness. He is found writing big letters on road. He also has a dog that is made to sully the clothes of the people by its droppings. Naturally, now people would not use them and therefore give them to Man-man who would wash them and sell them off. Naipaul does not resort to obscenity and ambiguous dialogues or double entendre. Rather, he generates innocent humour by comic situations and humorous dialogues among them.

In addition to the comic features there is "an essential pathetic note beneath the humour" (Ramraj 271). For example, Morgan can make excellent fireworks but none ever acknowledges it. One night, ironically, due to an accident it fires off, burning the entire house. Even Morgan never expected it. Ironically, he is homeless when his talents are proved. Thus, it arouses laughter and pity.

Majority of the characters of *Miguel Street* live in a fantasy world. Morgan thinks that on a day, the King of England and the King of America will place their orders for the fireworks with himself. Man-man feels that he is Jesus Christ and so he decides to crucifix himself and invites people to stone him. However, when the first stone hits him, he shouts:

> What the hell is this? [...] Look, get me down from this thing quick, let me down quick, I go settle with son of bitch who pelt a stone at me. (44)

B. Wordsworth imagines himself to be the spiritual brother of W. Wordsworth, because he can watch small flowers, like the morning glory. He tells the narrator, "Now let us lie on the grass and look up at the sky and I want you to think how far those stars are from us" (48). Naipaul later on brings a policeman to ask him what he is doing there. Mr Wordsworth replies that he has been asking the same question to himself for last 40 years! Both converse in different contexts that generates humour.

Naipaul's humour in the stories emerges not from the plots but from the matter itself. He makes use of what Linda Hutcheon calls typical post-modern paradoxical form of parody. "Parody both asserts and undercuts that which it contests" (7). She further states that parody "uses and abuses texts and convention of the tradition" (9). For example, he parodies the system of legislature, executive, judiciary, having a constitution to follow and then its implementation and the effect and impact of it on the people who are to abide by it.

In "The Pyrotechnicist," he gives a picture of a family that has its own written constitution—"Crime and Punishment"—which prescribes a code of conduct for the children and punishment in case they violate it. Naipaul humourously narrates the thing and raises the question of the state of constitutions in such countries. Secondly, he seems to be examining the fact whether the constitutions are effective at all, particularly, when the citizens are like these children, either adamant or insincere? He perhaps wants to convey that in the absence of true regards such a constitution solves no problem.

The things are legislated in this way:

For fighting:	(1)	at home	Five strokes
	(2)	in the street	Seven strokes
	(3)	at school	Eight strokes

(Naipaul: 1959: 67)

Then, Naipaul portrays the court scene. The father, every week, calls for a family court in which he plays the role of a judge and the culprits of the week are presented before him for punishment and nothing is brought to this court for justice.

The narrator portrays the proceedings in this way:

> [...] 'stand!'
> We all stood up, and Morgan appeared smiling all around.
> I asked Hat, "Why he smiling so?"
> Hat said, "That is how the magistrates and them do when they come in court."

> Morgan's eldest son shouted, "Andrew Morgan!"
>
> Andrew Morgan came and stood before his father.
>
> The eldest boy read very loudly, "Andrew Morgan, you are charged with [...]."
>
> Morgan, scribbling on a sheet of paper, looked up. "Have you anything to say?" (Naipaul: 1959: 68)

Morgan's sons take the things very jokingly. Though they keep a copy of the constitution in their pockets, they violate it without any sense of guilt, as if it is not meant for following.

These stories turn out to be social comedies, where the characters portrayed are not individuals. Therefore, their frailties are not individual frailties but social weaknesses, commonly shared by its members. The individuals represent different aspects of the society. Together they make the street complete and so the same characters occur in various stories.

The stories in the second collection—*A Flag on the Island* are heterogeneous in the thematic occupations, characterization, and narrative techniques among others. All these stories talk of different times and places. Hence the characters do not form a society-'street' but they remain individuals fighting their battles themselves. We find them struggling for their rights and identity. They are not free from the vices of the contemporary world either. Selfishness, superstition, intolerance, corruption, hypocrisy, and exploitation among other things are found in these persons. Hence, the common phenomenon in it is confrontation. The innocence of the earlier book is totally absent among them. Even the people are no more simple but complex individuals. The writer does not concern himself with the externally observable and social realities of life but with the inner, psychological realities of the minds. In the first book, the narrator is same throughout and his attitude to the street remains the same, whereas in this book, there is no common narrator. Rather the narrator changes from story to story. The stories—'The Enemy,' 'The Raffle' and 'The Perfect Tenants' have autobiographical significance, where the author mingles his own experiences with his fictional creations.

In 'My Aunt Gold Teeth' he deals with the superstitious nature of his society through the character of Gold Teeth, a childless lady from an orthodox Hindu family who indulges in superstitious Christian practices as well. Coincidently, her husband falls ill and everyone considers her following of Christianity to be responsible for the illness. But Pundit Ganesh does not mind her doing so and tells her that what is important is prayer and not the way it is performed. Poor lady continues to practice both the faiths. And suddenly one day her husband dies.

Naipaul narrates this pathetic story of orthodoxy and superstition in mock-heroic style. He mocks at the aunt as well as the society by using heavy words for petty things. The narrator states that his aunt ate little and prayed much, and became an 'addict' of Christianity. Her religious 'schizophrenia' grew. She felt then that her 'religious' transgression was responsible her husband's illness. She confesses her 'trafficking with Christianity.' The narrator observes that "she carried herself into the churchyard [...] feeling like an explorer in a land of cannibals" (19).

The author exposes the society for which religion remains confined to rituals only and the values upheld by it remain neglected. People are after convenience. If things run smoothly, there is no problem but if they go wrong, people blame the habit, person or institution.

The story, "Greenie and Yellow" is a metaphorical story told in the fashion of a fable. It is set in England. Naipaul attempts to narrativize slavery, frustration, hopelessness and the impossibility of creative work in the world. It is a story of three birds—Bluey, Yellow and Greenie. Bluey is a cage bird, all the time cheerful and zestful playing with its toys. Then another bird, Greenie is brought by the mistress. Greenie is a bully and makes lot of noise all the time since it has enjoyed freedom so far. It baits Bluey often and puzzles it. Bluey is incapable of resistance, so it remains resigned in the cage. Now the mistress brings another bird, Yellow, as a mate for Greenie but Yellow dislodges him. Yellow pushes him now and then, does not let him sleep also, but Greenie does not take interest in her. Yellow upsets him so much that he falls ill and then dies. Yellow also feels frustrated. Then Yellow is put with Bluey who takes interest in her but then Yellow shows no interest in him. Some days later, Yellow also dies.

Bluey is again all alone but then he is as fresh as he used to be in past. Naipaul in this manner reveals how creativity is misdirected in the world. The cage life has made Bluey incapable of living outside in free atmosphere. The cage metaphorically stands for the world devoid of opportunities for creativity. When some one digs out the skeletons of Greenie and Yellow, it is impossible to tell which skull belongs to whom, suggesting that the two birds are not different from each other.

"The Enemy" is an autobiographical account of the author's childhood. The daily quarrels of the parents have left the child unattended. He also receives a lot of thrashing everyday. All his efforts to draw his mother close to him fail. But once he gets wounded and falls ill, his mother is all for him. He innocently prays to the God to give him two hundred hands. He further wishes that all his hands get wounded, for then his mother would take 200 times more interest in him.

In "The Raffle," Naipaul autobiographically presents the memories of his school days. Even the name of the narrator is Vidiadhar Naipaul. Satirizing the teacher, he states:

> They don't pay primary school teachers a lot in Trinidad, but they allow them to beat their pupils as much as they want [...]. Mr Hind never beat me. He never made me clean the blackboard. He never made me shine his shoes with the duster. (Naipaul: 1962: 19-20)

"The Christian Story" is a satire on the hypocrisy and snobbish attitude of the people. Randolph, a converted Presbyterian of Indian origin and a teacher by profession, ruminates over his past. He is on the verge of retirement and is facing an enquiry on the corruption charges against himself. He ridicules his Indian counterparts, Hindu religion and all that belongs to the Hindus. Naipaul turns the satire on the narrator himself. Randolph considers Hinduism unfit for the modern world as it means 'animistic rites,' 'idolatry' and 'cowdung.' He hates rituals but himself goes to Church on all Sundays. He despises 'dhotis' of Hindus as they reveal the legs and make the person seem ridiculous. At the same time, he praises the Christian girls who wear short-frocks, leaving their legs totally bare. He praises the missionaries who work among the backward people but he himself does not sympathize with the backwards. Rather he despises them. While commenting on the Hindu wives, he despises them saying that he would marry an intelligent, educated and cultured lady. However, the readers know that his wife is neither intelligent nor cultured. She does not mind her husband's indulgence in financial irregularities with the school funds. Moreover, when an inspection committee arrives to investigate into the matter, she sets the very building on fire to hide the poor construction and thus destroys the evidence of financial corruption. Ironically, Randolph describes progress as an attitude of mind rather than an outward show and adds, "it was this that my religion gave me" (Naipaul: 1967: 27). The readers have already come to know about his attitude of mind. Further, whenever he ridicules the Hindus, he ridicules only the outward qualities and whatever he takes pride in regard to Christianity it is also outward.

In *In a Free State,* Naipaul's art reaches its maturity and attains a focused sharpness in his work. The book contains three stories—"One Out of Many," "Tell Me Who to Kill" and "In a Free State"—dealing with the same theme—freedom. Ironically, the protagonists of these stories are 'the casualties of freedom.' It projects individuals who are expatriates, staying away in an alien world. Ian Hamilton rightly states that the book offers a much grandeur, much more total vision of placelessness than offered before. The individuals are all alienated figures. They belong to different nations—India, Africa, Sweden, Germany, China and America. They always find the atmosphere around them to be hostile. Hence they are constantly on a move. Though the colonial period is over and the states are free, yet the psychological and cultural independence *i.e.* freedom has not come. "Santosh's loss of an ideal self, Dayo's brother's loss of a complete love and Bobby's sense of a loss of a supporting environment, all as a consequence of a growth in knowledge through disillusioning interaction with reality, reflect analogously the lonely tramp at odds with his environment deeply conscious of his vulnerability" (Kamra 148).

'One Out of Many' revolves around Santosh, an Indian immigrant in America who employs different tactics to get citizenship. He was a servant in Bombay and was comparatively happy also. He got a chance to migrate to America, his dreamland. He is however always under the tension of being deported. He had thought that in America he would enjoy greater freedom but it was not so. What he gains there is confusion and humiliation. He marries a black woman to seek citizenship. He realizes that his life had no dignity. He realizes with despair: "All that freedom has brought me is the knowledge that I have a face and have a body, that I must feed this body and clothe this body for a certain number of years. Then it would be over" (58).

The protagonist of "Tell Me Who to Kill," Dayo's brother also passes through the same sense of despair and loss. He is almost mad due to psychological set backs and is totally directionless. He feels that he is like a ship without rudder. He goes to attend his brother's marriage and in fact he has been relieved from the mental hospital for that day only. It is a pathetic story of a rural simple man who wants his brother to go to England and study for the better career and life. What he gets is painful disillusionment. The protagonist realizes that only he is responsible for his own fate. Nevertheless, he does not know the reason of it.

The third story is set in an English-speaking out-post in the midst of the African wilderness. This part of the world is a conglomeration of several tribes put together as a nation in making, with the Americans helping them to grow. The 'state' lacks in the basis for the unity among the tribes. The natives *i.e.* the Africans in the story feel that they have been making progress but the author reveals how they are mere products of the white civilization and are unable to think and act independently. They are just mimic men. It centres around two English characters Bobby, a civil servant and Linda, a wife of another English officer. They are together for a seminar on community development. Ironically, only a few Africans are participating in this seminar on their community development. The narrator states, "the Africans were well dressed and dignified, with little to say" (103). Both the persons observe the Africans on their journey back to the capital and discover that the political freedom has brought the tribal rivalry on the surface with greater intensity. The people have greater loyalty to their respective tribes than the state. Naipaul reveals a wide gap existing between the rural and the urban Africans. The rural folk is least concerned whether they are free or not. They are lost in their own traditional chores. On the other hand, the urban Africans are cut off from their roots. They imitate the American and the European life-styles. Naipaul reveals the fate of newly independent nations who do not know the significance of a 'Free state.' The forest Africans are having integrity and identity but they are illiterate, ignorant and poor. They, thus, cannot take up the responsibility of providing a direction to their state. The city Africans are rootless and sorts of parasites, concerned with their material prosperity and least dedicated to the cause of their state. All over, there are illusions. The state passes into chaos as the President and the King, belonging to separate tribes, pull it into opposite directions, making the situation worse. The Africans feel that the turmoil is because of the English people. So they attack the Whites. Bobby senses the African attitudes and tries to be African by adopting the external objects representing Africa. However, it does not save him from violence.

Thus, *In a Free State* reveals the sad fate of the post-colonial societies which attained political freedom without being socially, psychologically and culturally free. Freedom has no meaning when the individual is cut off from his communities. The writer states that it is dangerous to be free in an alien land, as it is likely to lead to perversion in the absence of any check on oneself.

All the three collections unfold the impact of colonialism on the minds of the people and on the society as well. *Miguel Street* reveals the fact of the hampering of the physical, intellectual, emotional and social lives of the people. In the second collection, he makes his observation more general in the sense that he does not confine his stories to the Trinidadians and to the slum dwellers alone but expands the scope and thus tries to convey the same phenomenon symbolically. The author reveals in his third collection what happens to the citizens from such a country when they are out of their ancestral lands and enjoy complete independence. The third collection is a more general exploration of the same phenomenon with reference to people who are displaced, irrespective of their nationality. It reconstructs the disharmony between the people and the places they live upon in fictional terms.

WORKS CITED

Derrick, A.C. "Naipaul's Technique as a Novelist." *Journal of Commonwealth Literature,* VIII, July, 1969.

Hutcheon, Linda. *The Canadian Post-modern: A Study of Contemporary English Canadian Fiction.* Toronto: OUP, 1988.

Kamra, Shashi. *The Novels of V.S. Naipaul.* New Delhi: Sterling, 1990.

King, Bruce. *V.S. Naipaul.* Hong Kong: Macmillan, 1993.

Naipaul, V.S. *Miguel Street.* London: Penguin, 1959.

____. *The Middle Passage.* London: Penguin, 1962.

____. *A Flag on the Island.* London: Penguin, 1967.

____. *In A Free State.* London: Penguin, 1971.

Victor, Ramraj. "Diminishing Satire: A Study of V.S. Naipaul and Mordecai Richler." *Awakened Conscience* (ed.) Narasimhaiah, C.D. New Delhi: Sterling, 1978.

White, Landeg. *V.S. Naipaul: A Critical Introduction.* London: Macmillan, 1975.

22

A Critical Examination of the Sense of Detachment in the Selected Fictions and Short Fictions of Naipaul

S. KANAKARAJ

> I [Naipaul] find I have, without effort, achieved the Buddhist ideal of non-attachment. I am never disturbed by national or international issues. I do not sign petitions. I do not vote. I do not match. And I never cease to feel that this lack of interest is all wrong.[1]

Naipaul gets identified as one of the outstanding Commonwealth writers in English. He gets bracketed with the great African genius-artists, Claude McKay and Chinua Achebe, by his range of vision, language mastery and imaginative depiction of characters and situations. But he differs from the other intellectuals by marking a clear line of demarcation between personalism and impersonalism. In other words, never does Naipaul allow subjectivism to obtrude on his objective reportage of his feeling, thoughts, and experiences. In this respect he invites rich comparison with the American woman writer, Eudora Welty.

Naipaul is always able to operate between the two worlds—personal world and the world he describes and defines. It is in this context one examines his sense of detachment. He recognizes in Indian life elements of himself, a detachment, a denial of concern that matches his own existence in London. But he remains an outsider. Landeg White offers a pertinent remark, which is to the point in the present context:

> A Brahmin-cum-Englishman in Trinidad, a European in India, an Indian in London: one wonders whether such

> detachment, such seizing of the opportunities for retreat, is less a source of regret to him than a precondition of his writing life.[2]

In this respect, the travel books, *The Middle Passage* and *An Area of Darkness* project the novelist's sense of detachment. Both the works share Naipaul's eye for character and revelling incident, an alert style and a marvellous sensitivity to landscape.

The Middle Passage retains something of a diary's shapelessness. There is the balancing of the beginning of West Indians pouring into London against the ending with Americans pouring into the Caribbean. But there is little sign of organization, ideas and topics recurring spontaneously as from day-to-day. *The Middle Passage* is the brusque response of a man who denies that he has anything to do with what has irritated him.

And *An Area of Darkness* concerns itself with experiences in India. It is a polished and a calculated work. It channels its strongest criticisms through quotations from Gandhi. There is the thoroughness with which it balances specific encounters against general commentary, and glimpses from a train against residence in Kashmir.

The important point that is made here is the Indianness in Naipaul against the India that he is rejecting. The consequence is that he always remains an outsider and it is because he prefers detaching himself from the people that he mixed with and the places where he lived, whether in India, London, or Trinidad. Landeg White makes a pointed observation, which is worth quoting here:

> There is detachment [...] but it draws on different resources. The detachment of *The Middle Passage* takes the form of resistance to any circumstance which threatens Naipaul's composure. The author [Naipaul] is at war with his subject, and the irony diminishes and is ultimately self-destructive. But the irony of *An Area of Darkness* is a kind of perspective. It allows for self-discovery, for a constant revelation of new dimensions. It returns constantly to that personal crisis which is at the heart of

> the experiences recorded. *It depends on the fact of distancing in place and time.*[3] (My Emphasis)

In these two books, *The Middle Passage* and *An Area of Darkness*, Naipaul remains insulated, isolated and detached. He reports on India where he has lived but only by distancing himself. Similarly whether it is London or Trinidad that he reports there is the plus point of objective reportage, but the sense of detachment surfaces. In fact, he has the unique knack of operating between two worlds one that his is first environment and the other is the Bellowean second environment that he creates. His admission about his statements concerning India are worth recording here:

> And in India I was to see that so many of the things which the newer and now perhaps truer side of my nature kicked against—the smugness, as it seemed to me, the imperviousness to criticism, the refusal to see, the double-talk and double-think—had an answer in that side of myself which I had thought buried and which India revived as a faint memory, *I [Naipaul] understood better than I admitted.*[4] (My Emphasis)

On the whole Naipaul is a shaping rather than an inventive imagination. He does consciously use the novel to define his position in the word, to give back the past, to impose order on his history. The product remains fiction, but the discipline is not fundamentally opposed to that involved in writing.

For Naipaul the problem of form becomes the problem of establishing the right perspective. Only by placing himself as author accurately in relation to his material, but, of course, with a sense of detachment does he convince the reader that his vision is complete. And in Naipaul, as a writer of commitment, there is the quality of self-consciousness, a nagging awareness. Naipaul makes a pertinent remark in this regard:

> There's something absurd about the fictional form: it's an artificial activity, made-up of people taking part in invented actions. The first thing for the writer is to understand why he's setting all these people in motion. Which leads to the second problem: I [Naipaul] didn't know who I was.[5]

There is that sense of detachment when he traces his childhood. In fact when he is writing about childhood feelings of injustice he writes with a cynical lightness with a direct denial of the emotions involved. In this respect he distances himself from his narration. Landeg White makes a pointed observation, in this context, which is worth quoting here:

> We are left with a sense that something is being evaded, a feeling that all these details have for the author [Naipaul] a much deeper significance than is brought out by the story itself. Yet it is interesting to be able to read it now, not least because it illustrates the enormous advance in Naipaul's art.[6]

Two passages, one from *A House for Mr Biswas,* and the second from the short fiction, "Enemy," once read in conjunction with other argues to the points adduced thus far. The first passage runs thus:

> Mr Biswas opened the box and showed Anand the sharpened crayons. "Take them. They are yours. You can do what you like with them."
>
> Anand shook his head.
>
> "You don't want them?"
>
> Tarzan, between Anand's legs, held up his head to be stroked, closing his eyes in anticipation.
>
> "What do you want then?"
>
> Anand shook his head. Tarzan shook his.
>
> "Why did you stay then?"
>
> Anand looked exasperated.
>
> "Why?"
>
> "Because—" The word came out thin, explosive, charged with anger, at himself and his father.
>
> "Because they were going to leave you alone."
>
> For the rest of the day they hardly spoke.[7]

Compared to this, the version from "The Enemy" is tightly buttoned-up and stilted in its cynicism, and it runs thus:

> My mother decided to leave my father, and she wanted to take me to her mother.
>
> I refused to go.

> My father was ill, and in bed. Besides, he had promised that if I stayed with him I was to have a whole box of crayons.
>
> I chose the crayons and my father.[8]

With virgin imagination, and immense writing capacities, and rich language skills, and verbal brilliance Naipaul reminisces. But he does present feelings, thoughts and experiences with a sense of detachment. A significant and relevant passage from *A House for Mr Biswas* makes the point clear:

> Occasionally, a nerve of memory is touched—a puddle reflecting the blue sky after rain, a pack of thumbed cards, the fumbling with a shoe-lace, the smell of a new car, the sound of a stiff wind through trees, the smells and colours of a toyshop, the taste of milk and prunes—and a fragrant of forgotten experience would be dislodged, isolated, puzzling [...]. So later, and very slowly, in securer times of different stresses, when the memories had lost the power to hurt, with pain or joy, they would fall into place and give back the past.[9]

On this textual passage Landeg White argues pertinently thus:

> The subject is the children's memories of everything that has gone before, and one reason why the passage is so very moving is that the reader can identify all the images and relate them to their context [...]. Anand is, of course, the author—not Anand as he appears in the book but Anand as he has since become, Anand who has grown up into V.S. Naipaul, and whose memories, at first puzzling and disturbing, have through time and distance lost the power to hurt and—as he writes—are falling into place and giving back the past.[10]

Incidentally, one of the most remarkable features of *A House for Mr Biswas* is its solidity and comprehensiveness. There is so much of the personalism of Naipaul. But by distancing himself and by detaching himself from all that is narrated, Naipaul conveys the impression of decades through objective reportage.

There are references to the global confrontations, and the coming of motor cars, and cinemas. He notes the effects of economic transformation. Mr Biswas returns as a reporter to his birth place. He witnesses the change in the character of Tulsi. Mrs Tulsi, the supreme monarch is changed into Mrs Tulsi the cantankerous invalid. She regrets that the old ways have become old fashioned pretty soon. Mr Biswas chronicles the stages in the loss of India, the sift from country to town, from Hindi to English, from a preoccupation with Fate to a preoccupation with ambition. Thus, it is not the life of a man but the history of a culture.

Though the special quality of Naipaul is his unique ability to distance time and place and take recourse to a sense of detachment, his talent is not reductive and excluding. On the other hand he remains throughout his writing career sensitive to the meaning of history and landscape. It is in this respect one appreciates Naipaul's ability to introduce a comprehensive setting for a comprehensive history. A magnificent description in *A House for Mr Biswas* argues to the point:

> Towards the middle of the morning the sky lightened and lifted, the rain thinned to a drizzle, then stopped altogether. The clouds rolled back, the sky was suddenly blinding blue and there were shadows on the water [...]. Roads and roofs dried, steaming areas of dryness spreading out swiftly, like ink on a blotter. And presumably roads and yards were dry, except for the depressions where water had collected. Heat nibbled at their edges, until even the depressions failed to reflect the blue sky. And the world was dry again, except for the mud in the shelter of trees.[11]

And in its context, the descriptions of the drying sunny morning carries implications of the restoration of sanity and calm after the disorder and collapse of the night before.

And *A House for Mr Biswas* and *The Mimic Men* are the acknowledged masterpieces of Naipaul, the Commonwealth writer. Apart from his sense of detachment there is range of characters of Dickensian memorability. There is the technical accomplishment and elegance of style. But the point that ought to be stressed here is that there is the achievement of loving detail in all that he narrates. But the greater achievement lies in his artistic capacity to strike the celebration of escape.

Landeg White makes a pointed observation, in this context, which is worth quoting here:

> *It is his recognition that he is writing about societies to which he cannot belong that govern his approach to the problem facing himself, as author or narrator, accurately and honestly in relation to his material. It is his deepening understanding of his own displacement that makes possible the broadening of scope.* From frivolity to despair, from homelessness as the affliction of East Indians in Trinidad to homelessness as a universal condition—the gap is measured by his own gradual emergence from the security of colonialism.[12] [My Emphasis]

It ought to be stressed that Naipaul, the Commonwealth writer could fit into any existing society, whether a longing for other places, other circumstances, is not his strongest urge. But this urge is purely and comprehensively qualified by his sense of detachment. A passage from *An Area of Darkness* testifies to the fact that what one sees is just the tip of the ice berg, and the remaining part is deliberately concealed for he wishes to sound detached in his narration:

> An oblong of stiff new cloth lay before me, and I had the knowledge that of only out of this I could cut a smaller oblong of specific measurements, a specific section of this cloth, then the cloth would begin to unravel of itself, and the unravelling would spread from the cloth to the table to the house to all matter, *until the whole trick was undone.* Those were the words that were with me as I flattened the cloth and studied it for the clues which I knew existed, which I desired above everything else to find, but which I knew I never would.[13] (Italics as in the Original)

As such, Naipaul's fictions and short fictions are deliberate acts of satiric detachment.

Yet again, in *Mr Stone and the Knights Companion,* and in "A Flag on the Island," Naipaul qualifies two kinds of placelessness which is a further dimension of his detachment. There is the placelessness of a man who owns a house in London and yet finds that the physical world quite irrelevant to his humanity. Then there is the placelessness of people who, in the acquiring of a political identity have become uprooted within their own land.[14]

In the short fiction, "The Perfect Tenants" he presents Mrs Cooksey as the landlady, and traces her behaviour towards the Dakins. And the Dakins are welcomed initially, hut expelled after a long war of nerves. This story is successful because Naipaul accepts readily that he is dealing only with externals and the role he assigns himself as a detached storyteller.

REFERENCES

1. Naipaul, "London," in *The Overcrowded Barracoon.* London: Macmillan, 1972, 16.
2. Landeg White, *Naipaul: A Critical Introduction.* London: Macmillan, 1975, 7.
3. *Ibid.*, 23.
4. Naipaul, *An Area of Darkness.* London: Macmillan, 1964, 7.
5. Naipaul, "Interview with Francis Wyndham." *Sunday Times,* 2 January 1966, 9.
6. Landeg White, *Naipaul: A Critical Introduction,* 36.
7. Naipaul, *A House for Mr Biswas.* London: Macmillan, 1961, 230-31.
8. Naipaul, "The Enemy," in *The Flag on the Island.* London: Macmillan, 1967, 127.
9. Naipaul, *A House for Mr Biswas,* 523-24.
10. Landeg White, *Naipaul: A Critical Introduction,* 86-87.
11. Naipaul, *A House for Mr Biswas,* 267.
12. Landeg White, *Naipaul: A Critical Introduction,* 3.
13. Naipaul, *An Area of Darkness,* 280.
14. Landeg White, *Naipaul: A Critical Introduction,* 39.

CONTRIBUTORS

Rafe Dalleo. Department of Comparative Literature. Suny at Stony Brook, Stony Brook, New York, 11794, USA.

N. Sharada Iyer. Head, Department of English, Vasant College for Women, Rajghat Fort, Varanasi, Uttar Pradesh.

Prakash Chandra Pradhan. Senior Lecturer in English, K.B.D.A.V. College Nirakarpur, Khurda, Orissa.

Amar Nath Prasad. Lecturer in English, Jadgram College, Chapra, Bihar.

Santosh Chakrabatri. 19 P. Sil Lane, Kolkata, West Bengal.

Bhagabat Nayak. Lecturer in English, Kandarpur College, Cuttack, Orissa.

S. Kanakaraj. Professor and Head, Department of English, Directorate of Distance Education, Madurai Kamraj University, Madurai, Tamil Nadu.

J. Samuel Kirubahar. Department of English, VHNSN College, Virudhunagar, Tamil Nadu.

Sabita Tripathy. Reader, P.G. Department of English, Sambalpur University, Sambalpur, Orissa.

Jagdish V. Dave. Professor of English and Head, Department of English, North Gujarat University, Patan, Gujarat.

David Malcolm. Department of English, University of Gdansk, UI, Wita Stwosza 57, PL-80-387 Gdansk, Poland.

Emilienne Baneth-Nouailhetas. University of Paris III-Sorbonne Nouevelle, CNRS—Laboratoire Intermedia, Institut du Monde Anglophone, 5 rue de l'Ecole de Médeine, Paris, France.

Hiren Gohain. Former Professor of English & Dean of Arts Faculty, Gauhati University, Guwahati, Assam.

Nanda Kishore Mishra. Reader, Department of English, G.M. Autonomous College, Sambalpur, Orissa.

Veena Singh. Professor of English, Panjab University, Chandigarh, Haryana.

Aida Luz Rodríguez Colón. Department of English, College of Humanities, University of Puerto Rico, Rio Piedras Campus, P.O. Box 23356, San Juan, Puerto Rico 00931-3356.

Alpana Mishra. Lecturer, Behind Raghuraj Stadium, Imlipara, Bilaspur, Chhattisgarh.

Santwana Haldar. Reader in English, F.M. Auto College, Balasore, Orissa.

Aswini Kumar Vishnu. Head, Department of English, Sitabai Arts College, Akola, Maharashtra.

Nidhi Tiwari. Assistant Professor of English, Govt. Post-Graduate College, Narsinghpur, Madhya Pradesh.

Kamal Mehta. Department of English & Comparative Literary Studies, Saurashtra University, Rajkot, Gujarat.